FLASH IN THE PAN

THE LIFE AND DEATH OF AN
AMERICAN RESTAURANT

DAVID BLUM

SIMON & SCHUSTER

NEW YORK LONDON TORONTO SYDNEY TOKYO SINGAPORE

SIMON & SCHUSTER

SIMON & SCHUSTER BUILDING

ROCKEFELLER CENTER

1230 AVENUE OF THE AMERICAS

NEW YORK, NEW YORK 10020

DESIGNED BY

BARBARA M. BACHMAN

Manufactured in the
United States of America

1 3 5 7 9 10 8 6 4 2

Library of Congress Cataloging in
Publication Data
Blum, David
Flash in the pan : the life and death of an
American restaurant / David Blum.
p. cm.
1. Falls (Restaurant) I. Title.
TX945.5.F35B58 1992
641.5′09747′1—dc20   92-14649
CIP

ISBN: 978-1-4391-9377-8

FOR TERRI

CONTENTS

PART ONE: SMOKING

PART TWO: NON-SMOKING

Author's Note

Bruce Goldstein and Terry Quinn generously gave me complete access to their thoughts and actions as they created their restaurant, The Falls. They asked for nothing in return. In the beginning, they believed this book might promote their new restaurant; later, they were simply two honorable people ready to stand by their commitment. Were it not for their honesty and integrity, this book would not exist.

Both men talked to me at great length about their inner thoughts and feelings throughout the process. When you read such thoughts in the text, they reflect my best effort to describe their thinking at the time.

Beginning in February, 1990, I observed virtually all of the events described in the book. Where I did not, I have relied on at least one reliable source to re-create the scene or conversation.

Readers of nonfiction "process" books often wonder—rightly so—whether a reporter's presence has altered the events described. Their concern is that characters might be performing for the reporter. To guard against this, I spent hundreds of hours at The Falls over a fifteen-month period so that I would become, as much as possible, a part of the background. I often did not carry a notebook or tape recorder. When incidents appear in the book that I observed without the subject's knowledge that I was a reporter, I have concealed their identity. No one is quoted by name in the book unless they knew I was—at all times—a working journalist on the premises, a fact I made everyone at The Falls aware of as frequently as I could.

All the characters are real. There are no composites. The names of some characters have been changed, along with some identifying characteristics. In some cases, people asked for anonymity; in others, I gave it because the people were involved with The Falls for only a short time. Where a character's full name is given, that is their real name; when only a first name is given, that name has been changed.

Tomorrow is a busy day.

We got things to do;

We got eggs to lay.

We got ground to dig, and worms to scratch—

Takes a lot of sittin' gettin' chicks to hatch.

    —L o u i s   J o r d a n
        "AIN'T NOBODY HERE BUT US CHICKENS"

SMOKING

PART ONE

HAVE YOU MET

MISS JONES?

ONE

Monday, March 4, 1991, 7:15 P.M. The war is over. War is not healthy for restaurants and other living things. But The Falls has survived.

And tonight . . . tonight is going to be hot.

Danny Aiello is coming. He is going to be here any minute for dinner. A table is being held.

Danny Aiello is tonight's featured performer in the Lush Life Lounge. Otherwise known, to whomever it is known, as The Falls. Recently the place has taken to calling itself the Lush Life Lounge on Monday and Tuesday nights, because when The Falls was just calling itself The Falls on those nights, it was damn lucky if it got twenty customers for dinner all night. It is named for an old John Coltrane tune. It probably ought to be called the Last Ditch Lounge, since Aiello's appearance on the marquee (actually there is no marquee; hell, there isn't even a *sign* out front!) tonight comes at a moment of complete and total desperation—a final, wildly chaotic effort to inject new life into a restaurant that has just passed its first birthday, but hovers constantly near death.

A commercial storage facility has just opened up across the street. They are no doubt counting on some business from The Falls. Maybe they've noticed how goddamned dark it is inside there; is it to save electricity, or to make it look more like a wake? How about calling it the Lack of Life Lounge? The Lust for Life Lounge? One of the owners was moping around a few hours ago, talking about turning the entire place into a strip joint. That would presumably be called, simply, the Lush Lounge. If the Grim Reaper called for a table tonight—not so farfetched a possibility, really, not in New York City in the 1990s—they'd give him the corner banquette, ply him with free champagne and hope for the best.

Aiello shares a Sinatra obsession with The Falls; so it was discovered by Bruce Goldstein, the restaurant's proprietor, who heard Aiello sing Sinatra in his movie, *Once Around*, one night when he probably should have been at work. The actor has been convinced by others, including *Once Around* producer Griffin Dunne, a pal of the management, to take the stage in a benefit. We are told the cause is a Bronx Catholic rest home, but if it saves the life of a trendy downtown restaurant gasping its final breath, surely the nuns won't complain.

What is truly amazing about tonight is how, on the verge of catastrophe, The Falls is alive at all.

These days The Falls is getting five letters a day from its neighborhood bank. None of them are invitations to a cocktail party.

The venetian blinds look like they could use a dusting; so could that hot pink neon bulb that circles the window panels and gives off a cheesy afterglow. Even those overhead art deco light fixtures, four of them, hanging over the room like missiles, seem aimed directly at this restaurant's heart. They point downward, those monstrous lights, and even through the dust they cast a luscious hue—though they never stop looking like they're about to crash directly into the table below.

At least the waitresses look good. Human beings like to keep themselves dusted. Tonight it's a gathering of Falls Stars, a constellation of beauties in tight black miniskirts, bending, touching, stroking, leaning. Only hot lookers need apply. Why the hell not? They go well with the place. Since opening night, it has been the firm policy of The Falls to have a Firm Policy. If someone is going to serve me the wrong order, an owner of The Falls said once, *I'd rather get the wrong order from a pretty girl than a fat guy.* The waitresses oblige this sexism, or maybe it's just the recession and they need the money. One of them likes to keep two pens planted firmly between her breasts; is that so we *will* look at her breasts, or so that we won't?

Hundreds of hours of jazz and pop standards sit on a shelf behind the bar, back where Bruce Goldstein likes to spend most of his nights, and it is a strict Goldstein rule that music be played at all times, no exceptions. Tonight we are hearing a preponderance of Sinatra, in anticipation of the arrival of many Italians, including an actual friend of Sinatra named Jilly Rizzo, who used to own a 52nd Street jazz joint named Jilly's. Yes, Jilly is coming tonight, and he will want to hear Sinatra being played on the sound system. Jilly has a decided preference for the works of Sinatra.

So it is now 7:15 on an otherwise deadly quiet night in early March in the Year We Won the Persian Gulf War. No one was murdered in New York City on this night, not even an innocent by-stander.

The Falls is open for business.

And tonight . . . tonight is going to be hot.

/Hot nights come and go in the life of anyone, anything. The Falls has proved to be no exception. We are here, a few days into its second year of life, marveling at its defiance of the laws of business. By those laws, this restaurant should already be dead. And yet, when its first birthday went by a few nights ago, the blessed event did not warrant so much as a candle. (Odd, isn't it, when you consider what horrors most restaurants inflict when it's *your* birthday?)

Restaurants are not, either in the traditional or metaphorical sense, conceived or born. A seed is not planted and allowed to grow. There is no wonderful, charmed period where they come into the world all wrinkly and cute and cuddly. Friends and relatives do not make pilgrimages with little gift-wrapped presents to a restaurant upon the announcement of its birth.

Restaurants, alas, come to life fully formed, ready to deteriorate and wither away almost instantly. They must, from the day they face the world for the first time, act mature and sophisticated and wise. Frankly, it's a lot to ask of anything, even an institution—and maybe that is the reason we are dealing here with a perilously fragile enterprise that is, perhaps, analogous to nothing. A moribund movie lives on in the video store, passed over thousands of times by discriminating renters; a novel gathers dust on a library shelf, a burial ground for obscure chapters in our culture. No such luck for restaurants. They live and then they die. They get no funeral plots or obituaries. There's no place to put a wreath, or page to place a black-bordered announcement.

Depressing, isn't it?

Which is why it is impossible to review the events on this particular corner of the earth—the corner of Varick and Vandam streets in lower Manhattan, a corner not known even to the vast majority of New York City cabdrivers let alone the nearly four billion people on this planet—without thinking about death.

Restaurants are not only mere mortals, but they suffer an infant mortality rate that—in human terms—would lead to the immediate end of civilization. Only one in four restaurants in New York City makes it past its fifth birthday.

Imagine! Would you have a baby if you knew it would be dead within five years? Forget human comparisons; would you start a business facing those daunting odds? Invest money? Place a bet? Is there anything in the world, really, that you would do if you thought that it had a 75 percent chance of failure within five years? Some people— were they to be told that they themselves had a 75 percent chance of dying within five years—would probably lock themselves in a garage with their car engine running.

But other people thrive on the very threat of failure that others find so daunting.

Dances With Wolves. Anybody wanna see a three-hour movie about Indians? Apparently so. The Gulf War. *Big* risk. Turned out to be a pretty damn successful idea.

It would make for a simple explanation to suggest that in the fall of 1989, nearly two years before Danny Aiello took the stage at the Lush Life Lounge, we lived in a more hopeful time—and that when Bruce Goldstein first pushed forward with the idea for The Falls, he managed to tap into the positive vibes of the late 1980s, the burgeoning affluence of the postwar baby boom generation that still had money to spend. Sure, the market had crashed—but that was two years before, we'd all had some time to get our shit together. We stopped taking drugs, didn't we? Think of how much money we saved right there! In the late 1980s we became, as one wise member of this generation recently put it, "drugless home addicts"—doomed to covet apartments and houses larger than our own. We could no longer stop ourselves from marching into banks and requesting loans, loans, more loans; we mortgaged ourselves.

For what? For an apartment with a view of a filthy river called the Hudson? For a house with a pleasant yard and a quality school system? For convenient access to a grocery store that charges $8 for a six-pack of beer, and a dry cleaner that gets $4 to press your pants?

But it's not that simple. Never is.

• • •

/We all know where babies are conceived.

In case you were wondering about restaurants, they are conceived in the mind.

It was the summer of 1989, and Bruce Goldstein was only just re-covered from the death of a loved one, a restaurant that defied all odds and lived from 1978 to 1988, yes, an entire decade, making it by in-dustry standards a miracle. A thriving restaurant! Its name was Cen-tral Falls; and The Falls got its name from that illustrious predecessor.

But The Falls is not what Bruce Goldstein would have called his new restaurant had it been *his* decision. It never is when Other Peo-ple's Money is involved.

It would have been called Miss Jones. Not Miss Jones Café. Not Miss Jones's Place. Certainly not Ms. Jones.

It seems that Bruce was driving along the highway from the luxuri-ous beachfront community of Sag Harbor, about three hours from New York, after a weekend of summer sun. His skin was dark; his mind was wandering. As always, Bruce was thinking, mostly about the new restaurant he had been saying he might want to start. He popped a Bobby Short tape into the tape deck, and hummed along with one of his favorite nightclub crooners.

Suddenly, as in stop-the-car-I-gotta-make-an-important-call sud-denly, Bruce had it. The name.

"Have you met Miss Jones?" Bobby Short was singing.

Miss Jones! What a great name for a restaurant! Full-blown fanta-sies projected themselves in Bruce's mind. He saw a beautiful, glam-orous, rich, sexy couple. Probably in black tie. They were stepping into a taxi. "We're going to Miss Jones," the handsome young man instructed the driver. Without hesitation the cabbie drove off in the direction of Varick and Vandam.

I've got it, Bruce thought. People will drink champagne out of ruby slippers. Bobby Short will sing, models will dance, everyone will eat. Yes! Miss Jones it is!

"Hmmmm," Terry Quinn said.

Bruce had, indeed, pulled off to the side of the busy highway, found a phone and called his partner on their new, unformed restaurant idea. This is what happens when you have a partner. You call him up with your epiphanies.

"I'm not sure I get it," Terry Quinn continued.

What is Terry talking about? Bruce cannot believe that he doesn't get it. It's *perfect*. It's got mystery . . . romance . . . style. Hell, *I* want to eat at Miss Jones. I want to *say* Miss Jones. I want to know her, to have her . . . she is my mystery woman.

"Nobody will know what it is," Terry Quinn said.

It's a restaurant! Miss Jones is an idea . . . and I will plant that idea in their minds. They will want to come visit Miss Jones. They will become obsessed with her, as I have. They will keep coming back, coming back, coming back . . . oh, it will be wonderful.

"It's too confusing," Terry Quinn said.

Too confusing? Two words? Come on, man! Miss Jones is the answer to so many questions in my life, the answer to so many problems. I *know* it will work. I am not wrong about this, believe me.

"You're crazy," Terry Quinn said. "Goodbye."

Bruce Goldstein got back in his car. Okay, so I'm crazy. But it's a great name for a restaurant.

VARICK AND VANDAM

TWO

You know your life is devoted to restaurants when you are eighteen years old and you want to work in Rose's Restaurant on Cape Cod for the summer and they'll never hire anyone under twenty-one because they serve liquor. So you go in with your phony ID card that says your name is Joe Rose. They look at you kinda funny but they figure, why would he lie? And they give you the job and it works out great and you're learning the ropes and you know this is what you want to do, you know it so much that one day, when your mother wants to visit you at your restaurant, you say, okay Mom, but you'll have to be Mrs. Rose.

That's the way it was for Bruce Goldstein. All his life. Getting ahead, telling a story, making it work. He spent most of his early years in Rhode Island working relentlessly toward his goal. After he got out of high school in the Providence suburb of Pawtucket—where the yearbook predicted Bruce Goldstein would become "a swanky nightclub owner"—and a year at the University of Rhode Island, he moved to Boston. There, during every spare minute, he worked to fulfill his yearbook prophecy in restaurants and bars. Daisy Buchanan's on Newbury Street; The Kenmore Club on Kenmore Square. First he went to Bentley School of Accounting and Finance, then to Suffolk

University, where he got a degree and even spent a year going to business school.

But at heart Bruce was a kid from Rhode Island and he wanted to go home. When Bruce was growing up, his dad—whose nickname was Goldie, and whom Bruce now describes as "a Jewish gangster"—owned a few private gaming clubs and was suspected of bookmaking on the side. Bruce remembers being a little boy and having the police raid his house, looking for evidence that his dad was a bookie. When Bruce was twenty-three his father died; so he left Boston and went back home. It was 1970 in America and for a young man on the make, that often meant the music business. For a couple years he promoted concerts and did pretty well. But he wanted back into restaurants. He figured out the best place in Providence for a restaurant and he got the money—earned some, borrowed some; it's always the same—and he just did it. He met a man named Morris Nathanson, a designer who looks exactly like Mark Twain, who helped him put it together, and who became a lifelong friend.

And so, by the time Bruce was twenty-four, he'd gotten himself his first place, called the Incredible Organ, and what people remember about it was that Bruce thought up the idea of a trolley car that would bring people right to the door of the restaurant from wherever they were. Location, location, location!

But after a while Bruce wanted a trolley car to take him out of Rhode Island. He didn't like being a big fish in a little pond. He loved his mother and Carol, his sister, and his sense of family is strong; so that was the tough part about leaving. But he knew he had to. He wanted to go somewhere pretty and nice. He took his Incredible Organ profits—must have been $50,000 or so—and went to the Caribbean. First to St. Martin, then to St. Bart's, and in these glamorous French resorts he wheeled and dealed till he had himself restaurants; in all, five successful places that catered to tourists and locals and anyone looking for a meal. They were packed from the moment he started them. Bruce began to believe he had the magic touch.

For almost a decade Bruce remained there—a man with a tan and a plan. He knew it didn't take much to get a couple of beachfront joints together. Sure they were nice, his pal Morris came down to help him with the decor; but there were other fish to be fried, so to speak.

So one day in 1977 he sold all his interests in the Caribbean and walked away with more than $200,000 in profit, and came to New York. He got himself an apartment and immediately had visions of restaurants; maybe one could go right here on Union Square—right across from his new bachelor pad. But eventually he found his way to new neighborhoods and new vistas, and discovered new opportunities waiting wherever he looked. This was the 1970s, after all, and he had a six-figure bank account.

Thus, in 1978, Central Falls was born, with the design of old friend Morris Nathanson, and the irrepressible spirit of Bruce Goldstein.

Central Falls struggled through the first several months, but by the end of the first year had become a hit—a restaurant and watering hole for the rapidly growing population of a New York neighborhood just beginning to prosper at the end of the 1970s: SoHo.

Technically it means South of Houston Street, but SoHo means much more than that. For a decade it was the undisputed center of the New York art world; as home to galleries owned by prominent dealers like Mary Boone and Holly Solomon and Leo Castelli, it was where you could go on a Sunday afternoon and find a large piece of black metal, what it was exactly no one knew, that cost $20,000. Artists like Vito Acconci, famous for having masturbated for hours in a gallery, would show his work in SoHo. So too would more conventional painters like Robert Rauschenberg and Jasper Johns.

If SoHo were a microcosm of New York City, then its Fifth Avenue would be a two-lane, ten-block boulevard called West Broadway. If, on a Sunday afternoon in 1982, you wanted to spend a few lazy hours gallery hopping in SoHo, you started and finished on West Broadway. What it lacked in outer beauty it made up for in a vibrant inner world. It seemed as though every nondescript four-story loft building had five or six galleries, each with its own distinct vision. You would ride in a cavernous elevator or march up wide, dark stairs, and discover a world of modern art that you could actually buy. It was the world Woody Allen portrayed almost without parody in *Hannah and Her Sisters;* painters like Max von Sydow were refusing to sell canvases according to size and color, but collectors like Daniel Stern were still going to take a limo down there and try.

If you were visiting, or if you were lucky enough to actually *live* right along the cutting edge of American modern art—either way you needed a place to eat. And Bruce Goldstein had just such a place. The amazing thing about Central Falls, at 478 West Broadway, was that it practically *preceded* the SoHo boom; it opened in September of 1978, and from the day it opened, Central Falls had it. Location, location, location!

But by 1989, Central Falls had closed, the victim of rapidly rising rents—his had climbed from $2,200 a month in 1978 to $18,000 a decade later—and a gradually declining economy.

Bruce Goldstein retreated to the shadows. Having declared bankruptcy—enabling him to escape without having to pay several out-standing bills from food purveyors—he didn't see the point in remaining. So he went back to the Caribbean for a while, which is where he had his first serious conversation with a friend of Central Falls regular Matt Dillon, a very nice guy named Terry Quinn.

/You get used to crowded rooms when you grow up with nine brothers and three sisters, and the nine brothers and you all sleep in the same bedroom, doubled up in beds and fighting and giggling and all that stuff. That's how Terry Quinn grew up, and if he seems exceedingly comfortable working a crowded room, that's because he is. They grew up in a small house in Brooklyn, and Terry commuted to Catholic schools, first in Brooklyn, then in other parts of New York; one in Queens, then, after he got thrown out of that one, a place called La Salle on Second Avenue in Manhattan. La Salle specialized in Catholic kids who got thrown out.

Terry spent a lot of those years reading all kinds of magazines. He loved to read articles about guys who came up from nowhere and made it big. Not guys who got success handed to them on a plate, like movie stars; more like businessmen and entrepreneurs, men who had an idea and made it work, and made lots of money, too. He knew he wanted to be that kind of guy, the kind that got written up in maga-zines; he liked the pictures, too. To this day he keeps a large collection of private shots of himself on the beach here and there with Matt Dillon and other friends, cavorting.

He graduated from high school, finally, a football star with no par-ticular ambitions. He went to St. Francis College in Brooklyn Heights, but by the time he was twenty he was married and had to drop out. By the time he was twenty-two, he had two sons. He found his family a nice, small apartment in Queens, rent-controlled, for $200 a month, and worked a variety of odd jobs that got him enough money to buy a car. He needed a lot more, though, he knew that. In 1982, after his second son was born, he took the civil service exam to become a fire-man. He passed, but it was going to be a while before he got on the city payroll; in those days, he says, "They were trying to hire mostly women. A guy didn't have much of a chance."

So he decided to tackle Wall Street. A few of his brothers had al-ready made the plunge into the world of money, and they brought him into it. He found it exciting—and he had enough of an aptitude to have passed the stockbroker licensing exam on his first try in 1985.

But the more time he spent around money, the more he wanted to earn it for himself. He was working for a Wall Street brokerage house when part of it moved to the corner of 57th Street and Fifth Avenue, the center of the universe for a young man on the way up in the world of money, fashion and power. He'd stayed friends with a boyhood pal, Patrick Fahey, who now worked in that neighborhood as a fashion model—and together they scanned the city for opportunities.

"I'd read in *Interview* magazine about those outlaw parties that happened in the streets. By word of mouth, or by phone calls, someone would get a crowd of people on the street, on the West Side, get a deserted street in a commercial area, and a truck would pull up and serve drinks and stuff. People would gather. I went to one or two. The cops would always come and break them up. It gave me the idea. With word of mouth I could gather a bunch of people, too."

So Terry and Patrick scanned the classifieds for the right kind of space to open a nightclub—one that would appeal to the young crowd of actors and models that Terry and Patrick now counted as their friends. Finally, through *The New York Times*, they found a space in Greenwich Village, an Israeli restaurant that had just gone under, and they knew it would be just right. "Some girl had lent us money," Terry says. "I had not a cent. I was living paycheck to paycheck, no matter what I was doing. It wasn't enough." She lent Patrick and Terry each $15,000, and another investor borrowed $40,000 to make up the rest of what they needed. They named it Peggy Sue's, though not after the movie or the song. "I thought a woman's name was good luck," he explains.

Peggy Sue's took off; but right as that happened, the Fire Department phoned. They had a job.

So Terry went to work as a fireman.

He was probably the only fireman in New York City who also owned a trendy Manhattan nightspot on the side.

It was right around this time that Terry separated from his wife, and began living in a lovely West Village walk-up.

It was at Peggy Sue's that Terry first discovered models and movie stars, the formula for a club's success, not to mention his own.

"I knew them personally. I knew all the girl models and I knew guy models. You meet more and more, you meet the bookers, and they want to know the people who own the clubs because they want to be taken care of. It's a circle. They want to know you, and you want to know their girls. And they're always bringing whoever's new in town. There's always new young girls coming in. And they're all twenty years old, nineteen, twenty, twenty-one. And that's what makes a crowd."

The formula for a successful New York nightspot is simple: If a beautiful girl comes up to the velvet rope, you let her in immediately.

"Right away," Terry says. "I don't think any club will ever leave beautiful girls standing outside. I was buying bottles of champagne for some of these girls. Six or seven beautiful girls can keep a hundred guys. It'll keep me in a place. Seven beautiful girls. They never do think about being used . . . they're too young, or not that smart. They don't really think about it. They get jaded after two years and then they don't go out anymore. You don't see 'em around. They get hooked up with some famous actor or musician, a wealthy guy, a banker or something, and they disappear into the sunset.

"And then the new ones come along and take their place."

/In 1989, as Peggy Sue's grew more successful, Terry Quinn and Matt Dillon looked inside the window of a restaurant named La Gamelle. It doesn't exist anymore, now it's a hot joint called Lucky Strike, but at the time it was for sale and Terry was thinking of buying it and maybe getting into the restaurant business. It wasn't a very nice place, though, at least not at that time. It had one big problem, something about raw sewage coming out into the street. Not good for a restaurant.

As they stared into the window, Matt said to Terry, "You should get together with Bruce."

So they went to St. Bart's and they kicked back a few and became friends and decided to open a restaurant.

They came back to Manhattan and combed the city together. They looked at a place on 13th Street, off Sixth Avenue. They looked at a place on Avenue A. It had to be cheap, of course. Very cheap.

The best place they saw was a restaurant on Varick Street that had seen better days: J.S. VanDam. Both Bruce and Terry had been there as customers, and each remembered it as the darkest restaurant they'd ever seen. "I didn't like anybody in there," Terry says. "People have these fond memories of the place, but I think it was drug induced. It was a place to drink and do coke." But as Terry and Bruce and Matt continued their search of Manhattan, their minds kept coming back to it, and to the mysterious magic that once lured crowds to the corner of Varick and Vandam.

Varick Street is a one-way, three-lane downtown thoroughfare used mostly by traffic headed to the Holland Tunnel and New Jersey. Pedestrians keep their distance, especially at night. The street has been there since the 1700s, named for Richard Varick, an early mayor of New York. Vandam is a short side street best known to New Yorkers as the home, until recently, of the Thalia SoHo repertory theater. The spot now for sale had always been a restaurant; for more than two decades before J.S. VanDam it was Villa Varick, a cheap neighborhood hangout where a chicken dinner cost $3 and beers were a quarter. Before that—when the space first opened in the 1940s—it had possibly been a private gambling club, with dark curtains protecting its customers from the authorities and the street.

The "J.S." in J.S. VanDam stood for Jim and Susan, two waiters at Raoul's, a nearby French bistro that had been popular for years. But Susan had died a year ago, and Jim had put the place on the market. It did have one major advantage: the room itself. It was large, almost cavernous; extremely high ceilings; a corner location with lots of windows; right on a major downtown thoroughfare; and, most important, one of the longest, finest bars in New York City. "I thought that it was the perfect space," Terry says now.

After much haggling—matters became more complicated when the VanDam owner declared bankruptcy—Bruce and Terry negotiated a rent of $5,416.67 a month. Armed with a deal, Terry and Bruce cemented their relationship into a company called 150 Varick Inc. Terry Quinn was its president.

A friendship had become a partnership.

"I got to know him better," Terry later said of those months. "After we first met we went out a lot. I'm a pretty good judge of character. I knew that you have to sacrifice some things for other things. No partnership is going to be perfect, no person you're going to find is going to be the perfect guy, deaf and dumb, he does all the work for you. Bruce was the best at paying attention to a lot of the small details. He had better taste than most restaurateurs. Better taste in music. He's obsessed with music . . . I think it's one of the things that makes the place. The music and the lighting . . .

"He's got a lot of experience, Bruce. He's an older guy, he's been around, he's done restaurants all over the place. It's hard to find people that have that kind of taste. The knowledge of how to work things out. He doesn't pay attention to the accounting, things like that, but he knows how to work things out."

MISS JONES

THREE

Somewhere a man is melting.

This man thinks that Kimberly Jones finds him attractive, or interesting. And this is exciting news, because Kimberly Jones is attractive and interesting herself. She is turning up the volume on her lilting Arkansas twang, and the gentleman in question falls completely. He is a total sucker for a twang. And so Kimberly—not Kim—Jones brushes her bangs off her forehead, laughs and continues the meltdown.

She parts her hair on the side—thin, wavy brown hair, often pulled back, sometimes left unwashed. That is the only part of her physical appearance that would occasionally not be described as well scrubbed, which is her calling card. She dresses demurely. She walks demurely. At least for an Arkansas girl who used to write restaurant reviews about Italian joints she thinks were run by mobsters in the witness protection program, or else why would they be so good?

She came to work for Bruce Goldstein in June of 1989. She met a man at the Ambassador East Hotel in Chicago who suggested it. They met in the hallway or the elevator or something. It was a food convention. The next thing she knew she was getting off a plane at Kennedy Airport with two apple pies she had baked for Bruce Goldstein, because her mom told her it was polite to bring people a pie.

28

First thing she did was get an apartment on the Upper West Side, with a doorman. It cost a fair amount but then what doesn't? Then she got a boyfriend. This being New York City, she found herself a celebrity, Rich Hall, a comedian who had done commercials and TV shows and perhaps even Vegas for a night or two. She was happy.

Bruce gave her work right away on his pet project, the Central Falls Road Show, a business he spun off his old restaurant, Central Falls. It was the ultimate enterprise for a man who believed in catering to the stars: what else? They made lunches for Meryl Streep and dinners for Roseanne Barr (though Roseanne sometimes preferred to get burgers and fries from Wendy's), and Kimberly—her Arkansas training as a chef serving her well—cooked and cleaned and arranged and drove and just about everything else, though when asked her official title, much later, she would report simply, "I was the chef."

In August Kimberly had to go home—she needed surgery on her knee. By the time she came back in September, wearing a leg brace she thought was positively hideous, Bruce had rounded up his investors, some of them at least, enough of them for now. Things were starting to happen, and Kimberly was going to be there for it all, wearing this stupid brace. Damn!

The thing about Kimberly Jones is this: She is not from New York. She is not *like* New York. Dad's retired, used to be an agricultural resource economist . . . Mom inherited some farmland in Louisiana. They farmed cotton till the mid-1970s, must have been where that voice of cotton came from; then soybeans. In the off-season? Winter wheat, of course.

"I used to think it was the new thing when we'd go to my friend's house and they'd have canned string beans," she remembered. "All our green beans were frozen or jarred. They'd get to open the cans. I thought it was the neatest thing to eat canned vegetables." Kimberly grew up eating black-eyed peas and butter beans. Mom would stew tomatoes and peaches, and it's so funny, even now Kimberly will be at the grocery store or the farmer's market and they'll have a good deal on okra, and Kimberly will go home and stew a bunch of it and then freeze it for later.

"It's like my grandmother did," she says, "and like my mom did, but growing up, I thought, I'd love some canned soup or a TV dinner."

And so, to the people who made up the core of this nascent restaurant project, Kimberly was part of the allure, the mystique. How many women do you know from Arkansas? You needed something answered, you called Kimberly. She needed something done, she called you. Always friendly, always warm, always sweet. You looked forward to your interaction with Kimberly. This was going to be *fun*—having Kimberly Jones on board—something told you.

Bruce Goldstein recognized her value immediately. Certainly it was well beyond the $10-an-hour wage he was paying her, for hours well beyond the forty or so she billed him for on small pieces of yellow paper she kept in a file.

Her first important task was to coordinate what was about to become a massive flow of official paperwork produced by a new restaurant. This meant keeping track of the lawyers, the investors, the applications, the phone . . . Bruce was obsessed with that damn phone. By the time March 1, 1990, rolled around, Bruce and Kimberly had spent hours on the phone on the simple matter *of* the phone. Bruce cared deeply, passionately about the nature of phone service to be provided at The Falls for its management personnel. He wanted to be quite certain that his needs would be covered. He found the bureaucracy of New York Telephone to be a continual annoyance—although Kimberly, in fact, was the one who fought the red tape on a daily basis.

The Falls's headquarters in those days was Bruce's apartment on Mercer Street, a quiet side street in a part of Greenwich Village that could be described as upscale—even if it was so close to the wretched strip of retail excess known as 8th Street. To anyone who has visited New York since about 1965, 8th Street is a familiar nuisance; shoes and more shoes, pizza and more pizza, crap and more crap. There is the occasional bright spot in this madness—a store or two with genuine bargains, not rip-offs, a halfway decent video store—but generally speaking, Bruce looked out from his twenty-fourth-floor vista onto just another reason to hate New York. Perhaps he felt an occasional twinge of bitterness that the restaurants in his immediate vicinity, most of them second-rate if not third-rate, nevertheless managed to do gangbuster business.

Kimberly worked at Bruce's desk in his pleasant, if crowded, living room. It had a colorful feel. Posters hung on the wall from early glory days in the Caribbean. They crowded each other to the point where little wall space remained, an effective way of camouflaging the fact that this was, after all, one of those uncomfortably boxy apartments one finds in New York City high rises. The low ceilings and flat walls and undistinguished layout did not parallel Bruce's mellow, exotic tastes. The furniture, modern and sleek and comfortable, improved the picture. It gave the place a distinctive warmth, a friendly glow.

His obsession with music filled the place, and he had clearly designed the room with listening in mind. There was an enormous collection of records, CDs, and tapes, and a comfortable sofa faced the speakers, big enough to be slept on. Which it frequently was. Matt Dillon, among others, was known to use Bruce's couch overnight. Comfortable. Centrally located. You could call at the last minute and there was room available.

For months, The Falls used Bruce's address as its own. Stationery was printed. A rubber stamp was made. The Falls's phone number was Bruce's phone number. Investors sent their checks to Bruce's. Lawyers called Bruce's. (You'd think he might have progressed beyond call waiting, wouldn't you? But he didn't, and one rarely called Bruce's without getting the story that someone's holding, gotta go, sorry.)

Mainly it was Kimberly on the phone.

"I just did a lot of calling people," she remembered much later, with the edge of bitterness in her voice one comes to associate with former employees of Bruce's. "Finding out what needed to be done. Working on the liquor license. It was incredible. He"—the lawyer they'd hired to work on getting the license—"must have been so sick of me because I was up there almost every day." Up there literally. The lawyer who eventually handled their liquor license, David Korngut, works out of the Empire State Building.

Kimberly handled the fingerprints, the checks, the forms, all the requisite crap one needed to assemble for a liquor license. It was a tough job for anyone, and it didn't make it any easier that Kimberly —sweet, lovely Kimberly—had to do all this schlepping in a hideous leg brace after her surgery. Pretty girls from Arkansas don't do much schlepping.

THE SLICING OF THE PIE

FOUR

On October 9, 1989, The Falls officially became a celebrity restaurant.

For it was on that day, a Monday, that a handsome movie star from the tony New York suburb of Mamaroneck opened up his large notebook-sized checkbook from Barclay's Bank of New York and wrote out a check for $10,000 to "150 Varic Inc." (Movie stars don't have to get names right, do they?) At the bottom of the check was his characteristic simple scrawl, practically printed out so there was no mistaking it, and at the top was his name and his parents' address in Mamaroneck, where this young stud still spent much of his time, a good hour's drive at least from the southeast corner of Varick and Vandam.

Matt Dillon had never invested in a restaurant before.

But then again, neither had his pal Terry Quinn.

They'd been friends for a while, Matt and Terry, basketball buddies and then genuine good friends. They traveled together to Europe and the Caribbean. They hung out together with beautiful women in skimpy bathing suits on sandy beaches. There would never be any question that when Terry referred to "Matt" that he meant this Matt, movie star Matt. The one who you immediately noticed looked one hell of a lot like Terry Quinn, or the other way around, depending. Which must have made their friendship easier. Terry needed nothing from Matt. Terry had looks, charm and money. Okay, so Matt was famous. But Terry, in his own way, was famous, too—not movie star famous, but famous enough to get into VIP rooms and gossip columns and fancy parties.

Terry Quinn looked famous.

But the idea of this check—of finally, irrevocably altering the nature of their friendship by allowing a five-figure sum of money to change hands between them—was to do for The Falls what Terry Quinn, alone, could not. To be a celebrity restaurant, after all, you need a celebrity.

Matt Dillon would definitely do.

As September rolled into October, Bruce needed the money to get things moving. He glowed from four months of natural sunshine. By then Bruce's plans for The Falls had crystallized to the point where it all got put down on paper in a three-page document, bound in a brown cover with a title page and *everything*, though Bruce is later quick to point out that this was not an official offering. It was merely designed to give investors a clear picture of exactly what they would be getting for their money, aside from the privilege of saying, "I'm an investor, and I'd like *that* table, please."

It was called "Restaurant Investment Projections," and it contained but one cream-colored sheet of text. Apparently it does not behoove a restaurant to make too many promises in advance of opening night. Here is the full text:

ALLOCATION OF TOTAL INVESTMENT

The total capital requirement is projected to be $180,000. Said investment shall be allocated as follows:

Down payment of purchase price	$75,000
Renovations of restaurant	$60,000

Legal and accounting fees $10,000
* Working capital $35,000

* A portion of the working capital fund shall be used towards the purchase of a computer system which establishes sales and inventory controls. The use of a computer system is expected to reduce the projected labor costs and accordingly increase profits.

CAPITAL STRUCTURE

The corporation shall issue ten shares of common stock, no par value. Nine shares shall be offered to investors at a value of twenty thousand ($20,000) dollars for each share. One share shall be issued to the organizer/developer, Bruce Goldstein, in consideration for the discovery and development of the business opportunity.

As additional consideration for his ten percent (10%) interest in the venture, Bruce Goldstein has agreed to contribute the profits that will be derived from his catering business which operates under the trade name "Central Falls Road Show." It is anticipated that the gross revenues of said venture will exceed the annual sum of $300,000 and will substantially increase the projected profit distributions to investors.

Page 2 was entitled "Projected Weekly Net Profit for Restaurant Operation":

PROJECTED WEEKLY NET PROFIT FOR RESTAURANT OPERATION

SALES			
Food Sales	9,000	12,000	18,000
Beverage Sales	6,000	8,000	12,000
Total Sales	15,000	20,000	30,000
COST OF SALES			
Food	3,600	4,800	7,200
Beverage	1,800	2,240	3,360
Total Cost of Sales	(5,400)	(7,040)	(10,560)
Gross Profit	9,600	12,960	19,440

OPERATING EXPENSES			
Rent	1,250	1,250	1,250
Gas & electric	300	400	600
Water	100	150	200
Insurance	400	400	400
Accounting	200	200	200
Advertising	100	100	100
Rubbish removal	150	200	300
Telephone	100	100	100
Amex/MC/Visa charges	40	60	100
Exterminating	50	50	50
Licenses & permits	75	75	75
Linens & uniforms	75	100	150
Salaries—officers	1,200	1,200	1,200
Salaries—others	1,600	1,800	2,500
Payroll taxes	300	400	500
Maintenance & repairs	150	150	150
Misc. expenses	250	300	400
Total Expenses	(6,340)	(6,935)	(8,275)
Net Profit	3,260	6,025	11,165
Note payment			
(principal only)	(284)	(284)	(284)
Net Profit before			
income and sales tax	2,976	5,741	10,881

What all these tiny little numbers basically mean is that The Falls believed very strongly . . . very *early* that it would be a profitable venture. The little numbers would become big numbers. Bills would be paid. Money would be made. To underscore this notion, the restaurant provided on page 3 the numbers that investors truly wanted to read: "Distributions of Weekly Profit."

DISTRIBUTIONS OF WEEKLY PROFIT

The Corporation will be making distributions to the shareholders after retaining a portion of the profits for contingencies and to establish a working capital fund. The following is a projection of distributions based upon a retention of 0%, 25% and 50% of net operating profits in retained earnings:

PROJECTED WEEKLY PROFITS	2,976	5,741	10,881
RETAINED EARNINGS (0%)	-0-	-0-	-0-
DISTRIBUTIONS TO INVESTORS	2,976	5,741	10,881

PROJECTED WEEKLY PROFITS	2,976	5,741	10,881
RETAINED EARNINGS (25%)	⟨ 744⟩	⟨1,435⟩	⟨ 2,720⟩
DISTRIBUTIONS TO INVESTORS	2,232	4,306	8,161

PROJECTED WEEKLY PROFITS	2,976	5,741	10,881
RETAINED EARNINGS (50%)	⟨1,488⟩	⟨2,870⟩	⟨ 5,440⟩
DISTRIBUTIONS TO INVESTORS	1,488	2,871	5,441

Investors love to see the word "profit." They especially love to see the word "net profit." Without much difficulty, Bruce and Terry were able to market and sell the rest of the available shares. Those left over after Bruce, Terry and Matt, that is. As the prospectus mentioned, Bruce got 10 percent of The Falls in exchange for his work. One of the principal investors in The Falls, a woman named Carol Silverman, also happened to be Bruce's sister. This essentially gave Bruce control of 20 percent of the stock—two slices of the proverbial pie.

Terry, in return for $20,000, got 10 percent.

Matt's ten grand got him five.

Other celebrities signed up for the rest, including Alan Parker, the British film director best known for *Mississippi Burning*, his longtime producer, Bob Colesberry, and ice cream heiress and Goldstein pal Edie Baskin, art director for *Saturday Night Live*. Each of them owned 10 percent of this freshly baked pie.

/Michael Sebastian is a talented and successful record producer, not a celebrity or anything, but with good green money. In the fall of 1989 he put $20,000 into the pot, got ten shares for his money and thought, "This is gonna be fun."

Michael Sebastian is not his real name. Restaurant investors tend to be shy. They invariably come, as Sebastian does, from the small, elite world of discretionary income earners—men and women whose livelihoods don't depend on the vagaries of the economy.

In restaurant investment, Sebastian thought perhaps he might have found a perfect calling. Especially since, when you get right down to it, there weren't all that many restaurants in New York City he really liked. Oh, there were restaurants near his home . . . restaurants his friends liked to frequent . . . restaurants he felt he *had* to visit just to maintain his regular table. But he needed, no, *wanted* something better. He wanted a place he could call his own.

He'd heard about the deal at a party hosted by Bob Colesberry. Bruce Goldstein was there. "Sure, I'd love to invest in a restaurant!" were the words he uttered, impulsively perhaps, but heartfelt nonetheless. He signed on immediately, even helped out by fronting $2,000 for an escrow account with a lawyer.

Did Bruce mention that night about the Liquor Authority? Probably not. There's a state agency that regulates restaurants selling booze, a tough one with investigators and forms and interviews. It's called the New York State Liquor Authority, and it would become the most difficult and unexpected part of the process for all the investors. Each of them would have to go and be fingerprinted. Each of them would have to demonstrate that the money they invested in The Falls was their own. If necessary they'd have to produce bank statements and tax records. At the very least they had to disclose the sources of their investment funds and go through rigorous, legal checks.

"Pain in the ass," Sebastian recalled.

"An absolutely necessary protection that keeps criminal elements out of the restaurant business," Richard Chernela, a spokesman for the Liquor Authority, explained.

It is a process that takes an ill-defined period to complete. Oh sure, the forms are clear enough—the background checks, bank statements, all that. But what happens after that gets a little murky. Will the application go on the top of the pile or the bottom? *That* is the question. And to answer this question a restaurant owner can try all sorts of maneuvers. The most frequent is to locate a lawyer with experience at working through the bureaucracy. The Falls began this process with a lawyer named Mel Altman. After several weeks in which little work was done, Bruce and Terry abruptly changed lawyers.

They turned next to David Korngut, the man in the Empire State Building and an experienced hand in the license game. While no one will admit that connections matter, they seem to; Korngut likes to assert his ability to reach people inside the authority by phone, find out what's going on and report back to the client. Korngut—with the helpful assistance of Kimberly Jones, the dutiful check collector—put together The Falls's application by November of 1989, plenty of time to get open by the first of March.

According to the statement of finances filed with the authority, eighty shares in the company were sold at $2,000 a share, with the additional twenty shares split between Terry and Bruce as president and secretary/treasurer, respectively, of 150 Varick Inc. The largest shareholders held ten shares, bought for a $20,000 investment. That list included Alexandra Brochen, a model; Terry Quinn, who put borrowed money from his brother for an investment; and Carol Silverman, Bruce's sister, who also reported to the Liquor Authority that she had borrowed the money to invest.

The total assets of the investors was put at $1.02 million, and the total cost of opening The Falls at $123,866.67, with $75,000 of that going toward fixtures already in place, such as the kitchen, the air conditioning, the bar equipment, even a few leftover plates and cups. J.S. VanDam was known as a turnkey operation, meaning that those fixtures need not be bought. All the new owners needed to do was, you got it, put the key in the lock and walk right in.

All in all, The Falls was a low-cost venture that, on paper at least, looked like a surefire winner—bound to return heaps of profits to all slice owners of this tasty pie.

WHY DID HEMINGWAY

LOVE FISH?

FIVE

There is a wonderful restaurant in New York City called L'Acajou, which is French for mahogany.

If the guidebooks bothered to write about L'Acajou, which they don't, which is good, they would say that L'Acajou is a great restaurant, with wonderful coffee-shop-style booths and good French bistro food and a great wine list, supervised by a true connoisseur of wine named Danny, and a warm atmosphere and two terrific waiters, Brendan and Patty, and there is even a rumor floating around that Bruce Springsteen likes to eat there all by himself in a rear booth, facing the back wall, and that he likes the flourless chocolate cake.

Brian Moores used to be the chef at L'Acajou.

Like Terry Quinn, Brian had a tiny little scar on his face, though it didn't quite suggest menace; it made you think he must have slipped chopping an onion.

He sparkled.

Little brown eyes, an unkempt pile of brown hair he'd always push back, and a small, compact body that fit perfectly between the frying pan and the fire.

A voice that twisted and curled.

Hands that whipped and basted and chopped and tossed. You would watch Brian Moores toss a salad and think, aaah . . . so *that's* how you toss a salad!

He could tell you something about wine, but he didn't. Instead he would tell you something about a guy he once knew who thought of the telephone before Alexander Graham Bell, or was it Brian who had the idea? He had dreams, and you could taste them in his capon breast and in his squid ink capellini and in his Icelandic langoustines.

Or hear them in his stories—long-winded ones, the kind that make you think about your laundry or your bank balance or why you're not getting enough iron in your diet. He was the opposite of a natural storyteller, but that did not prevent him from thinking of himself as Will Rogers. And he was just so goddamned sweet you didn't care.

He got married not long ago. They lived together in the Pennsylvania countryside, and Brian Moores took the bus to work every day, three hours back and forth—time to read, he said; time to dream. He read Hemingway and mysteries and novels by his father and his sister.

Why do all chefs love fish? Why did Hemingway love fish?

/Bruce and Brian met in the fall of 1989. A drunk named Robert introduced them.

Robert claims to be a writer, and there are those who will confirm that he has written a novel or two. A living is earned. Enough for Robert to drown himself in only the finest French wines. Even through the blurriest of vision he can make out the difference between a Margaux and a Côte du Rhône. On an average night Robert will order a Black Label on the rocks, a bottle of Muscadet, a Martell cognac and a glass of ice water, with some food mixed in here and there to break the flow. "You just can't get great wine by the glass," Robert says, and will offer anyone a glass from his bottle to prove it.

Robert likes to find himself a comfortable barstool and then stay there. The ones at Central Falls were particularly comfortable and he did a lot of drinking there. He also had a fondness for the cozy seats at L'Acajou's long bar, but stools with backs were his decided preference. He could stand. Heavy drinkers generally prefer to sit, though, and you can't really blame them. After much sitting at the bar of Central Falls, he came to know Bruce Goldstein, and after not so much sitting at L'Acajou, Brian Moores.

Bruce, he said one day, you should really meet Brian Moores. He was at L'Acajou awhile, a *long* while, now he's living in Pennsylvania, may I have him call you?

But by then Bruce had already put an ad in *The New York Times*, looking for a chef. It cost him $542 and ran one Sunday in September of 1989.

"A new restaurant will be opening in SoHo. Emphasizing healthy lighter fare, de-emphasizing cream and butter sauce. . . ." And a phone number. Lots and lots of people called. Three chefs from the Russian Tea Room alone called. The personal cook to Ethel Kennedy called. Macrobiotic chefs who misunderstood the ad called. A guy named Tony called from an overpriced gourmet food shop in the Hamptons, the Barefoot Contessa, and of everyone who called, he was the only one who ever stood a chance. The goal was to pay somebody $40,000 or maybe $50,000 if they had to, so, sadly, the guys from the Russian Tea Room were just not going to work out.

Although it did raise an interesting question: Can you make borscht without cream?

Kimberly interviewed the applicants, five of them in person, and met Brian, too. He wasn't really an applicant but he *was* somebody to consider. Bruce had eaten Brian's food, and liked it. Bruce figured Brian would be pretty good on TV, and, of course, with a place like The Falls you had to count on some television exposure. The chef might be called on to appear on the morning shows in an apron and toque. This was going to be tough. Brian was good. Tony was good.

What if we hired both?

An interesting idea. Brian and Tony would be the co-executive chefs of The Falls. Brian the loud one, Tony soft . . . Brian the classy French chef, Tony the family Italian . . . Brian the chief cook, Tony the bottle washer. Yes, it just might work! The more they thought about it, the less they wanted to think about it. Yes, let's do it. Two is better than one, and not really that much more expensive, actually.

To celebrate this decision with a public act of boldness, Bruce and Kimberly and Brian and Tony went to the New York Hotel and Restaurant Show at the Jacob K. Javits Convention Center, all together, one huge display of friendship and camaraderie that would introduce the world to The Falls Foursome. We have arrived! No more butter and cream!

They bought a smoker while they were there. And so Brian started talking about smoking. Smoking everything. Smoking oysters. Smoking cheese. Long stories. Kimberly wanted to strangle him. But that was Brian's style. He didn't *mean* to bore you. He believed, in some fundamental way, that what he had to say was compelling. And though his stories weren't, he was.

But as they walked up and down the aisles at the Javits Center—Bruce marveling, as people tend to, at the union clout in convention centers that pays five hairy-knuckled guys to eat donuts—Brian riffed and riffed. Tony listened, of course, being the junior member of the team. Part of the job to listen. Everybody just thought Tony was quiet and shy, and Brian a tad chatty.

Up and down, up and down. Brian told them about ovens and broilers and grills. Chicken and burgers and fish. He talked while he walked. He talked while they talked. He talked and talked.

It was a very long day.

A few days later, Brian and Tony were supposed to meet and talk again. Brian went to the appointed place at the appointed time. Tony did not.

He disappeared.

So Brian became the executive chef of The Falls, all by himself.

This was going to be great, Brian thought. Bruce says he'll really get going on the opening in February, and start serving in March, so that's pretty soon. I'll leave L'Acajou at the end of January and start my new life. A hot new restaurant with celebrities will attract a lot of attention, I bet. Matt Dillon's a good guy. And it means I'll finally get reviewed by *The New York Times*, right? They never came to L'Acajou. They go for this kind of place. They'll be here the opening week. What a mess that will be. I don't like this no-cream-sauce business, but I'll get around it, the menu will be good, very good, lots of pastas, lots of game, lots of fish. Weird fish. Funny fish. The critics love funny fish.

THE PRICE OF EGGS IN SOHO

SIX

Bruce is mad. Furious. No, just kidding. Not mad. Bemused.

He arrived this morning, as usual, must have been ten or so. Via the usual route by Mercedes sports car, he can go home to restaurant in ten minutes, passing through the high points of Greenwich Village and SoHo as he speeds along. His car enables him to move throughout the city at the speed of yellow light. He notices, as always, streets and avenues filled to overflowing with *restaurants*. Too many damn restaurants. Who the hell is eating there? Nobody he knows. Nobody anyone knows.

And not just pizza places—though God knows there are too many of them. Ray, Original Ray's, Ray Bari, Dough Ray Me . . . say it loud and there's music playing! In the old days a slice of pizza was something worth caring about. Once upon a time we really did want to know if there was a Good Ray and a Bad Ray. Now it's just Ray, the man who claims to be Italian but is no doubt from Queens just like everybody else, and who makes Greasy Pizza. The other day Bruce had a slice on 8th Street, and it simply amazed him how far the standards had slipped.

"Pizza isn't what it used to be." Bruce loves nothing more than a simple declarative statement. The kind that says, I have extremely high standards when it comes to pizza, and, naturally, to restaurants.

Like for example:

He notices, during his frequent jaunts through lower Manhattan this second month of the first year of the new decade, that everything in the world has recently gone completely to hell in a handbasket.

Or maybe he just said everything sucks.

The other morning, Howard Stern was talking on his very popular morning, drive-time WXRK radio show, to his sidekick, Robin Quivers. After a long pause of silence, he remarked to Robin: *"Everybody's a jerk."* Robin, who normally agrees with Howard about everything, said, "Howard, what am I supposed to say to a statement like *that?"* And yet, Robin, that is precisely what Bruce Goldstein is saying, basically, about the world around him. And you have to admit, it is a popular position these dark days:

You've all heard the chorus.

Movies aren't as good as they were in the 1970s. TV is stupid, except for *thirtysomething*. Magazines aren't what they used to be. Broadway costs too damn much. The cartoons in *The New Yorker* aren't funny anymore. Dry beer is ridiculous. Bubble gum costs fifty cents.

Get me out of here!

But Bruce has a job to do. He is opening up a brand-new restaurant, in the face of the most resounding chorus of backlash on this list: That restaurants are no fun. That we are mad as hell and we are not going to wait at the bar anymore. That we are sick and tired of getting the bad table by the kitchen. That we like getting our dishes at the same time, damnit, not whenever it's convenient for *you*. We want something for our hard-earned money, damnit!

Oh boy does Bruce hear this chorus. It reverberates in his ears at every turn. He must make something of this place, The Falls— he'd *better*—or else he will be just another target of animosity. He sincerely wants his restaurant to be good. And if he doesn't know exactly what he means by *good*—well, he will figure it out. He has some ideas, of course, and they will be presenting themselves at the appropriate time, but for the moment he is content to do the things one does in the normal course of opening a new restaurant—ignoring, for the moment, the highly unusual, profoundly negative and deeply pessimistic mood into which this restaurant will soon be launched.

But he has more important things to think about this Monday morning. Like the fact that he wuz robbed. He's barely even *in* the joint. Practically just signed the lease. Has the insurance even kicked in yet?

"Looks like the thieves threw a brunch." Bruce observes that they had or took several bottles of red wine, including a couple of special vintages. They didn't steal the phone, another big component of Bruce's life, but they did manage to break it. Or was it somebody else? Anyway, it's broken. For some inexplicable reason the thieves left behind some expensive tools, and the radio.

"Maybe some executive winos did it." Bruce is joking around now. This is the bemused part. He cannot comprehend why someone would spare the radio. He lives for music. It goes wherever he goes. Up to the roof of his building when he is catching rays. In the car, on the beach, walking, running, sitting, standing: He must have music.

The opening of The Falls is now less than one month away. Although Bruce knows the dangers of picking an arbitrary opening date—he has yet to get a liquor license; or how about even tables and chairs?— he has happily and irrevocably settled on March 1, 1990, as opening day. A Thursday. You don't want to open a restaurant on a weekend because it might get *too* crazy. Mondays—too slow. Tuesday or Wednesday? Might be okay, but why open on February 28 when March 1, the next day, is a *Thursday?* Thursday is party night.

Today is February 7, 1990.

On this particular morning, The Falls is little more than an empty space. The main dining room is a vast expanse of garbage. The only functional object to speak of is the glass reception desk at the front door, where the phone sits. The bar is littered with paper HAVE A NICE DAY coffee cups. As workmen wander in between ten and eleven this morning, they carry with them the official workman's meal of a buttered bagel, not toasted, and coffee regular. (In New York, for some reason, "regular" means with milk. Whether this means that black coffee is somehow irregular is not clear.) It certainly seems odd for so many people to be bringing food into a restaurant.

Bruce is here to oversee. Over the next three weeks he will be making dozens of choices, answering countless questions that will ultimately chart the course of The Falls. He is . . . what? The owner? Not really. Several people own shares in The Falls equal to Bruce's, so his voting power is not nearly enough to control—although he will, in future months, protest to the contrary. And the president of 150 Varick Inc., the business entity that owns The Falls, is Terry Quinn.

Proprietor is probably the best word for Bruce. Which admittedly is a difference of nuance, since a proprietor is technically an owner; but the word also implies presence, and . . . yes, that's it exactly. Bruce is a *presence*. If you are looking for Bruce these days, you will find him at The Falls. Friends of Bruce stop in to say hello. The phone rings, it's invariably for Bruce. Studies show that the word most frequently uttered at The Falls is Bruce.

At around 11:15, a saleswoman named Betsy comes in looking for Bruce. She is carrying bread. It is actually a comforting sight. Food in The Falls. She represents a company called Eli's Bread, a well-known name in New York City because Eli's last name is Zabar, and Zabar is an *extremely* well-known name in New York City. Zabar is the last name of an old West Side family that owns several blocks of real estate along upper Broadway, including, of course, Zabar's—the enormous, wildly successful gourmet food retailer synonymous with Sunday brunch since the 1960s.

Betsy has bread to sell. She has spoken with Brian Moores about her bread, and of course, he is ready to buy, but he must have the approval of the proprietor, mustn't he?

Bruce, Brian and Betsy greet each other warmly. Betsy is wearing a long black leather coat and black Reeboks. There is a pencil in her hair. She is a saleswoman, and as such she has more than the requisite amount of warmth. Even her bread is warm!

She lays out her goodies on a part of the bar that has yet to be littered with coffee cups and bagel wrappings. Her fingers are experienced at handling large amounts of bread, and so she is able to quickly display loaf after loaf after loaf. Bruce's fingers are experienced at taking samples of food provided by salespersons, and eating them.

He goes straight for a baguette and gnaws off a piece. Bruce is quite fond of bread. As he chews, Betsy goes into her preprogrammed pitch.

"This is our pecan-raisin roll." She speaks proudly of her product as she holds it up for inspection. Bruce takes it from her and bites into it.

"Mmmmm. You could heat them up like muffins."

Brian winces. That is not what a highly trained chef would do with a delicious pecan-raisin roll!

"Here is what we call our heartland roll," Betsy says, showing a large, round, aptly named hunk of bread that Bruce is now fondling.

Bruce turns to Brian and suggests hollowing them out and putting beef stew into them. This is an even more disgusting idea that Brian will try desperately to discourage.

They do agree that The Falls should serve Eli's sourdough baguettes. These are delicious; and as Brian and Bruce munch away, the subject of price comes up. Betsy's non-negotiable price for the baguettes is $2 a dozen.

"Is there any way I can get a better price?" Bruce asks. It is not haggling, exactly, because he has no leverage. He is merely asking because it is some kind of instinct.

Her dark eyebrows rise. "At that price I'm—"

"You're losing money, right?" Bruce smiles. He likes to smile. It is not an act for him to smile. Oh, sure, his smile *means* something; like in this instance, his smile means, You will not leave the premises until I have had my way with you. You will leave here begging for mercy. Please, Mr. Goldstein! I can't lower the price anymore! Help! Stop smiling! But he will not; Bruce has been blessed with pretty good teeth, maybe not *perfect*, but as the front end of a smile they work well. It is not uncommon for people with a broad, healthy smile to be perceived as charming, and Bruce falls squarely into this category.

"You're losing money, right? We'll order tons, and put you out of business." A quick smile combined with a quick wit. Betsy is momentarily rendered speechless.

However, being a shrewd businesswoman—you don't get a long black leather coat for nothing, right?—Betsy will not budge on the price. She has seen a thousand smiles. "How about these health rolls for burgers?" she suggests. Bruce takes another bite. This is turning into lunch.

"Mmmmm. Who's eating burgers and worrying about health?" Bruce wonders aloud. And chews aloud. He's back to the baguette, and may well finish the whole damn thing. After all, he likes Eli's bread, he likes this lady in the leather coat, and he likes this baguette.

"Brioche buns . . . organic rye . . . sourdough." Bruce dictates his bread order and she jots it down. Hands are shaken. Loaves are left. A deal is done.

After she leaves, Bruce turns to Brian and says, "Good bread is important." Brian agrees.

/Brian has completed the first draft of the menu, and will give it to Bruce today. It is divided into two categories: From the Grill, and The Lighter Side.

Bruce has always intended to give The Falls menu a healthy tone. He has encouraged Brian to exclude all cream-based dishes, including soups. This will be part of what makes The Falls special. People are sick and tired of cream. They want cream out of their lives forever. They do not want to be fat.

Bruce knows this, because he was once fat himself.

Sometime during the mid-1980s—no one can pin down the date exactly, though it definitely coincided with his ownership of Central Falls—Bruce got fat. Not overweight. Not paunchy. One hates to report these sorts of embarrassing personal details, but to understand exactly why this man is, now, so passionately opposed to butter and cream, one must know that, yes, Bruce used to be fat.

Fat enough to be nicknamed the Fat Man.

"We could never tell him that he was getting fat," remembers one former longtime employee of Central Falls. "I was shocked. We used to tease him. He'd call right before he'd leave his apartment. We'd be setting up, doing stuff. And he'd call and we'd all scurry. 'Beware, the Fat Man's coming. The Fat Man's gonna show up.' But never, never never would we say that to his face."

But fat he was, and fat he remained—in all ways except his mind. It was widely believed that Bruce could not acknowledge being fat, could not accept it . . . despite overwhelming physical evidence to the contrary.

To look at Bruce now—even when he's munching, no, make that gnawing at baguettes—it is hard to imagine him in the mold of Pavarotti or Prudhomme. The Fat Man! It seems ridiculous now. Bruce is your garden-variety middleweight, a cream sauce guy. He pores over pasta cookbooks like a five-year-old reads *Playboy*, touching the pages, wondering if the food could ever taste as magical as it looks.

It also seems so sweet, so innocent . . .

But a former Fat Man knows what can happen. A few too many fettuccines; a well-marbled steak or five; crème brûlée after crème brûlée after crème brûlée; watch how fat a man can get! No, it will not do for The Falls to be anything but a health-conscious food emporium. Brian's mandate must be to remove all temptation from the menu. *I will not become the Fat Man again,* he thinks. No butter, no cream.

Here is what Brian has come up with, as it appeared on a typed piece of paper he brought with him from home this morning, and proofread this morning on the bus.

FROM THE GRILL

Atlantic Swordfish
Golden Trout
Pacific Dolphin
Yellowfin Tuna
Icelandic Langoustines (with white truffle virgin olive oil) with

choice of sauce: pico de gallo; chien; oriental black bean relish, Provençale [crossed out in pencil], other sauce

Capon Breast, marinated with pesto and served with angelhair pasta
Baby Boneless Chicken glazed with fresh herbs
New York Strip Steak with handcut fries
Prime Lamb Chops with rosemary and dijon mustard sauce
  above served with choice of starch and vegetable

THE LIGHTER SIDE

Pheasant Pot Pie with wild mushrooms
Buffalo Burgers topped with choice of three cheeses
Open-faced Chicken Salad on 7-grain bread with eggless mayonnaise
Vegetable Plate
Agnolotti with tomato and wild boar prosciutto
Squid Ink Capellini with garlic, tomato and olive oil, hot peppers

DINNER MENU

SALADS
House Salad: romaine, Boston, and radicchio with house vinaigrette.
Arugula and Asiago: arugula with shaved Asiago cheese dressed with extra virgin olive oil and champagne vinegar
Oriental Grilled Chicken Salad: watercress, romaine, snow peas, scallions and grilled chicken breast with soy sauce, ginger and sesame oil
Endive and Walnut: Belgian endive and chopped walnut and strawberry vinaigrette [marked "OUT"]
Low Fat Mozzarella with red and yellow pear tomatoes and braised leeks (virgin olive oil)

APPETIZERS
Pacific Oysters on the half shell: varieties vary with availability
Grilled Sea Scallops with fennel and saffron compote [crossed out: marked "special"]
Crabmeat Wontons with sweet and hot pepper relish
Peppered Smoked Salmon with leeks vinaigrette
Asparagus hot or chilled
  hot: virgin olive oil and lemon

chilled: house vinaigrette
Marinated Pure Beef Tenderloin with three peppercorns, olive oil
   and grated Romano
Soup of the Day
Hot appetizer?

"That's it." Brian is going over it one last time. He stands at the bar. He has cleared a space for himself amid the cups and wrappers. There are other changes he wants to make, but he cannot find a pen or pencil. Who keeps taking all the pens and pencils?

"It's not the menu *I'd* put together," he says, fingering the document one last time, "but it's not my restaurant."

The capon breast in particular bothered Brian. It was, quite simply, not his kind of dish. "Bruce served that at Central Falls. It just doesn't fit on this menu. I guarantee you, it'll be gone before we open."

There goes his hand again. Through the hair, through the hair; he can't help himself. It happens whenever his conversation pitch reaches any sort of passionate level, which is maybe once every ten minutes. This habit has ended up leaving Brian with a sort of permanent cowlick in the front. In 1964 Brian would have been described as a mop top.

"This place . . ." He has to look around it as he says this, maybe just to remind himself that, yes, this *is* a restaurant, after all. "This place will be getting a lot of press. The reviewers will be all over it. And they'll pick at things like that." That capon breast, he means. He taps his finger against the menu.

Bruce wanders by—something he does so well; wander by—and Brian hands him the document for a quick look. His eyes stop at the mention of Icelandic langoustines.

"Better say *fresh*," Bruce says. "When they see Icelandic, they think frozen."

By the way, Bruce: Who are *they*?

He has something he wants to sell here in this room, and it has nothing to do with langoustines, or brioche buns, or the price of eggs in SoHo.

He will make these choices today, and tomorrow, and for the next three weeks; he will pick the wines and the flowers and the plates and the cups. He will order the light bulbs and flush the toilets and run his index finger along the bar. He will do everything a proprietor is supposed to do. This is right; this is what he is paid to do.

Bruce says there will be something here on March 1, 1990, that cannot be ordered from the store, or found in the Bowery, or cooked on a stove. Not everyone who comes to The Falls will notice it. Quite possibly no one will. Bruce is, after all, a man of many secrets, and this is one of them.

But it will be here.

"Listen," he says.

HEY BARTENDER

SEVEN

Legend has it that somebody once forked over $10,000 simply for the privilege of being a bartender at a fancy New York restaurant called the River Cafe.

Said ten grand went directly into the pocket of the former bartender, who then recommended the well-oiled replacement to his boss, who then hired him.

Within three months, said replacement earned back his ten grand, plus another, plus another, plus another.

Think about it. You give a bartender a buck every time he pours you and your pals a round of drinks. So does everybody else. That adds up to a lot of bucks, perhaps ten thousand bucks if you're behind the right bar at the right time.

Which is why everybody who has arrived at The Falls today, in response to its ad for waiters and bartenders in the current issue of *Backstage*, has indicated to management that they would prefer to be hired as a bartender, although, of course, they would consider a waiter's job, naturally, not wanting to seem *picky* or anything.

Kimberly Jones isn't into picky and for the moment she gets to choose who shall get hired and who shall not; who shall pour drinks and who shall wait tables; who shall carry and who shall wash; who shall wear miniskirts and who shall wear pants. Kimberly heard that *Backstage*, the bible for would-be actors and actresses, would reach New York's finest service personnel—the supposed army of glamorous show biz types willing to serve food for tips and a small amount of cash up front.

But it isn't working out, now, is it?

Kimberly has positioned herself at a corner banquette—boy, wouldn't it be nice if there was one lousy table or chair in this joint already!—and has folded her legs neatly so as to balance a pad of paper on her knee. This will enable her to properly peruse résumés and make occasional notes.

So in walks applicant ... no, make that supplicant number one. Eric Stern. (No real names here, of course.) Is this the last job in America or something? This guy is actually leaning toward Kimberly as he walks across the empty restaurant toward her, clutching his bulging briefcase under his arm (what could possibly be in that thing?), his eyes darting around the room, noting (as they all do) the vast expanse of bar and salivating at the wonderfully enticing prospect of all those drinks, all those tips, all that cash.

Down, boy. Be subtle. Kimberly is watching you.

"It's not as if I'm tied to bartending," Eric says. It's the first thing he says after sitting down, handing Kimberly his résumé and watching her eyes scan the record of bars tended over the years. Pathetic. Of *course* you're tied to bartending. Admit it. His hairline is receding; he is old. Too old. He does have a pleasant face, no argument there. However, The Falls is not about Pleasant. It is about long legs and square jaws and black shirts.

Eric knows this. He is sweating now as he watches Kimberly cross him off her mental list. Go for it, man! Try something else!

"I'm not tied to days or nights." Okay, okay ... flexible. That's good. She's warming.

Kimberly has spotted a relevant detail on Eric's résumé. He has been through the opening of a restaurant. When you get right down to it, that's something Kimberly hasn't been through. Uh-oh. He's more qualified than her. Forget it, buster.

"Yes ... that's a nice place." Kimberly nods. She continues to read. She must be reading the part about my acting, he thinks. Better say something. Better cover my flank.

"I've been an actor ... I'm not into that now. I'm looking for a management position."

She smiles sweetly. *I'm* the goddamned manager around here, Kimberly thinks. Plus she has noticed something else: this guy's a father. He has an actual child. While this may be very sweet and lovely, and it may be something Kimberly wants to pursue as a line of conversation, it most definitely removes Eric from consideration as an employee of The Falls. We don't want any Daddies around here. Bruce is Daddy enough. He is Daddy Dearest. Big Daddy.

"Thanks for coming in, Eric. You really have excellent qualifications. We don't know exactly what our needs are but we should have it worked out soon and we'll call you. Do we have your number?"

In other words: Sorry, Eric. Go home and play with your kid.

Kimberly is momentarily discouraged. This is not working out. She has not taken a single note. And by the way, where is everybody? Where are the multitudes of people we had been led to expect from an ad in *Backstage* that cost $400 and change?

In walks supplicant number two. This job seeker has taken a different approach. She is wearing black leggings, calf-high black boots and a black leather jacket that offsets her pale, luminous skin and jet black hair. As she walks over toward Kimberly, Bruce eyes her figure from behind. He is pleased. He smiles and makes a gesture toward her that Kimberly notes. It says, in essence, *You got the job.*

/It has been decided already that the bar at The Falls will be managed by a man named Henry.

There is this theory: When you meet a man named Henry, and he likes to be called Henry, you know you have met someone slightly out of the ordinary but nonetheless interesting and probably very, very smart.

When you meet Henry Hauck, you know your theory is correct.

What does Henry Hauck do? He opens bars. This is not a living, you think to yourself. And you are right, which is why Henry Hauck has been living on or near the edge of fiscal respectability for years now. One suspects that Henry Hauck has a very bad filing system and probably doesn't save his receipts for unreimbursed business expenses, even though he has quite a few.

Henry Hauck is what you would call gangly, if you liked that word; slender is what his mother would call him. He's tall and pale with deep-set eyes that do a lot of staring.

The man can *pour*. He knows a shot, could measure one in his sleep; probably has.

Started bartending in Boulder. Cool town. Mork and Mindy. Good-looking girls. Everybody there drinks to get warm, or to get hot.

Moved to New York City. Early 1980s. It was all happening then. Drinking, dancing, snorting, fucking. Henry Hauck in hog heaven. He liked it behind the bar.

By 1990 he was bored shitless, but what was he going to do? He needed money. He knew the tricks. His pal Brian from L'Acajou told him about Bruce and Bruce about him, which is how it works, and he got the job at The Falls.

No application necessary.

Now here it is, practically Henry's first day, and already it's beginning. This guy Bruce has got some crazy ideas about how to run a restaurant. Henry will listen, of course, having all those years of experience as an employee. He knows his place. But he is also one of those people you meet practically every day in this business, the type that say to themselves, *I can do this.* And occasionally add: *I will do this.* It is believed that if you repeat this enough times, someone will believe you and give you the money to open a restaurant yourself. It has been known to happen. And Henry, being a bit of an entrepreneur, thinks it will happen to him. He has been around cash, this one, and he has learned some valuable lessons, the most important one being, *get some.*

Meanwhile, he must listen to Bruce ramble on—God, is he tedious! —about the nature of drinking in America.

"You know what I like?" Bruce asks. Henry is behind the bar. Bruce leans up against it.

"No, Bruce, I don't."

"Hennessy VSOP. You'll enjoy pushing it." Bruce is referring to an expensive brand of cognac, the kind that is special-ordered after dinner by those with *class.* "You go to a French restaurant," Bruce goes on, "and you know what they got?"

Henry is apparently not one for rhetorical questions.

Bruce continues. "They got Rémy. You ask for another one? They got Rémy." Rémy is short for Rémy-Martin, a perfectly good cognac, not fancy but good. Plenty good for Henry. You can see plainly on Henry's face his response to this suggestion, observation, whatever it is, and it is something ugly. Henry must restrain himself. The opening of The Falls is still three weeks away, and he would like to hang on to the job at least that long, maybe longer.

Fortunately, Bruce has been distracted by Franco, the painter, who is working on the trim at the ceiling. He is a hardworking man in his twenties who cannot speak a single word of English. He understands nothing, which is probably why he works so hard.

"Stop dripping the paint!" Bruce yells. There is no indication that Franco either knows or cares that he has been spoken to.

"I've got to learn Spanish," Bruce mutters, walking away from the bar toward the door. "I can speak a little French . . . but nobody French does any work."

Bruce disappears.

This happened yesterday, too, and the day before that. In the middle of a sentence, as a thought trails off, suddenly, without a trace, Bruce disappears. He gets in his car, drives off, and doesn't return for a half hour at least, maybe forty-five minutes.

Is he catching some rays at the tanning salon?

Is he eating a cheeseburger deluxe at some greasy spoon?

Is he going home to watch *Jeopardy?*

For the first time, but certainly not the last, the question is asked:

Where in the hell is Bruce?

AMERICAN BUFFALO BURGER

EIGHT

There comes a time in a restaurant's life when one must set the price.

It is an act of colossal egotism. Oh, sure, you can convince yourself it has something to do with food costs and percentage of revenues and projected incomes. Go right ahead. You're kidding yourself. Maybe there are restaurants, somewhere out there, where we do not know, and they are consulting mainframe computers and Lotus spreadsheets and profit gurus on the proper price for red snapper almondine. Proper meaning maximum, of course. The maximum price we can charge without fear. Remember this: All restaurants adhere to an important economic principle, which is simply, How much can I get away with charging for this crap?

Such as the day in May of 1991 when Michael's Restaurant in midtown Manhattan set the price of two eggs scrambled at fourteen bucks. For shame! Were they thinking, twelve dollars just won't be enough to cover our monthly nut? Ten bucks sounds cheap, Michael thinks. It insults our customers. Those bastards, do they honestly think so little of the breakfast-buying population? In the restaurant business, arrogance is bliss.

Questions, questions. That's all it is. Nobody has any answers. There are no rules. No government agency regulates the profit margin, thank

God. Go buy eggs and scramble 'em yourself, Michael's is saying. See if we care.

But most restaurants never quite reach such heights of attitude. They seek a middle ground between ego and success. They calculate positive vibes into the price. There has to be some imagination involved, after all; before a restaurant opens its doors, there's no way to know whether anyone will open their wallets and bleed a little. That's what you want, by the way: blood. You want to see them sweat. And that's *after* their little wait at the bar. Drips of sweat must fall onto the menu itself. Everything must be slightly more expensive than it should be, *would* be if you were cooking at home. For this there is a formula. Not cooking at home is a numerical factor to be multiplied times the wholesale cost. Having a fellow human being ask you what you want to eat, write it down, deliver your dinner and—if they're at all decent—refill your waterglass; now that's got to be worth something, right? Of course right. Pay up.

Which is why, when Bruce and Brian sat down to discuss the most sensitive issue of money and its relationship to meat, carbohydrates and cheese, and how much of it they would be asking for, some mighty bizarre things got said.

The discussion began simply enough, in the basement. Bruce and Brian had, by this time, formed a relationship that enabled decisions to be made quickly. This resulted from Brian's amiable nature. He didn't mind agreeing. Seemed to prefer it, in fact. Obviously, his thoughts diverged significantly from his actions; if they didn't he wouldn't even *be* here.

For example, french fries do not figure in his thoughts. "I have served *enough* french fries in my time," he remarked once. But he was to serve many thousands more at The Falls. He had accepted this already, resigned himself to it. He would make them with skill and serve them with pride.

Therefore he would not like to charge money for them. They would be his little gift to The Falls. Take my fries, please. They're good.

Bruce has a different idea. Which is not to say he disagrees with Brian. Don't forget, he likes to give things away whenever possible. And french fries rank high, probably throughout the Western world, among the foodstuffs most frequently provided at no charge to paying customers. But don't forget that Bruce would like to make as much money as possible, very quickly.

How to reconcile? This tortures Bruce. He must think. But he must also speak. So, rather conveniently, he thinks while he speaks.

"I think," Bruce said, in trying to calculate the proper price for a chicken sandwich, and explaining to Brian why it should be $6.50 and not $7.50 and definitely *not* serving french fries for free along with it, and developing a larger philosophy to govern the use of french fries in general, "We ought to start figuring out whether we want to start having people pay for french fries or not pay for french fries. I think that they should be paying for french fries."

Bruce has once again put his finger on the pulse of humanity. He has raised a question and damn well answered it.

"I'll tell you one thing," Brian says. You know he'll probably tell you three things, but who cares, he's a nice guy. "I really don't want to get into the deal where I'm making french fries all the time and custom orders for people. That hangs us up when we're busy."

"You mean side orders?"

"If you have a side order written on the menu that's one thing," Brian says. Oh, he's got this all worked out, doesn't he. "We know that, we got it. But we designate what things get it, so that's always a constant. And then if you want to have it as a side deal."

This won't do for Bruce. "I think nothing should get french fries, except the steak," he says.

These men come from different worlds. In Brian's world there are plates and plates of pommes frites. They come free of charge.

"And the burger," Brian counsels.

"And the burger. That's it."

"And then," Brian says, and *then*—"just put it as a side order."

"Yeah."

"Yeah," Brian says, relieved, finally, to have gotten through to this knucklehead, " 'cause the least amount of things is easier."

Now Bruce's mind has gotten what it needs: an electrical charge that comes from challenge. He must be right. As the boss, he must make decisions, act forthright, *command*. He must have theories. Ramble. Pontificate. Justify every dollar he wants to get.

"I think it's crazy," Bruce says. "Sandwiches? If you're going to have those big sandwiches, I don't think the sandwiches should get anything with 'em. A sandwich for $6.50—"

Hey wait a minute! "That's a good price," Brian says evenly. He has worked all this out, too, remember. "You can hardly get one at a deli—"

"Yeah. That's lunch. That's what lunch is."

"Yeah. Exactly."

Thank goodness we're agreed on that!

"For that stinking sandwich that I paid in that sandwich place on Greenwich Avenue," Bruce says, "is $5.50. Tuna and nothing. Six dollars for turkey and cheese." Brian wants to interrupt. He leans forward, the words ready to fly out of his mouth: *That's exactly my point, Bruce! Let's beat the delis at their own game!* But he is not allowed to speak. Bruce continues: "Let me ask you this. Hold it, hold it, hold it. Let me give you a question."

"Yeah." I should stop being so fucking amiable, Brian thinks.

"You want to do the grilled chicken sandwich and have a regular sandwich like smoked turkey breast or something like that? Smoked turkey breast and avocado, something like that—as a special? Or do you want to have a sandwich like a smoked turkey breast and the chicken be the special?"

That Brian can deal with. "Well," he says expansively, "I'll tell you what would be cooler. You got a chicken salad sandwich already. Now I think it's a little redundant to put a grilled chicken salad. Why don't you have grilled smoked chicken or something? Or something a little more interesting? I don't think we're gonna need two chicken sandwiches. Two out of four sandwiches—"

"You know what? Take off the hot sandwich."

"And just do it as a special?"

"Do that as a special. Come up with an interesting sandwich like smoked turkey breast with a nice cheese and avocado."

Okay, okay . . . but Brian cannot resist a little dig. "West SoHo style," he says, smiling, knowing that Bruce loves to think of this location as something he calls "West SoHo," but alas, nobody else does. Brian knows that Bruce would like The Falls to be the anchor of West SoHo, the watering hole to an entire new neighborhood. But Brian also knows that there is no such thing as West SoHo. It is a figment of Bruce's fertile imagination. Still, he will be pushing it. Yes he will. And he will be damned if he will laugh at or ridicule his idea.

Bruce says simply, "I think it's a great sandwich." He will not be taking any shit, thank you.

/In the restaurant business, there is an axiom that applies in every case, except those where it doesn't.

The axiom is, if you cover your nut at lunch, dinner will be your profit. The way to make it work is to get yourself a large, steady lunch business that comes back every day. Those regular customers will pay your bills. They will be the customers you depend on. It's only fair, when you think about it; the people who depend most on you—the lunchers who need their entrées fast; the regulars who want the same food every day, no changes, no exceptions—become the people you depend on the most. This business reality shapes the strategy of every restaurant in the world, from the Four Seasons to the Four Brothers. You scratch my back, I'll scratch yours.

So when it comes to pricing lunch, Bruce and Brian share a desire to accommodate. Why not be nice to the lunch crowd? Let's give 'em cheaper prices for the same food. The sandwiches will be cheap, of course, but so will the steak. There will have to be ways to make money, but they will be slippery, hard to notice. There will be nuances—fifty cents here, a dollar there. Nothing visible to the naked eye.

Dinner is different. Land of the Big Money.

"Oysters vary with prices," Brian says. He wants to be fair. "You want to put, 'by the piece'?"

"Yeah," says Bruce. That's how everybody does it. That's how *we'll* do it.

"I can tell you they're going to be about fifty-five cents apiece wholesale right now." Brian is attempting to set the tone. "You're never gonna make money on 'em," he says.

"It's a pain in the ass." Bruce gets the hint. His head hurts. "I think $1.75—"

The strategy worked! Bruce can be manipulated, just as Brian thought. "That's what I would go with. That's what you used to go with as well. You even went higher than that at one time."

If we keep going, Brian thinks, maybe this will actually work out. "Peppered smoked salmon . . . it's $12.95 a pound, you're going to get less than a two-ounce portion. You're going to get—"

"More than a two-ounce—"

"That's a lot," Brian says. "I would go $5.50."

"I want people to get this, and that's a dinner for some people," Bruce explains.

"I'm going to make it $6 then."

You understand! "Yeah," Bruce says.

The rhythm has been established. Charge more and you will make more. "The crabmeat wontons are relatively cheap," Brian says in a quick gear-switch. "Crabmeat's not cheap but we don't use that much in it."

"Four dollars?"

"Four-fifty," Brian counters.

Kimberly Jones, who has been paying respectful silence throughout these high-level negotiations, swings her head around. "I'd say you could probably get five on those," she offers.

"No—four-fifty," Bruce says. Kimberly, take a note—you're not here to give your opinion. To Brian he says, "You're gonna get six, right?"

He nods. "I wrap 'em on my fingers, so they look like a tortellini, almost. You know what I'm talking about?"

"They're not like that big greasy thing." Bruce shakes his hands as though they are suddenly swathed in grease.

"No," Brian says. "We don't want a humpy thing."

Bruce continues his questioning on the quantity. "How many do you get, like, six or eight on a plate?"

"Yeah, like eight."

"Okay," he says, "and you put what kinda sauce with those?"

What is this—restaurant school? They're crabmeat wontons, boss. No milk on these babies. "Hot and sweet pepper, diced up real fine. It's like a relish. It's a hot relish. It's good."

"All right."

"So we're saying what for that? Four-fifty? We can make money on that, for sure."

Oddly enough, Brian has proved to be the capitalist profitmonger in this discussion. It's not that his income depends on that of the restaurant. If anything, bargains would work to his advantage—the bang-for-the-buck equation being among the most popular in recessionary times. But he realizes how important it is to cover the wholesale cost of food. Everything on the menu, with the possible exception of steaks and chops, should be at least three times the wholesale cost, otherwise you're going to go broke. And hey, if you can charge an arm and a leg for a breast or a thigh . . .

But meat is hard to price. More people eat meat than anything else. People like a good steak. They love a cheap good steak.

"The marinated tenderloin of beef. What did you used to get for carpaccio? Seven dollars?"

"More, we used to get."

"We can establish a price right here and now," Brian says. "What do you think? I say we go at least $7.50."

"I got a feeling that'll cost you at least $2, $2.50 a portion."

"It'll probably cost $2 a portion. And then you figure you probably want to make 30 percent—that'd be $6.75, so you want to make more than 30 percent on it."

"Let's go $8 on it." Bruce says. "I'll tell you why. That's a dinner."

"Yeah it is. And people—"

"People will have that as dinner."

A system has been developed. First, Bruce says what he wants to do. Then Brian explains whether it is something they should or should not do. Then Bruce says what he will do. This will often have nothing to do with what Brian has said. Unless they are in agreement; then it will. It is clear that inside Bruce's head an image is growing. It is of The Falls at its peak. People are ordering appetizers and steaks and french fries. It really doesn't matter, does it? As long as the room is full and the plates are white and the skirts are short and the music is loud and the tables are black.

/Can you fool some of the people all of the time?

"You know," Brian says, as they work their way through the dinner entrées on the menu, "theoretically you shouldn't have your highest price last."

He points to his list. At the moment, the $18 swordfish is the final item. This will be a mistake. Bruce appears unconvinced, though. He has a look that perfectly conveys this: a blank, head-scratching stare directed at the wall. Brian is not terribly good at pulling the focus toward himself. Too damned sweet.

"That's sort of—you should throw it in the middle."

Finally Bruce eyeballs the list. Does he really care about what goes where? "All right, throw it in the middle then," he says. "All right."

Victory at last! It's not much, but with this guy you gotta take it wherever you can get it. So Brian is feeling generous. "I can do the trout for fifteen bucks. Easy. I can even do it for $14."

"Let's do $14 for the trout. I want trout to be like chicken."

Trout like chicken? Brian ignores him and presses happily on.

"You're going to get away with reasonable food costs," Brian says. "We don't have a big expense on expensive ingredients. Tuna's running fairly high now, it's about six and a half a pound now, it'll go down to four by mid-season, by April or May."

"Everybody in this fuckin' city is getting $22 to $25 for tuna. I'd like to sell it for $16, $15."

"*Sixteen* dollars."

"I really would." Bruce, you're a wild man . . . $16 for tuna! You're a revolutionary!

Anticipating the dangers of this strategy, Brian nods gently but adds, "Lamb's gonna have to be $18. I think we have no choice on the lamb. Lamb has skyrocketed."

Eighteen, okay, all right, but—"We're not going for that New Zealand frozen shit, are we?"

"No," Brian says. "We're going for good."

More fish, lots of fish, too many fish . . . will it matter if it's cheap? Does the price of mahimahi vary according to demand? Do people know a good deal on Icelandic langoustines if they see it? Bruce loves fish, loves too many fish; but lurking in his mind is a vision of what all these numbers mean:

Nothing.

"Here's what I'd like to do," he says. He wants to get this vision off his chest. He wants Brian to know what will happen, what to expect. What he will do.

"Here's what usually happens. You open, you do this. Your realistic food costs come in and you say, well shit, this is stupid, this is costing so much a pound, and this is costing us more a pound, and we're charging the same money, and you'll make some adjustments."

Brian hears him. He has been buying food for years, wholesale, retail, you name it he's bought it. "The best rule of thumb . . . I've maintained as low as 33 percent in French restaurants, it's hard to do, let me tell you. What you gotta do is take everything times three. Your costs. Forget about labor. It's negligible. Usually. Unless it's something really complicated. So take it times three and I'll give you 33 percent food cost on it. Right? And that's in the ballpark. You're gonna have a couple items you're gonna make a killing on."

"Like chicken."

"Pasta, chicken, soup . . ."

Yes! Pasta, chicken and soup. Bruce and Brian are finally singing the same song. Brian cannot resist throwing in a little professional expertise. "Those will accommodate your more expensive things like lamb that you're not going to make as big a profit on . . ."

Listen to these boys, horns in hand, Bruce leading the way: "I'll bet you could see lamb in a restaurant for $24. I want to ruin the restaurants that are doing it for $24. I want people to say, what am I doing paying this over here when I could pay for it over there. And theoretically if your drink prices are priced where you're getting a good markup, of four or five to one on drinks, you'll make it up. I think the key is not to look for one shot for nine o'clock for people to eat. It's to get people in here all the time."

"Now the lamb," says the ever-practical executive chef. "We're going to have to go $18 on the lamb. People are willing to pay it. That's the deal on lamb. That's the most expensive thing we're going to have, and that's not bad."

"And when you describe it," Bruce says, "I want you to say what kind of lamb and all that stuff. What is it, local? That New Zealand frozen shit is just a promotion. It's all frozen."

"It bleeds too much when you cook it."

"It bleeds, it's full of *water*."

"Shell steak's gonna run us about $2.55 untrimmed for shells," Brian says. "By the time I trim it it's gonna cost us $5 a pound. A little over. All right? A ten-ounce steak?"

"A twelve-ounce steak."

"Actually it's gonna cost us about $5 for a steak. We could do it at $15. I'd go $16, but you can do it at $15."

"That's with the fries, right?" Bruce and his french fries; give the man what he wants. Brian nods.

"Sixteen dollars. I want it less. That's what I want. I want people to have a nice steak and fries for $16 and a glass of wine, and I also want to appeal to those people that are comin' in alone, who are sitting at the bar."

There Bruce goes again . . . lapsing into reverie. Now he sees the bar. Long and strong. Men and women filling the stools. Laughing and talking. Drinking and eating. There he is, at the end of it, watching, waiting. Some nights he will be hungry, and he will want an appetizer, maybe two, perhaps even an entrée. He will order himself dinner and eat it, right smack at the bar, surrounded by people—happy, comfortable people who come here night after night, for the steaks and the girls and the drinks and the music.

And the french fries will be free.

/All that remains now is the chicken.

"The poussin, the baby chickens, are going to cost us about $3.50 apiece," Brian says. "So I would say you can go $15."

Bruce shakes his head. "Fourteen."

"Let's think about that. I'd go $15." Brian's had pretty good luck. Now he's going to try toe-to-toe combat.

"Fifteen?"

Bang! You're dead. "We'll go $14," Brian says. He knows when he has no chance. "I can do it," he adds with supreme confidence. And he can.

Bruce wants to explain. He has just vetoed his chef, he knows a toe or two has been stepped on, and he'd like to give a reason.

"You know why? Chicken is—let me tell you something. Here's what's going to happen. This is a crazy thing. Women go out on a date—and *you* can bear this out," he says, gesturing at Kimberly Jones, "sometimes they're thoughtful enough to always order the lowest-priced thing on the menu."

"I always do," Kimberly purrs, and you can believe she does. "I *do*."

"They *do*." Bruce has been affirmed. "They always order the lowest-priced thing. It usually ends up being the chicken. I think that there should be another entrée that should be the same price as the chicken—"

Kimberly says, "I agree completely—"

". . . so that women don't have to feel that they have to order the cheapest thing, it'll always be chicken. They always look to it and say it's the lowest—"

"All right," Brian says wearily. He's not here for a seminar on what women want. "That's fine, but you got a little deal here that's not normal."

"You got a piece of fish here that's fifteen bucks." Bruce is guessing.

"I got one for fourteen bucks," Brian says.

"You got a fourteen-buck?"

"And there'll be specials for that."

"Make this $14.50 for the chicken," Bruce says, before returning to his initial point for a final hammering in. "I'd like to really see women order better food for less money. But it really happens . . . I've noticed it, it's unbelievable. Especially on Valentine's Day you look at the orders and it's always chicken-pasta-chicken-pasta for the women. Chicken and pasta, chicken and pasta."

Brian had better agree or he'll be here all night. "That's a generalization but you're right," he says.

"Except," Bruce adds softly, too soft to be sure he knows what he means . . . "except for some kind of women."

The meeting is over. Brian has to go home. There's a bus to catch; a child to play with; a wife to kiss.

WHAT ELSE IS A CEILING

BUT A WALL

TURNED UPSIDE DOWN?

NINE

Matchboxes. Phone booths. Candles. Light bulbs. Forks and knives. Cups and saucers. Things must be bought. Deals must be struck. Cash must be spent.

The phone man comes. He needs no identification. You know him because he has a big huge yellow phone strapped to his leg. The phone man always makes it look easy. He knows which colored wire goes where. Bruce is happy to see the phone man, we know he is extremely passionate about phones, almost as passionate as the phone man himself, probably. Bruce would have made a great phone man.

Bruce explains to the phone man that his phone was stolen. Which it was. Except it wasn't. A phone was broken during the robbery so it was deemed wiser by somebody to report it stolen. However, it was not stolen, it was broken, and Bruce would now like the phone man to please fix it.

The phone man shakes his head.

"I'm just here to tell you," the phone man says, "that if the phone was stolen then we need a police report or we can't do anything." Is *that* not a good answer. "Okay," seethes Bruce. He is burning now. "It *isn't* stolen. Here it is. My phone. It isn't working. Can you fix it?" Bruce hands the phone man his telephone, a standard black-and-gray

AT&T phone that sits at a slight angle to a flat surface, an exemplary instrument in all ways except that it doesn't work.

No, explains the phone man, he cannot fix it. The phone man sees he is needed. He is asserting himself. You have to admire just how well adjusted he is. "Because you reported it this way. I'm just here to *tell* you what you should do to get the phone fixed."

"So," Bruce says, "you're telling me that the truth is screwing me up here." The truth being that the phone was broken, and the sad reality being that the phone man is unlikely to provide much help.

"That's right," the phone man responds evenly. He is trained to avoid confrontation. Phone men and women rarely lose their tempers. Something to do with their wiring.

Bruce stands up. Until now he has been sitting on a stool behind the glass counter at the entrance. He presents a more imposing figure when standing, he is six foot three, remember, and even at his trimmest, weighing somewhere in the vicinity of two hundred pounds. He smiles a kind of half smile. It is not meant as a friendly gesture. He then walks out from behind the partition and moves around the phone man. Back and forth. Hard to follow. He's playing with his hair. There is some reason to believe that Bruce might be on the verge of a temper tantrum. The hair, the pacing, the smile . . . but he holds it in. He knows that he will get more from this phone man by the art of gentle persuasion than other, more hostile tactics.

"Here's who to call," the phone man is saying. "This man will help you."

Bruce is pleased. That's all he really wanted; a name, a phone number, some way to cut through the crap.

The phone man leaves, the matchbox guy comes.

This guy works upstairs. No surprise here. The Falls is conveniently located in New York's printing district, and printers make matchboxes. When he heard The Falls was moving into the space downstairs, he made a visit and offered Bruce a nice deal on matches. Bruce gave him the official logo for The Falls—a light brown background with black lettering and a green waterfall design. The matchbox guy made a nice little box, nothing fancy, with one-sided striking capability. The address and phone number on the back.

"It's glued by hand," the guy says. "It'll look better when it's glued by machine."

"I like it *this* way," Bruce says.

"Sorry, I'm not gonna glue all your matchboxes by hand," the guy says.

Inside the box are several examples of the kind of matchstick that

will be provided. They are short, wooden sticks with a green bulb at
the top. Bruce fingers the sticks, attempting to count them.

"What is the least amount of sticks I can put into a box?" Bruce
asks. Two dozen is the answer, an amount that sounds about right to
Bruce. No reason to give extra matches away. He gives the go-ahead
to the production of a thousand matchboxes. They *have* to be ready by
March 1, he says. Oh yes, Bruce, they will, the match guy promises. It
is too early for Bruce to panic, but you can tell this guy isn't really
sure that he can deliver, and Bruce isn't sure either, quite frankly.

He has other things to worry about.

He has made a list of them. He is prone to making lists on a small
lined yellow pad that he keeps inside of a black vinyl notebook. He
tends to scribble thoughts in no particular order, to remind himself of
what needs to be done. The only trouble with his lists is that he sometimes forgets to consult them. But they are there when he needs them,
and today he has made a list of several matters that need tending to.

BRUCE'S LIST

table for computer—18 x 18
candles—votive
change bulbs from flood to spots
outside—from frosted to clear
glass or black ashtrays?

Lights. Colors. Shapes. Sizes. Bruce has his little obsessions, yes,
and like everyone they are often most clearly revealed in the little
scraps of paper that surround him. Writers stuff their little notes in a
drawer and collect them years later into coherent form. Bruce jots
constantly, but he cannot afford to wait more than a day or two before
consulting his notes. The shape and style of the light bulbs are of
utmost importance to his vision of The Falls. Likewise the ashtrays,
the computer table, the waiters and waitresses, the matches . . . likewise everything that is not colorless or shapeless or lifeless.

/The Bowery is a part of Manhattan most commonly associated with
bums. To a lesser extent it is associated with restaurant and kitchen
supplies.

"Today we should go to the Bowery," Bruce says.

It is February 15, 1990. Two weeks away from opening night. Time
to start thinking about food and plates and glassware. Brian and

Henry and Bruce are beginning to sweat. Not a lot; two weeks is a long time in this business, you could open overnight if you had to, but two weeks can also be short, painfully short, when you want to do something right. And the personality feature that links these three men—they otherwise share nothing in common, *nothing*—is that they care deeply about doing things right. Each of them in his own way. Perfectionists. Determined and obstinate and dedicated and firm. You will not get any sloppy work past these guys. Perhaps they respect this characteristic, or perhaps they are each so determined that they see the others as lesser mortals. This remains to be seen.

They exit The Falls at 11:30 in the morning for the journey to the Bowery, a short, bumpy cab ride away. They pull up in front of Metro, a wholesale outfit with dozens of varieties of plates, glasses and other necessary materials that they intend to buy.

They are expected.

They move. They grab. They touch. A glass is held up to the light. A plate is turned over and inspected.

A salesman greets them.

"You know who we are," says Bruce.

"We come in droves," Brian says.

Bruce holds up a glass. "You have a highball glass that's similar to this one?"

Henry closes one eye and squints through the other. As the bartender he intends to be extremely particular about the quality of the glassware.

"Simple," Bruce says finally. "That's what I like. Elegant."

Bruce puts it down and picks up a teapot.

"This is the thing for the tea," he says. Bruce holds it in Henry's direction. "Is this too small for tea? An *order* of tea?"

Henry cannot believe this. Henry has a highly refined sense of taste, and the teapot Bruce is holding does not fit into it. He scans his brain for a polite way to express that thought. "It looks like Howard Johnson's a little bit," he says finally, not exactly a devastating slam, but it does get the message across.

"We want to look a little *like* Howard Johnson's," he says. Oh, so he *agrees* with Henry! "But 1960. You couldn't get this in Howard Johnson's today."

Brian is flipping over some plates. "Howard Johnson's doesn't exist anymore," he says matter-of-factly from across the room.

"No more HoJos?" Henry asks.

"No, they got bought out."

Bruce takes the teapot and the glasses and the shots and the plates that he likes and he buys them. Lots of them. They are not what Brian wants. Brian likes a simple, elegant plate with just enough room for an entrée. Bruce wants a big comfy plate that you can squeeze some mashed potatoes and a vegetable on the side. This is what he wants, and what he will get.

Henry likes a lightweight, long-stemmed wineglass. Bruce likes a heavy, short-stemmed glass. This is what he will get. He also likes small glass coffeepots with black plastic trim, individual portions to be served at the elegant brunch he has planned. He will get these, too.

What does all this say about The Falls? Henry is wondering this, watching nervously as Bruce picks out all the wrong glasses and plates and cups. He has seen the wrong glasses bought before. He has observed the choices of others, and looked on as the restaurant-going public has spurned the wrong-shaped goblet. Someday, he thinks . . . someday I will be here, selecting my own glasses, picking my own plates, charting my own, unique course. I will open a restaurant of my own. And at last it will be done right.

Brian does not share such dreams. Oh, sure, he would love to own his own place, why not? But he does not allow himself to obsess about the day when his own restaurant will open its doors. For the moment, perhaps forever, he is content to cook. He firmly believes in his art. Unfortunately, part of the art is the plate. He knows his plates and his place. He will not put up a fight, not just yet anyway, but he is nonetheless troubled. All that food on one plate . . . how *awful*. The sauces will clash. The look will be wrong.

Two weeks.

/The Bowery is not someplace you want to hang out. You want to get your shit and leave and get back to wherever it is you came from. "Let's go back and have a meeting," Bruce suggests. He likes meetings. Gathering the forces and telling them what to do and impressing them with his ability to make decisions, to know what is right. They return to The Falls. Still no chairs, still no tables, nobody said this was gonna be a comfortable meeting, did they? The floors have still not been cleaned. Soft lights camouflage the dirt. Classical music fills the air instead of the ubiquitous jazz. Why? No one knows.

Henry wants to take a nap. So he does.

Bruce looks at the walls. His eyes dart from wall to wall. They have finally been painted, everything but the mahogany strips on top, near the ceiling. It is good. The ceiling has been painted, too. It used to be black. Now it is beige. It looks much better, everyone agrees. The ceiling is important to Bruce. He wanted it to look nice, and is happy that it does. "What else is a ceiling," he asks no one in particular, "but a wall turned upside down?"

Henry awakens.

Now it is time for the forces of The Falls, Bruce, Henry, Brian and of course Kimberly Jones, to gather around the desk in the basement office for an impromptu, freewheeling discussion of what has been done, what has yet to be done, and what will never get done.

The Agenda:

I. Please Don't Buy Maraschino Cherries

"Cocktail napkins," Bruce says. Does he mean we need them? We want them? We have them? A long pause for nothing. "I ordered the toothpicks."

"All your bar dry goods are ordered," Brian says. Stop worrying, Bruce, we know what we're doing, we've done it before, it will all work out.

Oh, but I *do* worry. "Don't order any cherries," he says. "I *hate* 'em."

"I ordered them," Brian says.

"Can you cancel them?"

"I can cancel." Brian makes a note. Captain Queeg doesn't like cherries.

"Cancel the cherries. I hate them. And they're bad for you. Red cherries are the worst. You know what I'd like to do, Henry? The number of drinks that really require a cherry, like an old-fashioned, that *really* require it, I'd rather stop in the supermarket on the way in. And tell the bartender every time you see some in the market, bring some in. It looks nicer."

"I can cancel it." Brian would like to move to the next subject.

"Or when cherries are in season."

"July."

Is there anything else anyone would like to say about cherries? Yes. You with the tan.

"You know what I'm saying, Henry," Bruce says. "I just hate those candied things."

II. We Need Hot Water

"When are we going to have hot water?" Brian asks.

"Why *don't* we have hot water?" Bruce responds.

"I don't know," says Brian.

"It was either shut off, unplugged . . ."

"Is the gas shut off?" Brian asks.

"I have no idea," says Bruce. "Is it gas or electric?"

"Gas," Brian says.

"Gotta be gas," Henry says.

III. How to Get Ice in Hot Weather: A Pull-and-Tug Situation

This is something Bruce knows plenty about. He likes to have a lot of ice.

"When you lease an ice machine from Basic Leasing," he explains to his troops, "you lease ice. Basically. You lease the equipment, but you also lease the fact that if you run out of ice, the machine breaks anytime or is slow, they deliver ice. They have trucks roaming around the city waiting for them to call on the phone and say they have a problem. One of the advantages of Basic Leasing. So I always look at it like you're not paying $130 a month to lease the basic equipment . . . like you would be the leasing of a refrigerator . . . You're buying ice. It's a $130-a-month ice expense. And that's the best part of it. If it's inadequate at any point we upgrade the lease, put in another machine on top of it. They're not going to keep sending trucks here all the time.

"It's a pull-and-tug situation."

IV. Opening Day: A Hypothetical Scenario

"Let's talk for a minute," Bruce says. "We're opening on Thursday, March 1. Thursday will be a real run-through dinner."

"Do you want to open for lunch on Thursday?" Brian asks. You have no doubt noticed how extremely practical Brian's questions are. Brian is extremely proud of his attention to detail.

"I want this place operating, ready to go, Thursday, noon," Bruce says.

"I don't think we should serve lunch."

"Okay." Attaboy, Bruce, stick to your guns!

"We open the bar," Bruce says. "The bar is open. The waiters are starting to learn the machine. Everybody's running around a little bit. You can start popping out a few specials. The staff can taste. Serve each other. All that kind of thing. So that they start to get into it—to start pickin' on the help and that . . . I'd like to serve Thursday night, Friday lunch, Friday dinner . . . Saturday, no lunch. We want to have a bang-up dinner on Saturday night. We want to open for brunch the first week."

"I think we want to wait a week," Brian says.

"Okay," Bruce says.

V. The Waiters Should Start Working Now

No, they shouldn't.

"There's nothing for them to do until Monday," Henry protests.

"I'll find things for them to do," Bruce says. "I'll send them on errands. Henry, it's more for them to get a feel of the place. I wouldn't mind if they hung around tasting wines. I don't care. The more people that do that. The more people involved with what we're doing here . . ."

"People can't just stop their jobs . . ."

"I'm not saying to stop their jobs," Bruce says, "but I say that you have an hour or two in your day when you're not doing anything you should be here. I'm not tellin' 'em to quit their jobs, but they should be here. Because I want to know if in fact they are the right people, and I want to know it as soon as possible, and not after the fact, because just by having an interview and going through an application, doesn't really give you—"

"Well, you did tell me that Katherine was hired," Henry says. Henry is referring to a quiet, attractive young blond bartender Bruce approved.

"She is hired. But that's all I'm saying. She's hired because Brian knew her and she came down, she was good, she was cute, she had a nice attitude, she said she's a good bartender, but I don't know if she's a good bartender till I've spent some time with her, and neither do you. You can call references, but that's not going to . . . Relax. She probably knows how to tend bar, but does she know how to tend bar the way we want her to tend bar? Does she have good mobility?"

Good mobility? What the hell is good mobility? Yes, the girl can walk. She can probably even jog. She has two legs, Bruce . . . remember, you approved of her legs.

VI. In Conclusion: I Am David Merrick

"I'm looking at this like I'm putting on an off-Broadway show. You got a cast of characters here. Whether they got bit parts or nonspeaking parts, they're part of the production and they should be coming in trying to give as much energy as they can to make it a long-running hit. We're not just calling Central Casting and saying, go to the Belasco Theatre at 8:00 tonight. This is not what's happening here. We are a production company. Downtown. Some people are not going to get into that feeling because they either have a sour New York attitude or they have burnout factor. I don't cook. I don't tend bar. Although I've done bar, I've waited on tables, I've done it all. But I'm acting like a producer in a way, and I'm trying to get the best people in the best technical positions that you can. That's what a producer should be doing. That's the feeling we're trying to get across. I'm trying for people to get that feeling from me. All right?"

Henry says, "I understand your point. They have a point, too, that they just don't want to come down here—why should people get suckered into doing work for nothing? That's always the rap."

"Henry—I don't think that's the case."

"I know that's not the case for you, but that's that feeling, that's their thought. People are ambiguous about that."

Bruce is not going to respond to *that*.

"What else does anybody else want to talk about?" Bruce scans the room. "Because we're going to have this meeting tomorrow to see what progress we've made on the items. You've gotta start taking notes tomorrow about who's doing what. And we can have a progress report. And there's another thing. I think we're gonna have to start coming in at least one day on the weekend."

"We've only got one more weekend."

LET THE GAMES BEGIN

TEN

Ah, Philippe Dumont!

Your handsome face, your lilting accent, your cuddly poodle, your beautiful girlfriend!

You are the envy of all of us, Philippe!

You are the mysterious Philippe, the friend of Bruce, the soft-spoken gentleman whose job it will be to stand by the door of The Falls on opening night, kissing the girls . . . you will handle that, won't you? Kissing girls is what a Frenchman does best, and you are *so* French . . .

You are the son of a famous French singer, some call him the French Sinatra, but how can that be if no one but Bruce can remember his name? But he must be good, because you have money . . . money enough to drive a Jaguar, money enough to eat and smoke and drink, money enough to fly back and forth to your beachfront land in St. Bart's, where your idea of a job is to supervise the construction of a swimming pool . . . money for nothing and the chicks for free.

"My girlfriend, she has been working out with a trainer," you explain, lighting a Marlboro while your gentle voice strokes our ears. "She is hard, so hard . . . there is no fat on her at all." And as if you are not to be believed—you *are!*—you tell us to look in the catalog of

Victoria's Secret, and there we will find her, this no-fat girlfriend, Alexandra. To a Frenchman this is nothing, perhaps; but to us, a girlfriend from the Victoria's Secret catalog is something beyond reason, a genuine mind-blowing symbol of masculine achievement, something to be looked on with equal measures of envy, lust and profound bitterness. And you, Philippe, quite frankly—may we be so bold?—don't seem to be the type to have one.

How old are you, anyway? You look like a well-preserved forty-five-year-old, but in truth you are a wasted thirty-three-year-old. Bruce knows your secrets, doesn't he . . . maybe that's why you have this love-hate relationship with Bruce; this need to explain your anger at him, your theories about him, your love of him.

"I love Bruce," you say.

Do you know how to run a restaurant? Do you know what Bruce knows? One day you tell the staff to work harder—"I don't want to be a ball-breaker," you explain, "but I will"—and the next day you are gone. Perhaps your mystery explains something about you. Women love mystery, don't they? Or perhaps it is your well-shaped jaw, or the way you look into their eyes. You really *don't* want to be a ball-breaker.

You seem to believe in The Falls. You come there every day, your poodle on a leash. You wear structured jackets and flowing shirts and soft leather shoes, a full-scale commitment to the downtown New York life. You have worked in restaurants for years; you know what to do. As the glamour crowd begins to make its way to The Falls by cab and limo, you will stand by to greet them. "Hold table 40!" you will command, knowing that this-friend-from-Elite-Models-or-the-head-of-Ford-Models might enjoy the particular view afforded from that spot. And if perchance that table slips away, woe betide the one who makes the error. "I was *holding* that table, they *like* that table," you will quietly mourn.

Philippe, your job will be to preside over the days of heat. You will keep them tooling at the bar. "No tables yet, sorry," you will say to couples who can clearly see tables. "Reserved, sorry," you will explain, to those who question you. And then you will turn on your leather heel and kiss the pretty girl who just walked in, and a man at the bar will wonder just who you were, and who he was not.

/Bruce loves Philippe. He will never admit it. But there is something so goddamned *cosmopolitan* about the guy. It's that St. Bart's thing,

the love of a tan, the lure of a sandy beach, the dreams, the fantasies
. . . Bruce loves a fantasy. Like any red-blooded American boy.

"He's had a bunch of restaurants," Bruce explains. He feels compelled to explain, perhaps, the allegiance between a handsome French
rake and an open-faced New Englander, a friendship that looks as
though it might have been forged over too many drinks, too many
years, too much of everything. The years of excess were fun, weren't
they? Oh, who the hell can remember.

Now we are in the age of anxiety. In two weeks The Falls will open
its doors. Much is now happening of tremendous importance. Things
that happen now will have profound consequences later. Bruce cannot
count on anyone but himself.

"I feel like David Merrick," he says.

He is speaking of the staff that has begun to form around him. Now
Kimberly is no longer enough. Brian has the kitchen, Henry the bar;
but others will be needed. Philippe will be here. This is why he has
turned up in the final hours of preparation. He will be the man at the
door, the man Bruce should be; the man Bruce doesn't want to be. He
wants to be in the back, where David Merrick sits, in the last row of
the balcony. He will be casting the rest of the company. Waiters and
waitresses must be hired to present a pretty picture.

Bruce is worried. He doesn't want to lose his control. In a few minutes there will be a staff meeting, the first. The waiters and waitresses
he and Kimberly hired will be coming in to learn the ropes. Bruce will
lurk in the background of this meeting, not wanting to speak. He will
allow Philippe the honors, along with an old hand from Central Falls,
a young actor named Brian Wry, not currently employed as an actor,
who has agreed to return to work with Bruce for the opening. He will
be the nice guy. He will try to prevent his staff from more than a
glimpse into the dark side of this particular moon.

But Bruce will be watching, you can assume that. He is already
starting to let his positions be known.

"People start getting testier," he reflects before the meeting begins.
He is referring to his staff so far—to Kimberly Jones, to Philippe
Dumont, to anyone who challenges his view of The Falls, the hit musical that he is about to open, without previews, on the New York
stage. He is explaining his policy about the people he has hired, the
cast of his show. He is reserving the right to fire them if they do not,
at any moment, fit his vision of The Falls at that moment.

"I mean," he says—everybody listen, Bruce is going to issue a major
policy address—"I mean, Kimberly thinks we need to let these people

give notice. I don't believe in notice. When somebody quits they should leave. Otherwise they'll just steal from you or they'll just do a lousy job.

"If I fire somebody," he says, and now he *definitely* will, you know it, "I don't give them notice—I just fire them. I don't want them hanging around."

Let the games begin.

In walk two dozen men and women. Almost all of them in black. Four of them are black, two Oriental. The women are wearing, for the most part, black stockings and short skirts. There is a disproportionate number of people now entering The Falls with blue eyes. They assemble themselves along the banquettes. The tables and chairs still have yet to arrive. Bruce hovers by the bar, walking in and out. Brian Wry, dressed in khaki pants, blue shirt and a multicolored belt, begins the meeting by promoting the concept of team spirit. This prompts a number of the prospective staffers to place their chins on their hands.

Bruce must say something. Overcome that shyness and exhort the troops. There have been questions from some of the women about the look of the place, and of the staff, and Bruce has been summoned to give them a definitive answer.

"I want you to look like women, not waiters. It's a people-watching place."

A few more chins drop. Bruce nods goodbye and ducks downstairs.

Now Kimberly has something *she* wants to say. "Come in!" she says sweetly. "Show your enthusiasm!"

Brian wants to add something. "If you all, like, tell people the place has just opened . . . if Bruce hears that attitude . . . it's bye-bye."

Oh, and Philippe wants to contribute a thought. He doesn't want to be a ball-breaker, but, "You have to treat your friends like your customers," he says, "and your customers like your friends."

Any questions?

The men and women who are to be the first staff at The Falls, the opening night army of restaurant reservists, have questions that concern mostly their dress, their hours and their pay. Yes. They are normal human beings. They do not understand this David Merrick business. They're actors, if they want a job in a theater they'll audition, okay?

As they leave, Bruce and Philippe and Brian Wry huddle to discuss. They have now gotten a pretty good look at them—and had a chance *to* evaluate their attitudes, their questions and their legs.

"Most of them won't make it," Philippe says. He is drawing on one

of his ubiquitous Marlboros. "As professionals. You can tell by looking. Anybody can be a waiter, but only some people can be a good
waiter." Brian basically agrees. "Some you can tell right away that
they won't work out."

He singles out one woman in the crowd—a twenty-three-year-old
actress with thick black hair, and equally thick legs, who asked a
number of questions about the appropriate dress for The Falls. "You
can tell she won't work out," Brian says, to the agreeing nods of Bruce
and Philippe.

"She's too uptight," Brian explains. Now we know why Bruce likes
this guy. "If she's so worried about her appearance she can't be confident enough to be a good waitress. A few of them will make it. It was
an okay-looking bunch. Not great. It should be. You go to a restaurant
and you want to be around good-looking people. You're putting things
in your mouth that they're giving you. It's easier that they're good-
looking."

Bruce has joined the conversation. He nods. Up and down. That is
exactly what I have been saying, he thinks. Nice way to put it, too, that
things-in-your-mouth idea. Now I'll say it myself. It's *my* philosophy.
To hell with labor laws and women's liberation and the whole damn
thing.

"I want them to be sexy," Bruce says. "Okay—so that makes me a
sexist. I don't mind. I like women to be sexy. To look good. Why not?"

An excellent question. Answers to follow.

/Eleven days . . . ten days . . . nine days . . .

And the damn place still isn't even clean!

After much procrastination, several boxes of old junk from the previous tenants are gone through. It is quickly apparent that the folks at
J.S. VanDam did not put too much stock into the beauty of things.
Bruce, Henry and Brian plow through the plates, cups, bowls and
other assorted crap left in the basement. They decide to keep one
water pitcher and three sauce boats. Bruce wants to keep a case of
simple white coffee cup saucers. There is much disgusted shaking of
heads by everyone. A puppy dog face appears on Bruce.

"Are they too ugly to get change and a check on?" he asks.

"Yes," everyone answers.

It's all right. If Bruce really cared, then the saucers would stay. He
picks his fights carefully and wins them.

A potential floor cleaner arrives a few minutes later. He is a black man in his forties, wearing a suit. He looks very clean. Bruce has found him in the Yellow Pages.

Bruce truly believes in the Yellow Pages. He buys into the concept completely. He especially likes the second volume of the New York Telephone Yellow Pages, which are business-related listings. When he needs something done, he looks it up in the Yellow Pages, calls the first listing that catches his eye, and frequently hires them to do the job. In this case, he has looked under "Cleaning Services" and found Will, professional floor cleaner, who has arrived late in the afternoon to give Bruce a free estimate.

"I'll do it for $1,200," he says after a quick look around. "That will include washing the floor, polishing, cleaning the kitchen, the bathroom and the lights."

Too much, says Bruce.

"I'll take $1,100 in cash," Will says quickly. He's used to this, planned for it, figured it into his first offer. "Plus an invitation to your opening night party."

Bruce has a better idea. He walks behind the bar, opens a refrigerator and pulls out a mysterious brown bottle he placed there earlier. He holds it up in Will's direction, and shakes it enticingly.

"How about some Jamaican sea moss that'll give you a hard-on when you go home to your wife?" Bruce has gotten this bottle from the Jamaican painter.

"Talk to me!" Will says. The two shake hands. Bruce pours him a tall, cool glass of Jamaican sea moss. The deal is done.

/The bills have begun to pile up. People want cash, it's the best way to get things done, but it doesn't exactly help the overall financial picture. The Falls is still nine days away from making money.

And so, the question arises: Is there enough money?

"I have enough money," Bruce answers. Ah, the confidence! The bravado! Has he been drinking Jamaican sea moss? "But some people haven't actually put in enough money yet," he adds as gently as possible. No names are mentioned. The investors must be treated nicely at this point. It would not do to be pointing fingers at the ones who have failed to write their checks. Don't forget, these investors are going to boost the cause, bring in crowds, help out in the press and, of course, eat here all the time.

These investors—will they make money on the place, Bruce?

"I think we can pay back everyone's investment in eighteen months.

That's doubling your money back plus you've still got your invest-ment."

/The awning goes up. A simple gray with white lettering, widely spaced, on the front. Nothing on the top. Nothing on the side. Bruce doesn't want to scream the name.

There's also a neon bulb installed that goes around the full length of the window, front and sides. It casts a bright pink glow.

"Is it too . . . pink?" someone asks.

"As long as the strip goes around, it's nice," Bruce says. "It's a continuous line. As long as it doesn't look cheap."

"You think it's too . . . dinerish?"

"It'll look rich," Bruce says.

The neon strip cost $1,958. Wow. What's the resale value of a hot pink neon bulb?

"If someone wants to buy it," Bruce says, "they can."

/How much are drinks going to cost? Henry is starting to wonder. He asks Bruce.

"Should drinks be tax included?" Bruce asks. "If you go into the Sheraton, they charge you tax."

"No way," Henry says. Bartenders do not want to deal in pennies.

"Can you round it to the nearest nickel?" Bruce is looking for an angle on this. But Henry shakes his head. Bartenders aren't too fond of nickels, either.

"Someday," Bruce says, "there's going to be a revolt. People should be paying taxes on drinks at the bar. It's only fair." The bills are adding up. The cash is flowing out. Bruce is starting to think of ways to make more.

Eight more days.

/At 3:30 in the afternoon of February 21, 1990, a week before opening night, the phone rings in the basement office. It is a gentleman named Sanford, calling to make a reservation. He would like to book a table for six at 10:00 P.M. on March 1, which is the opening night of The Falls.

In smoking, of course.

THE EVOLUTION AND

DEVELOPMENT OF A

BOTTLE IN SPACE

ELEVEN

The eggs are being cracked.

On the cutting table in the kitchen, Larry Mebane, one of the cooks, who used to work with Bruce at Central Falls, is getting ready for the opening of The Falls, now only forty-eight hours away, by taking them out, one by one, from the cardboard containers, six dozen of them, and separating the whites from the yolks. An egg is one of nature's products one has to particularly admire—the amazing fact that an egg, one simple little Grade A farm fresh egg, has three distinct elements to it, if you count the basically useless but highly entertaining shell. Larry is getting ready to make the desserts. This requires a substantial supply of whites and yolks.

Brian would also like someone to peel carrots. This would be a simple matter except that The Falls does not own a carrot peeler. The restaurant *does* have a cordless cellular telephone, which Bruce has had glued to the side of his head since it arrived last week, but it does not have a carrot peeler, or even a can opener, for that matter.

The place isn't ready.

The tabletops have not been attached to the bottoms, which arrived on Monday, along with the chairs. The waiters have not looked at a menu. There's no cold water in the kitchen, and no plumber to explain or repair it. The floor is dirty again, the bar is a mess, the stereo system still hasn't come . . .

So why does Bruce appear so calm? Is it merely a facade he is wearing to get the job done? What the hell is going on underneath that tan?

No one knows. There isn't even a liquor license yet. This could be a problem, you know. There's a law in New York State, and the idea of it is to keep restaurants from serving booze until they have a license —*in hand*. The law applies to liquor salesmen, who cannot sell liquor to a restaurant unless they can physically *see* the license. The New York State Liquor Authority has been around since just after Prohibition, and their rules are rigidly enforced.

Except, of course, when they are not.

To hear Bruce and Terry tell it, the New York State Liquor Authority can be handled. And they are working on it, yes they are. I know a guy who knows a guy who's a friend of a guy. I got this pal in City Government. I got a lawyer who can get these guys on the phone. They tell me it's all set, we got it, it'll be ready, no sweat. Just gotta pick it up. Bruce has made a call to his pal, see—a High-Ranking City Official who likes to drop by a restaurant now and again and be treated like Number One. Bruce met him years ago, during the heyday of Central Falls.

So Bruce is calling the High-Ranking City Official. The guy's gotta be able to grease things, help get people liquor licenses, he's very powerful, right?

We shall see.

Meanwhile, as the day goes on, as the hours pass and the carrot peeler isn't bought and the light bulbs don't fit and the tabletops sit, still, waiting to be attached, and the floor gets dustier and the phone gets busier, Bruce begins to show signs of wear. He is waiting for that goddamned license and it isn't here. He wants the place clean and it's a mess. He wants twenty people working day and night to get the place ready, not one.

His tan is turning red.

By 5:30 in the afternoon, so little has happened that Bruce is at the end of his rope. A prospective waitress has walked in the door to pick up a menu, and instead Bruce hands her a rag and tells her, "Dust the lights." Kimberly has questions, but he will not hear them. Brian and Henry have concerns, both of them, matters that need to be attended to now, *not* tomorrow, *not* after the opening . . . *now*. So when Bruce ducks downstairs to the office, to escape the demands, the questions, the unfinished tasks that remain to be done in the next forty-eight hours, they follow. Brian. Henry. Kimberly. The whole damn lot of them follow right behind Bruce, down the stairs, through the storage room, past the freezer, and into the inner sanctum Bruce has kept for moments like this, moments when the sight of so many remaining tasks becomes too much to bear.

He's on the edge. Ready to explode.

At which point Brian Wry enters the room, holding a bag of light bulbs.

Bruce takes the bag, looks inside, and sees the bulbs Brian has brought. He is not pleased. The room falls silent. Brian Moores and Henry are sitting on the couch. They watch carefully. They know that Bruce is . . . tense. Irritable. Kimberly is sitting at the desk. She knows what is about to happen. She has seen it before. Something is in the air, it is going to be terrible. She can feel it.

"This is the wrong kind of light bulb!" Bruce screams.

"What do you mean this is the wrong kind of light bulb?" Brian Wry asks.

Brian is trying to diffuse Bruce's temper. He knows what can happen, half expected it. Two months later, reflecting on this fateful afternoon, he is saying of Bruce, "He's fanatical about lights. Fanatical. Lighting's gotta be exactly right. The bulbs, the wattage . . . fanatical."

But he knows there is nothing he can do. The wick has been lit. The flame is burning.

"What do you *mean?*" Brian is grumpy and irritable himself. He had been expecting to stand on a ladder and install these lousy bulbs this afternoon, not argue about whether they're the right ones.

"You're not dedicated, you don't care about doing the job right," Bruce yells. "You're fucking lazy!"

To which Brian replies simply, "Bruce, that's not in my job description."

That's it for Bruce. He's got enough on his mind. He doesn't have to listen to some young actor feed him a line about job descriptions. That little jerk! Out pours a string of epithets, fucker, asshole, back and forth, back and forth . . . with Henry and Brian Moores and Kimberly as witnesses, shocked, scared but most of all *distant*, thank God, thinking: He's not yelling at me.

"Get out!" Bruce is yelling at Brian Wry. "Get out!"

"I'll get out!" Brian yells back. He's racing back and forth around the office, getting his stuff, preparing to happily follow Bruce's final orders. "I'll get out . . . I *quit!*"

Bruce has swung around to face Brian head-on. He will now deliver his famous knockout punch.

"You *won't* quit!" Bruce screams, fire in his eyes. "You're *fired!*"

Brian Wry went home. He took his things with him and never came back. Oh, he called Bruce to apologize, and it was accepted. And he came by to visit on opening night, marveled at the crowd and offered the opinion that The Falls would be a raging, huge success. But it would be, for the moment, the end of his relationship with Bruce, a relationship that began in 1980, and what is it now, 1990? A decade.

Long enough.

"I'm thinking of writing a wonderful play about a restaurant," Brian was saying a couple months later, over lunch at a restaurant just two blocks away from The Falls. Perhaps the dust had long since settled, but not the feelings left unresolved. "With Bruce as the archetypal leader. There's a lot of stuff you can do. Set it up so that you can have people coming in and out of the kitchen. The life of the bar, the life of the kitchen. Not like a TV sitcom. You'd have a real family . . . dealing with that. There's a lot of symbolisms and stuff.

"I have a great title. You know that sculpture—*The Evolution and Development of a Bottle in Space*? That's the name of this play. Of being contained, and being bought up, and being bottled up. 'Cause I remember running 'round like a maniac and not having any identity except . . . doing what I did. I'm just formulizing. Figuring out characters. I can go in. I was always very good to him. I never stole anything from him. Always brought in interesting people. I was a good person to him."

/Henry has witnessed this fight, silently but intently. Thus it is no surprise to him at all when, the next morning—which is the final morning before the morning of the day of the night of the opening of The Falls—he and Bruce share a few harsh words.

Remember, Henry has a way about him. It is that of a man who believes he knows what is right. He has been here before; he has fought every fight. He knows exactly the way a bar should look. He has been behind too many to recall. But there is only one way to do things behind the bar, and that is his way. He will make this clear either by saying it or showing it. There will be no mistake about it, though.

This morning, as Henry scans his bar and envisions the crush of people tomorrow night, he realizes that a mistake has been made. There is no glass washer. A glass washer is just what you think it is. It costs $300 and you can buy it on the Bowery. You can also live without it, and send your glasses back to the kitchen for the dishwasher to clean. But if you want to be fast and cool and clean, you'll have a glass washer behind the bar. Or at least Henry would.

Henry leans across the bar to talk to Bruce, who is sitting at the far end by the kitchen. He must tell Bruce how he feels. He must demand the washer. Otherwise he feels he cannot be responsible.

"You need a glass washer," Henry says.

Bruce shakes his head.

"You send the glasses into the dishwasher!" he says.

"What is this—a shot-and-beer joint?" Henry takes a towel and starts furiously wiping down the bar. He can barely stand to look at Bruce.

"Look," Bruce says, trying to calm Henry down. He knows he can't afford to spend $300 right now on anything—especially something that duplicates what he already has in the kitchen. "We don't need it," he says.

"I'm here to disagree. It's essential."

The fire in Henry's eyes is beginning to flame out of control.

"Then we disagree on what's essential," Bruce says. He will not be engaged in battle. Not yet. Not now.

But Henry will not let it go. He stands erect, opposite Bruce, the bar between them. His long arms swing in the direction of where the glass washer would be, but isn't, and never will be.

"This is 1990," Henry says. "You need a glass washer, we're not some beer-and-shot joint!"

Bruce smiles. "You ever see the movie *The Money Pit?* That's what this is. It's a cash-flow situation. Next week we'll have cash flow."

"But what about this week?"

Another smile. "I think in terms of *not* this week," Bruce says.

Henry begins to see that he will lose. He is not going to pay for a glass washer himself. Okay, what else? "What about pourers?" he asks. He is referring to those special caps on the tops of bottles used by bartenders to move the booze more easily from bottle to glass.

"All we need is plastic pourers," Bruce says.

That's *it*. Henry has officially lost it forever. This man is a *jerk*. You can practically hear the inside of Henry's mind, yelling at this guy, calling him a cheap bastard, planning to quit as soon as he can find something else . . . oh save me from another lousy bar!

But all he can muster aloud is a bit of annoyance; a shot of frustration.

"Oh Jesus!" he says, walking away. "This is supposed to be a class bar!" The further away he gets from Bruce, the less you can hear him mutter, but there he goes nonetheless. "Not a shot-and-beer joint!"

Henry, Henry . . .

Bruce is trying to draw the line. Too little money has been raised, that much is clear. Too much money has been spent. And no money, not one lousy dime, has yet been earned. Bruce has been here before, too, he has seen the Henrys come and go, the know-it-all bartenders, the chefs who would be king, the waiters with a dream. We all have dreams; Bruce knows this most of all. But this baby is his. He gets to dream *his* dreams here, and they don't involve glass pourers or glass washers or even Henry. No, damnit, Bruce is going to do this restaurant his way, and he will tell Henry what to do, and Brian, and Kimberly, and all the rest.

Somebody has to. Right? Somebody has to be the bad guy. Bruce knows that. He's been the bad guy before. He will be happy to take the blame if he's wrong. But right now, as the minutes click by and the opening is now a handful of hours away, Bruce thinks he's right.

/Bruce is not the only dreamer.

Last night, Brian Moores had a restaurant dream. He hasn't had one in years. But you know how it is, you get involved in something, it takes over your life, you're probably going to dream about it. And that is precisely the situation with Brian Moores and his subconscious mind.

In the dream, Brian had left the restaurant the night before and gone to take his bus home. This usually involves taking a cab uptown to the Port Authority Bus Terminal, then catching a bus that takes an hour to reach his destination. In the dream, he takes his standard journey home—and then realizes that he had left all the gas burners on, but not lit. The Falls was being filled with gas, ready to explode . . . and there was Brian, home, ninety minutes away. The place was locked. Only he had the key. He had to get back to New York and turn off those burners, save The Falls . . .

But he woke up before he could save The Falls. It burned to the ground.

· · ·

/Last-minute details must be taken care of:

11:00 A.M.: Bruce calls the woman designing the menu. "One change. Take out the word 'low-fat' before mozzarella. Make it 'fresh mozzarella.' "

12:15 P.M.: The garbage haulers come to pick up the last load of garbage before the opening. They've been coming for two weeks now. "Somebody told me the guys who run the garbage business are the ones who couldn't make it as wiseguys," Bruce says. "I believe it."

1:00 P.M.: The menu covers arrive. Simple tan heavy-stock paper with the green-and-black restaurant logo printed on it. "Isn't that beautiful?" Bruce says.

1:55 P.M.: The High-Ranking City Official finally calls Bruce back. It's forty-eight hours after Bruce placed the call to get his help on the liquor license. "He says, 'It's a state agency, not much I can do—but give the information to my secretary and I'll see what I can do.' "

2:25 P.M.: John Sheldon, one of New York's more experienced wine purveyors and a teacher as well, comes in to lecture the waiters on wine. He offers a few fundamental truths. "People like to hear the word *dry*," he says. "Most wines are dry, but it's important for people to hear it." Basically, Sheldon says, very few people know what they're doing when they order wine. "Most people order the *next* to the cheapest bottle on the menu," he says. "So it's a good idea to make that choice especially good."

4:00 P.M.: The liquor license matter is heating up. It's now needed in exactly twenty-four hours, or they cannot serve booze on opening night. "The guy who signs the license has a medical problem," Bruce says. Then he smiles. "Plus he's mad because nobody warned him how many people would be calling him." He got calls from the High-Ranking City Official's office, not to mention another former High-Ranker Bruce knows, plus the liquor companies *and* the lawyers. "So I got the name of a company that'll deliver the biggest stuff without a license."

A liquor company that will break the law! That settles that.

/Tonight the fire is going strong, the burners are on and Brian is standing over the flames. In a restaurant kitchen, the fire burns big and bright. A chef will let the burners go for hours, nothing on them, just there, hot, ready. Every so often a pot or pan will be needed, and the fire will be lit and going. Tonight Brian is making baby chicken and lamb chops and pasta, selections from the menu, and the principals of this grueling month at last sit down and eat dinner together. In other restaurants, the final night before the opening would be a chance for the waiters to learn how to serve others. But here it is decided that the waiters first need to learn how to serve their masters.

Brian and his cooking crew bring out platters of food as they finish them. Piles of mashed potatoes. Lots of lamb chops. A baby chicken, then another, then another. Wines are opened, good ones—bottles brought by potential purveyors as gifts. No longer is anyone using the pretense of tasting as an excuse to get drunk. Now it is a crying need to get plastered. After tonight, The Falls will no longer be the exclusive domain of its staff and owners. The kitchen will be open. Dinner will be served. And money at last will be made.

A waiter named Jonathan has recently joined the staff from a restaurant down the street. He has brought with him a technique for napkin folding that intrigues everyone. It involves creating the look of a ruffled fan, and it is precisely what Bruce is looking for. Bruce has spent the last half hour rejecting several suggested ways to fold a napkin—in the waterglass, along the side of the plate, he hates all that stuff. Not elegant enough. Not casual enough. The napkin is important to Bruce. Jonathan's solution pleases him, and for a brief moment he loves Jonathan, thinks he may perhaps be management material, and listens intently as Jonathan informs everyone how *he* would run things at The Falls.

Better, of course, than Bruce. Out of Bruce's earshot, Jonathan complains that the food just isn't that great. Nothing is quite right. "I make a perfect hollandaise," he says, referring to Brian's sauce as less than exemplary. In his early thirties, Jonathan is himself a playwright, though he has been working for years as a waiter. He is clean, fastidious, every receding blond hair on his head combed perfectly into place. He would like it very much if The Falls were equally well groomed and prepared. He sits and chews and sniffs and points out, to anyone who will listen, that what The Falls needs is more this and less that.

Who cares? Certainly not Bruce. Sure, he likes this guy, he likes anyone who is devoted enough to his work to care passionately about the napkins. But Bruce is much too busy tonight. *Much* too busy to care what waiters think about the food. Tonight he is on a mission to discover how to work the lights.

For the better part of the evening, as people move in and out and around the restaurant, eating, laughing, drinking, what amounts to an informal run-through of a hypothetical fun night at The Falls, Bruce is at the controls. Not in the figurative sense. The dials, the knobs and the switches—*those* controls, the ones that dim the lights and raise the sound and give the room its perpetual buzz and glow.

Bruce will work the knobs. Let others work the room.

Shenge the artist is here. He is African but has lived in New York for many years. He has known Bruce for all of them. This is SoHo, remember? He's eating and drinking and laughing. Yes, it is a party tonight. A party like the days of old. Those grand wonderful 1980s, they seem so long ago. Artists and musicians and actors, living on the fringes of life, food for nothing and the drinks for free. The politicians come, too, they are helping the cause, why not? Here comes the High-Ranking City Official. Give the man a drink! The lights are low and Sinatra is singing and Bruce is turning those dials.

Shenge is happy because he now has a painting on the wall of The Falls. He brought one in this afternoon and everybody hated it. It was ugly, and even worse, it was horizontal. He took it home and came back tonight with another one. This one is smaller and vertical.

Everyone loves it, especially Bruce.

OPENING NIGHT

TWELVE

You have to admire his passion.

Here we are just hours from the opening of The Falls, it's not even *noon* yet, and Bruce Goldstein continues his search for the perfect napkin fold. He will not settle on just an ordinary fold. Nor will he accept a napkin stashed in a cup. The napkin must be a statement in itself. The napkin is the first thing people will touch in The Falls. It better be nice and pretty. People like to touch pretty things. In Bruce's mind there is a picture of a napkin that is perfectly fanned. It is clean and white and pretty. It rests on a plate, and makes you want to touch it to your skin.

Is there no one here who can make Bruce the napkin fan of his dreams?

Perhaps Marcel can.

Marcel is a waiter, very cool, very French, a friend of Philippe, of course. Many years in the business. Here, there, back and forth. He's been around. Knows napkins pretty well. He is on intimate terms with napkins. Bruce suspects he will know exactly how to properly fold a napkin. He waves him over to discuss the napkin situation. Kimberly Jones, too. She is the closest thing in The Falls right now to a well-folded napkin.

"I did the fan," Bruce tells them. He waves a large, unfolded white napkin in front of him. "Now I can't remember how we did it." He futzes for a moment. "That's it. You gotta open it flat. No, it's too much work. You're basically going back and forth."

Marcel and Kimberly have each taken a napkin and are practicing.

"When you go to the nuthouse, you have to pay $1,500 a week to learn how to do things like this," Bruce says. Three grown men and women, folding, twisting . . .

As he folds, Marcel happens to mention to Bruce that he is upset about Brian Wry's departure.

"He doesn't want to work," Bruce says. He is yanking at the fabric. "He wants to—anybody who goes to a therapist twice a week doesn't know what they want."

"Bruce . . ." In Marcel's lilting accent, it comes out *Brooooze* . . . full of passion, devoid of grammar. "I want him. And Philippe want him, and you want him, but he love you so much, and you love him so much . . ."

"I don't love him that much . . ." Why can't I get this damn napkin to *fold?* Damnit! Do we *have* to talk about *him?* "There's a way to do a fan that I forget."

"You forgot," Marcel repeats. Thank you.

Bruce has finally gotten his napkin to roughly resemble the waiter's creation from the night before. "It should look eventually something like this. But I can't figure out how to do it."

Kimberly has been watching this conversation carefully. She has observed. She now with extraordinary calm and grace proceeds to fold the napkin perfectly. This will be The Falls's signature fold. At last.

"That's it," Bruce says. "How did you do that? That's it. And you do it where it comes out like this. Where one side sits down. Like this. That's it."

"There must be another way to do it," Marcel suggests bitterly.

"That's because it wasn't professional. She's been in the Ozarks too long," Bruce says.

Kimberly smiles. "We don't use napkins down there," she says demurely. "We just primp up our overalls."

Now it is a matter of pride for Bruce. As the proprietor of The Falls, he must be able to fold a napkin properly himself. "What did you do once you got it to this point?" he asks Kimberly. "Like this? Just tell me, when you got to this point, what did you do?"

Marcel walks away in disgust.

"I just went like that . . ." Kimberly demonstrates.

"Undo it. Let me see. That's it. But the napkins have to be very stiff." Kimberly looks nervous. Is he going to withdraw his endorsement? Oh my God . . . "Naaah, I don't want to do that. It's too much work."

What power! With one stroke of the hand, Bruce has managed to make Kimberly's napkin a star. And just as quickly pull her napkin apart.

/Across the restaurant, Terry Quinn is flipping through the newspaper. No, wait: he is *not* flipping through the newspaper. He is stuck on one page, reading an item on page 13 of *New York Newsday*, over and over and over again.

Here is the item:

> "BEFORE THE FALLS: Talk about hip and hot to trot before it even opens. Tonight, The Falls, the restaurant, will be unofficially opening in the space at 150 Varick St. that once housed J.S. VanDam, the restaurant. So why's it going to be hip and hot? Take a look at the owners/backers/players: **Terry Quinn,** co-owner of the downtown hot spot Peggy Sue's; **Bruce Goldstein,** who used to own Central Falls; **Allen Parker,** the director of everything from "Midnight Express" to "Mississippi Burning": **Bob Colesberry,** producer of "After Hours" and that "Mississippi" movie; fab actor **Matt Dillon,** Elite model **Alexandra,** and a few others. This group's good-looking enough to be its own modeling agency. . . ."

> —"Inside New York"
> *New York Newsday*
> March 1, 1990

To Terry, who is starting today by looking at the newspaper and who plans to end it with a hip, hot opening night dinner at The Falls, things look pretty damn good. The forecast is for sunny skies with brisk afternoon winds—a high of thirty-nine degrees. Not bad. In like a lamb chop, out like a steak. Tonight is supposed to be clear and cold. A glass of Moët champagne will take care of that. The likelihood of a major news event overshadowing the opening of The Falls seems fairly slim at this point, when you consider the lead story in the *Times* this morning had to do with Nicaraguan politics. And the most intriguing story being Washington mayor Marion Barry's not-guilty plea on perjury and drug counts.

Yeah, right, Bruce says, reading that.

The most interesting story in the paper, certainly to the relatively sleepless folks who have already shown up at The Falls by 10:00 this morning, was the one in *Newsday*, a respectable tabloid that is not above publishing a gossip column or two. Thank God. Where else could you guarantee a story announcing the opening of a restaurant on Varick Street with a couple of moderately well-known investors? This is not even the first item that has appeared in the press. *The Daily News* column "Apple Sauce" wrote about The Falls way back in January, the same month a photo of Bruce and Terry and some investors appeared in *Vanity Fair*, at this particular moment in history the most influential magazine in America.

A public relations man named Peter Himler has taken on The Falls as a pro bono client as a favor to his old friend Bruce. He used to do PR at Central Falls. He's been working diligently for weeks—mailing out menus, dropping items in various columns, he even got Brian Moores on a local talk show where he cooked some chicken. The host of the show couldn't stop drooling about the idea that Matt Dillon owned a restaurant, it was enough to make Brian sick. But a few people called after the show to make reservations, Himler was happy.

Terry Quinn is still looking at the item. There's his name in boldface, pretty cool, huh? However, he professes to be concerned. He keeps flipping the paper back to the page and he keeps reading it, over and over. He furrows his brow and gets worried and we're supposed to believe that Terry is pretty damn upset with all this attention. "Now that I'm in the paper," he says, "I'm going to get a million calls. Everybody's gonna be on my answering machine . . ." He imagines what they will say: "Why didn't you tell me you were opening up tonight?" And he will have to invite them, oh Lordie, how tragic it will be! Inviting a million people to The Falls!

/Michael Zimmer, another investor, has brought an original Keith Haring to hang in The Falls. He would like to see it on the wall in time for opening night.

Zimmer holds it up against the wall space near the front door, a high-visibility position right next to the bar. It is a huge black rectangular board, with small chalk figures drawn on it in classic Haring style. "It's a great piece," Bruce says, looking at it on a wall for the first time. But it won't work where Zimmer is holding it. "It won't fit over there."

"Five hundred fifty thousand dollars," Zimmer says as he carries it over to the other wall, by the staircase leading to the bathrooms. "It's a masterpiece."

This is where it belongs.

"Let's do it here," Bruce says.

/At 1:10 P.M., still five hours away from opening its doors, a liquor distributor turns up with two cases of Absolut vodka, four cases of J&B whiskey and several other cases of well-known brands of booze. The Falls still does not have its license from the New York State Liquor Authority to sell alcohol.

Calls are being made all day, a flurry of phone calls, to the state capital in Albany, to lawyers' offices, to friends at City Hall and of course to the Liquor Authority itself; but none of these calls has yet produced a license, a red-and-white document with an official seal that enables liquor to be bought and sold on the premises.

And yet . . . here is liquor being bought and sold!

Henry Hauck asks no questions. He knows better than that. He simply does his job, which is to take booze bottles out of boxes, put them on shelves and get them ready to be emptied. There is no acknowledgment from anyone that what has just taken place is against the law. There is only fervent hope that by 6:00 P.M., when Bruce hopes to open the doors of The Falls and let the customers pour in, he will have a liquor license in hand. Some risks have already been taken. No need to take any more unless absolutely necessary. When are these lawyers going to get that license?

"What a fuckin' asshole bunch of lawyers," Bruce says.

Glasses are unloaded.

Call the lawyers, call City Hall. We need that fucking piece of paper.

Flowers are being arranged.

Somebody tells Terry to go down to the authority. The license is ready!

Lemons are being sliced.

Terry goes downtown. That's where all the official pieces of paper are. Downtown. A lady makes him wait . . . what a bitch. Sit over there, she says. I'll see if the paper's ready. They told me to come right now, he says. The man *said*. Oh sure, she says, that's the standard line.

Just sit down. He's polite, he's sweet, he'll sit . . . but he'll *get* this
bitch. He reads upside down, you know, and he sees the license, there
it is, 150 Varick Inc., that's *us*, we're home free. It's late in the day,
too late says the lady, *not* too late, Terry says. I need the license, we're
opening soon. He checks his watch. Opening *now*. Wait here, she says.
Finally . . . *finally* she comes back with the paper. Here, Mr. Quinn,
sorry about that, didn't know who you were, very sorry, here's your
license.

I'm gonna get that bitch, he says to himself.

Terry walks in with the license. It's 4:28 P.M. Lemons are still being
sliced. Henry always says you can't have enough lemons. Terry smiles,
laughs, tells the story over and over, again and again—that *bitch*, she
wouldn't give it to me, but here it is, I got it, let's break out the booze!
Let's put it in a frame, Bruce says, somebody go get a frame, it's art,
we gotta hang this baby.

A bottle of champagne is uncorked. A toast is made.

"I feel great!" Bruce says. "How happy can you get?"

/The waiters and waitresses show up, one by one, a sea of black. Black
leggings, black miniskirts, black pants, black shoes. We are definitely
downtown.

Brian gathers them around the tables near the kitchen for a discussion of tonight's menu. This is standard operating procedure in
any restaurant—the inspirational speech from the chef. In other restaurants, the waiters might have had some kind of run-through,
or rehearsal. But The Falls's official policy is to wing it, and Brian
Moores has reluctantly gone along with this policy of semiorganized
madness.

Brian presents a marked contrast to the proceedings. He is wearing
all white. This is traditional for an executive chef. He is wearing baggy
white pants and white sneakers, a crisp new white shirt, high collar
and, of course, a perfectly starched white apron. The man is clean.

He begins his treatise on tonight's menu with the lettuce. He will,
as always, use more words than necessary; but he will also, as always,
reveal his passionate feelings about food. "The house salad is Boston,
romaine and radicchio, that's sort of self-explanatory. The house vinaigrette's like a creamy vinaigrette. It's got mustard and a little egg
yolk in it. The arugula and Asiago—"

"Is Asiago endive?" a waiter asks.

"Asiago's a kind of cheese. It's a really nice aged Italian cheese. It's

L U N C H

A P P E T Z E R S & S A L A D

MELON WITH DUCK PROSCUITTO $6.50

HOUSE SALAD $4.50
Boston, romaine and raddichio lettuces with
house vinaigrette.

ARUGULA AND ASAIGO $4.00
arugula with shaved asaigo, virgin olive oil
and balsamic vinegar.

**ORIENTAL SALAD W/GRILLED CHICKEN
$7.00**
watercress, romaine, snowpeas and grilled
chicken breast with soy, ginger and sesame
oil.

WARM GOAT CHEESE SALAD $7.00
New York State goatscheese served on spinach
with roasted pine nuts, spanish sherry vinegar
and walnut oil.

OYSTERS ON THE HALF SHELL $1.75 EACH

MOZZARELLA SALAD $5.00
with red and yellow pear tomatoes, extra virgin
olive oil and leeks vinaigrette.

PEPPERED SMOKED SALMON $6.50
garnished with lentils.

DEEP FRIED CHINCOTEAGUE OYSTERS $6.50
with cayenne mayonaisse.

SHRIMP AND FENNEL BROCHETTES $7.00
with creole spices.

CARPACCIO WEST SOHO STYLE $8.00
with three peppercorns, olive oil and grated
reggiano.

ASPARAGUS $5.50
chilled with vinaigrette or hot with olive oil and
lemon.

S A N D W I C H E S

SMOKED TURKEY WITH HAVARTI $7.50
with cayenne mayonnaise.

OPEN-FACED CHICKEN SALAD $7.50

BLACK FOREST HAM AND PROVALONE $7.50

GRILLED MERGUEZ SAUSAGE $6.50
with roasted peppers and creole mustard.

BUFFALO BURGER $10.00
with fries and choice of monterey jack, vermont
cheddar or havarti.

F R O M T H E G R I L L

ATLANTIC SWORDFISH $17.00

BONELESS ARCTIC CHAR $16.00

NORWEIGAN SALMON $16.00

PRIME NEW YORK SHELL STEAK $17.50

WHOLE SPLIT BABY CHICKEN $15.00
with fresh herb sauce.

fish served with choice of:
sauce chien,
salsa verde,
sauce provencal or
black bean and ginger sauce.

all entrees served with vegetable,
and mashed potatoes or
black beans and rice.

GRILLED BONELESS CAPON BREAST $14.00
marinated in pesto with room temperature angle hair pasta with fresh mozzarella, basil & tomato.

CAPELLINI W / SEA SCALLOPS $12.50
with garlic, tomatoes and olive oil.

BLACK LINGUINI SONOMA STYLE $12.00
with avocado, tomatoes, garlic and olive oil.

A P P E T I Z E R S & S A L A D S

SAFFRON AND SEAFOOD SOUP $4.00
with spicy garlic croutons.

HOUSE SALAD $3.50
Boston, romaine and raddichio lettuces with
house vinaigrette.

ARUGULA AND ASIAGO $4.00
arugula with shaved asiago, virgin olive oil and
balsamic vinegar.

GRILLED ORIENTAL CHICKEN SALAD $6.00
watercress, romaine, snowpeas and grilled
chicken breast with soy, ginger and sesame oil.

WARM GOAT CHEESE SALAD $7.00
New York State goats cheese served on spinach
with roasted pine nuts, spanish sherry vinegar
and walnut oil.

**PACIFIC OYSTERS ON THE HALF SHELL
$1.75 EACH**

MOZZARELLA SALAD $5.00
with red and yellow pear tomatoes,
extra virgin olive oil and leeks
vinaigrette.

PEPPERED SMOKED SALMON $6.50
garnished with red lentils.

SNOW CRABMEAT WON TONS $4.50
with sweet and hot pepper relish.

**FARM RAISED RABBIT TENDERLOIN AND
WILD MUSHROOM BROCHETTES $5.50**
with peanut sauce.

CARPACCIO WEST SOHO STYLE $8.00
with three peppercorns, olive oil and grated
romano cheese.

ASPARAGUS $5.50
chilled with vinaigrette or hot with olive oil
and lemon.

F R O M T H E G R I L L

ATLANTIC SWORDFISH
house cut **$14.00** full cut **$18.00**

**BONELESS NEW YORK STATE
GOLDEN TROUT $14.00**

NORWEGIAN SALMON $15.00

YELLOWFIN TUNA $16.00

ICELANDIC LANGOUSTINES $17.00
grilled with white truffle olive oil.

PRIME LAMB CHOPS $18.00
with whole grain mustard and rosemary sauce.

PRIME NEW YORK SHELL STEAK $16.50

**WHOLE SPLIT
BABY SPRING CHICKEN $14.00**
with fresh herb sauce.

all grilled fish served with choice

of sauce chien, salsa verde, sauce provencal

or black bean and ginger sauce.

all entrees served with choice of two:

vegetable of the day, corn on the cob, black

beans and rice or mashed potatoes.

GRILLED BONELESS CAPON BREAST $14.00
marinated in pesto with room temperature angel hair pasta with fresh mozzarella, basil & tomato.

PHEASANT AND WILD MUSHROOM POT PIE $14.00

BUFFALO BURGER $10.00
with homemade fries topped with choice of monterery jack, vermont, cheddar or mozzarella.

OPEN FACED HOUSE CHICKEN SALAD SANDWICH $9.00
on 7-Grain Bread

STEAMED VEGETABLE PLATE $12.00
with sea scallops.**$16.00**

SQUID INK CAPPELLINI $9.50
with garlic, tomatoes, hot peppers and virgin olive oil.

PORCINI FILLED HALF MOON PASTA $12.50
with plum tomato sauce accented with proscuitto and wild mushrooms.

mild, it's not real strong, but it's nice. Virgin olive oil, balsamic vinegar, it's very simply tossed together with the cheese on top. A couple of quail eggs on the side for garnish. A little pepper on top. You don't even need to worry about the garnish, that may change.

"Grilled oriental chicken salad is a boneless chicken breast grilled so it's warm, obviously, and it's served on top of romaine, watercress, snow peas and the dressing is soy sauce, ginger and sesame oil.

"New York goat cheese salad is a—oh, it's pretty self-explanatory. It's on spinach with roasted pine nuts with a sherry vinegar walnut oil.

"The oysters are $1.75 apiece, what I think we're gonna have to do on this for ordering is write down exactly the number—not like in orders of six. So if somebody wants eleven, you write eleven. If they want eighteen you write eighteen. Which would be three orders if you want to look at it that way."

"How small can an order be?" asks Jonathan, the napkin's architect, the man with the slicked-back hair.

"One, two. Bruce doesn't care."

"Are these Rock Point or Little Skokums?"

"Both. You got Little Skokums and Bay Bob Bays."

Jonathan turns to his fellow waiters. "It's important you know how to describe these oysters," he says profoundly. "They have characteristics."

Brian ignores him and goes on. "You can describe 'em, okay? These are very metallic, they're very mild, they're not milky or salty like Atlantic oysters at all. Little Skokums are smaller than the Bay Bob Bays but they're very similar in flavor. If anything the Bay Bob Bays are a little milder.

"The mozzarella salad tonight we don't have red pear tomatoes. We do have yellow pear tomatoes. And it's served with leeks fanned out on the plate and the house vinaigrette over it. Okay? You'll see it as it comes up.

"The peppered smoked salmon doesn't have red lentils tonight, it has green lentils. It's like a lentil with vinaigrette—it's like a lentil salad, except the salmon's fanned out across the plate."

"Serious recommendation," Jonathan says.

"This is Scottish smoked salmon. The snow crab wontons, they're wontons you can wrap around your fingers, they're not like a dumpling—they're like a tortellini, almost. But like a big tortellini. The crab meat is first cooked with a little bit of oil—there's no butter in it. We wrap 'em. We deep-fry 'em, and we serve 'em with a hot pepper relish.

It's like diced bell peppers and chili peppers. It's hot, and it has a little sesame oil in it.

"The rabbit tenderloins are little brochettes about that big, five inches long, we grill 'em, they have shiitake mushrooms and the rabbit on 'em, the peanut sauce is like a creamy peanut sauce, with peanuts pureed in it—it's real oriental-flavored sauce. I know it's beginning to sound like a lot of sesame oil, but that's the last one with it.

"The carpaccio is real thin sliced beef tenderloin marinated with three peppercorns and virgin olive oil, then we put grated cheese over it and we serve it. Green, black and white.

"The asparagus is either hot or cold. It's served with olive oil and lemon . . . the house vinaigrette is used for the asparagus, it's used on the mozzarella salad, for the leeks and it's used for the salad. Okay?

"You have from-the-grill items. Atlantic swordfish, the house cut is around six ounces and the full cut is around nine ounces. The boneless New York State golden trout tonight—I don't have it. Tonight I have Idaho rainbow trout, I'll have the golden trout tomorrow or Saturday."

"Is that with the head?" it is asked.

"I was going to serve it without head for the sake of fitting on our plates. So, you know, it's proper to serve it with the head, but what's the point? It'd be hanging off the plate, and I don't think that's very . . .

"The Norwegian salmon is cut in center-cut steaks. It has the center bone in it. Okay? That's the only bone.

"Yellowfin tuna, it's about a seven- or eight-ounce portion.

"Atlantic langoustines—what we do is we brush 'em with this white truffle olive oil, grill 'em, and then we serve a little dish of the white truffle olive oil on the side with it. First order comes up I'm going to make a couple extras and show you how to break 'em. I don't want to hand out crackers to do this, if we can avoid it. They're easy to be eaten with your hands. Are we going to do this towel deal or not? Bruce was talking about a finger bowl kinda thing for the langoustines. But I don't know. That's not important tonight.

"The prime lamb chops—you get three prime lamb chops—from the rack of lamb, they're the best possible meat, they're prime. The sauce is a reduction of lamb stock, so it's a brown sauce basically, with whole-grain mustard, and the flavor of rosemary. No actual rosemary. It's whole-grain mustard so you see the seed in it and the whole thing.

"The prime New York shell steak—that's just a ten-ounce strip, New York strip steak, grilled."

Jonathan has something else to say. "Is that marinated in garlic or anything?"

"*No*. Listen, I'll tell you something also. All the fish are going to be fashionably undercooked. I mean, people want 'em extremely rare, or whichever way they want to go. If they want them more cooked, the modifier's there. But you might tell them that the fish is kept slightly undercooked. I just leave a very, very slight amount.

"The whole split baby chicken, those things are about fourteen ounces and they kill 'em when they're three and a half weeks old . . . they're raised especially. The meat is much more tender and it's extremely juicy. What they do is they raise them to have juicier white meat. These are not fed anything. The sauce is an herb sauce it's got mint-basil, fresh thyme, rosemary, parsley and tarragon in it."

At last, a new voice in the wilderness. "Will the sauce come in a little bowl on the plate?" a waitress asks.

"Everything will have sauce on it unless you specify otherwise. Okay. There's four sauces—sauce chien. It translates as dog sauce. But what it is, is really made with Key limes in the Caribbean. But we don't have Key limes, so it's made with lime juice, it has pepper in it—hot peppers—basically water, lime juice, peppers, a little bit of oil and salt and pepper. It's like a wash. It's really nice, actually. It's about as simple as you can get, and there's zero calories. It *is* spicy, I'll clue you in on that.

"The salsa verde has tomatillos in it, it has cilantro, it has cumin in it, and onion—very fine—in it, and a little avocado. It's green, obviously, and it's got lemon juice in it. And olive oil. It's not spicy, really. It's not hot, I wouldn't say. It's nice. It's not what you'd expect to get at most Mexican restaurants in New York, though, okay? It's far superior. It's lighter than that.

"The sauce Provençale is a traditional French Provençale based with olive oil, tomatoes, chopped tomatoes, garlic, shallots, fresh thyme and seasoning, salt and pepper, that's it.

"The black bean and ginger sauce—black beans, ginger, sesame oil, soy sauce, ginger, obviously, scallions. What I'm going to do is ladle a bit on one half of the fish. That's the way it'll be served unless you want it on the side. It's not going to be swimming with sauce, so you might explain that we're not going in for—the only ones that are going to have a fair amount of sauce are going to be the chops and the baby chicken are going to have a fair amount of sauce.

"The vegetable of the day today is snow peas, we sauté it in olive oil, not butter, corn on the cob, we don't serve it with butter at the table."

A waiter asks: No butter, right?

"That's the main thing. Black beans and rice are with oil; traditional black beans and rice. Mashed potatoes are new potatoes—fresh new potatoes smashed down so they have the skin on them. Bruce used to have these at Central Falls. So they get a choice of either potatoes or rice or one of the vegetables.

"For the vegetable plate tonight there's going to be snow peas, zucchini, yellow squash, carrots, wild mushroom, rice, there'll be about seven things on it. We serve brown rice, always.

"The grilled boneless capon breast is marinated in pesto, it's grilled. We serve the pastas at room temperature. It's not to be served hot or cold. If someone says my pasta's cold I want to send it back, that's not the deal. That's not what's going on here, okay? It's meant to be served at room temperature. I don't want to hear about heating it up, either, because it's already in the sauce and everything else. It says room temperature, but just to be sure. It's tossed with fresh mozzarella and basil and tomatoes, chopped up. It's nice.

"The pheasant and wild mushroom pot pie is just a pheasant stock we use that's real strong, with the flavor of wild mushrooms, with pheasant meat, there's no other vegetables in it, it's pretty rich and it's pretty filling for what it is."

Pastry's only on the top?

"It's only on the top. Buffalo burgers—chock-full of Monterey jack, Vermont, cheddar or mozzarella, we have red onions, and romaine lettuce if they want it on it, and tomatoes. And they're served with fries."

And the fries are still free!

/At 5:00 P.M., as the waiters take their positions, the liquor license takes its place on the wall behind the bar, and the sun begins its final approach toward the horizon, Brian Moores and Bruce Goldstein go for a walk.

They exit through the front door of The Falls and walk together to the corner of Varick and Vandam. There they stand for a moment, searching the streets for people who might be walking their way. It is early. No one will be coming to The Falls at this hour, and surely not by foot. But they will be here soon. It is important for Bruce to have this moment in the sun.

For this occasion, Bruce is wearing a white pullover shirt—not

LaCoste exactly, but something like an alligator is crawling across the front of it. And on top of it he has on a baggy gray shirt with long red vertical stripes. He keeps a black pen clipped to the vest pocket of the outer shirt. He leaves this shirt open, and achieves a double-layered look he tends to prefer. The white shirt brings out the depth of his tan.

It's especially dark tonight.

"Take a good, deep breath," he tells Brian.

Brian is excited. For him, tonight will justify it all—the departure from L'Acajou, the tedious hours on the bus to Pennsylvania, the pointless debates over the price of fish. Tonight The Falls will come alive, and with it his career as a chef of significance. Fame! That's what The Falls is about, isn't it? The men and women whose money begat The Falls—they're famous, they're rich, they can create a restaurant with the stroke of a pen. After tonight, they will know me, too. I will be the man behind The Falls.

If only I had red lentils! How will the peppered smoked salmon taste without them? He is wondering, no, make that *obsessing* about those lentils. He actually sent someone to Balducci's, the fancy New York retail produce store, to buy some. They were out. They laughed at the question. *"Red* lentils? We *never* have red lentils," they said at Balducci's. Ah, the poor customers at The Falls—they have no idea what they will be missing, something so special they cannot get it, even at the beloved Balducci's.

"The place looks great," Bruce says. He puts his arm around Brian's shoulder, and together they go back inside.

/At 6:10 P.M., The Falls opens for business.

At 6:15 P.M., the first customers arrive for a drink. A man and a woman in their thirties. Already people are coming in that hardly fit the bill of The Falls. The man is wearing a hat, along with an outfit that strongly suggests a taste for Country & Western—tall boots, a vest, a plaid shirt. The woman looks more like a New York professional—long skirt, short boots and frizzy brown hair. She orders a club soda. He orders a J&B on the rocks. They whisper quietly to each other. They smoke. Every so often they turn around, and see that everyone in the restaurant is watching them. Bruce, by the stereo controls, keeps checking the level of their drinks. Brian stands by the back barrier between the dining room and the kitchen, waiting for someone to ask for a menu. The waiters wander aimlessly through the dining room—lighting candles, straightening forks and adjusting those perfectly folded napkins.

At 6:35, a man in a dark blue suit comes in by himself and orders a beer at the bar. Bruce is on the phone when he enters, but hangs up quickly when he observes the bartender—not Henry, he went home for a quick nap, the other guy, Gary—not putting down a coaster underneath the man's drinking glass. Bruce has gone to some trouble and expense to have coasters printed with The Falls name and insignia, and damnit, he'll have them used! Right after Gary finishes serving the beer, Bruce leans across the bar in full view of his three customers. "As soon as they sit down," Bruce says loudly, "put a coaster down in front."

If there were a clock in The Falls—and there was supposed to be, in fact, in an early design by Morris Nathanson, right above the bar—it would be ticking away the awkward, painful minutes that precede the arrival of the first customers to sit down for dinner. The candles are now lit, and the pink neon bulbs are doing their stuff. But it is an eerie, uncomfortable feeling. Sure, it's silly to think about—but what if nobody ever came to eat here? What if the restaurant died before it was born?

The first customers have arrived at 7:10 P.M., almost an hour to the second after the restaurant opened its doors, and they are whisked to a table for two. Bruce walks over to take a look. They have been given a decent though not particularly good table, the one adjacent to the big white post that holds up the room. The couple is dressed for a cold winter night—no black miniskirts or billowy silk shirts for these guys. The man is wearing a simple blue pullover and dark gray corduroy pants. He's youngish, perhaps forty, but prematurely gray. His companion looks younger; a blonde, she is wearing a soft white sweater and a charcoal gray skirt over her knees. "Should I buy 'em a drink?" he asks himself. But they've already ordered two glasses of white wine. Too late for grand gestures. He watches for a second as they scan their menus. Brian, meanwhile, scurries back into the kitchen. His job is about to begin.

They peruse the menu, slowly. Brian is offering three specials tonight:

Mesclun salad with sautéed sea scallops, olive oil and sherry vinegar . . . $7.

"Ehu" Hawaiian red snapper with sun-dried tomato, herbs and garlic . . . $15.

Grilled quail with rosemary sauce . . . $15.

The specials have been delicately handwritten on a separate menu enclosure, and written at the bottom are historic words chosen by Brian for this occasion: "OPENING NIGHT: 1 MAR 90: Thanks for Coming!"

A half hour later, the couple has made their decision. They have spent easily ten minutes intensely poring over the menu. Do they know they are the first customers ever to eat at The Falls? No one wants to tell them—no, that would be too pathetic. They nonchalantly

T   H   E
FALLS

SPECIALS

MESCLUN SALAD $7 00
     w/ SAUTEED SEA SCALLOPS
        OLIVE OIL & SHERRY VINEGAR

EHU: HAWAIIAN RED SNAPPER $15 00
     w/ SUN DRIED TOMATO, HERBS
                    & GARLIC

GRILLED QUAIL $14 00
        w/ ROSEMARY SAUCE

OPENING NIGHT: 1 MAR 90: Thanks for Coming!

wave over Jonathan, the controversial expert on napkin folding. He is crisp and clean in his white shirt and brightly colored tie. His hair has been expertly slicked back for this occasion. He has been poised, ready for action since they took their seats. "We'll have the peppered smoked salmon to start," the man says. Without the red lentils . . . oh *man.* "And for dinner, we'll have the half-moon pasta and the oriental chicken salad."

Appetizers for entrées. Damn.

Jonathan takes the order to the computer. This thing is going to be one major pain in the ass. After a misfire or two, he finally punches in the order properly, and sends it into the kitchen, where a small machine prints out the order on a slip of white paper. Brian is poised to receive, even though he's been monitoring the situation visually and knows the order already. The system works; that is important to him, he wants to reinforce it, and the only way is for the chef to remain in the kitchen and make what he is told.

"Come on, let's go!" Brian commands to his staff of four, three cooks and a dishwasher. He reaches for a plate, and begins the assembly process. Much has been readied in advance, and they can move quickly into put-on-the-plate mode if they want to. But it's cooking, finally, no more of that bullshit, no more staff meetings, no more listening to Bruce . . . this is what Brian does best, after all, this is what separates him from the rest of the staff. Bruce may run the joint, but Brian is *executive* chef—the only executive at The Falls.

Suddenly it explodes. Terry Quinn comes in trendy duds with four of his brothers. They are all classic Quinns. Handsome and virile and friendly. They assume a preferred table against the far wall. They order drinks all around. It is absolutely necessary for Terry to be in center position, though; he must be able to launch from his seat at any time to greet, to kiss, to schmooze. And within minutes, almost seconds, the opportunities come. Twos and fours and threes and sixes—groups of every conceivable size begin to turn up at the front door, looking for table at the newest restaurant in town. A few have reservations; most have been invited down by Terry or Bruce or Philippe, no reservations needed, just bring your pretty face down here and we'll make you happy.

By 9:00 P.M. it is clear that The Falls is a huge, unabashed hit. Yes sir. Every table is filled, every chair at the bar, and every conceivable space to stand in is taken. It is dark, it is cool . . . the men are handsome, the women beautiful. All of them. It is truly incredible. There is actually not one unattractive person here. The pink bulbs are hot, hot,

hot. The room glows from their heat. Is it that everyone here is beautiful, or that everyone looks beautiful in The Falls? Never mind, it's not important now.

Terry Quinn is responsible. When beautiful women and men enter The Falls and immediately begin kissing, you can assume that Fireman Terry Quinn is responsible. Yes, it really is true; that gorgeous hunk of manly junk was an Official New York City Firefighter! That Matt Dillon look-a-like was a fucking fireman! If you close your eyes and imagine him in big black boots, however, you will not be rewarded. At this moment, all that remains of his days on the force— halted at the moment by a long leave of absence—are a couple of extremely cool T-shirts, and hours of amusing stories about smoke and dalmatians and poles.

Terry Quinn was not put on this earth to put out fires. When you look at him glide across this now-emptying room, smacking lips and kissing cheeks and squeezing arms, you observe a man who was born to heat things up. Let's face it: This is Mr. Popularity you've heard tell about, a man who carries around the thickest Day-At-A-Glance you've ever seen (black, of course), filled to overflowing with phone numbers, oh yes, phone numbers of people you can only imagine, the kind of numbers most of us will never dial again.

Just look! There's that model, what's-her-name, you've seen her in the Victoria's Secret catalog . . . and her, and her, and her. They check their long coats and reveal very little in the way of clothing underneath. Cool guys, too—Richard Merkin, the artist; Eddie Hayes, the lawyer from *The Bonfire of the Vanities*; Reinaldo Herrera, what does he do? No one knows, no one cares.

/Bruce is at the dials. He cannot be bothered with kissing pretty girls. That is Terry's job. Philippe can handle that. He must dim the lights, darker, darker . . . And the music! He has to make sure that Sinatra is playing, because if you are a man over forty in this world, and you see a beautiful woman and you long for her and you dream of her, no man's music speaks to you like Sinatra. Bruce is happy, thrilled, overjoyed. The Falls is a hit.

"In the wee small hours of the morning . . ."

He turns up the music, ever so slightly, as this tune comes on. It is the first time he has played Sinatra since the doors opened, and it is a sign of success. It is an anthem of sorts, a statement that The Falls will be there when everything else is gone. He adjusts the lights one more time, then comes out from behind the bar to check out the kitchen. He pushes the swinging door and sees calamity. Brian is running, jumping, swirling; orders are pouring into the kitchen, the computer is cranking out little slips of paper, and plates are sailing out to their tables.

"It's a mess," Brian tells Bruce. "We're totally backed up, everybody's getting their order *real* late."

Bruce tells Brian what the chef already knows. The highly touted speed demon computer is slowing things up. "It's taking five to ten minutes for the order to get from the floor to you," he says. He has been watching the computers and the waitresses and the checks, and he has been around restaurants enough to know that if it were not opening night, if it were not his friends and if it were not . . . oh, forget it, we'll work this out later. "So *push.*"

But Bruce doesn't care. Not really; not now. He watches Brian for another moment, tears off an oversized piece of a long, thin baguette and puts it in his mouth. Then he turns. He pushes the swinging door and leaves the kitchen behind, to go back out and survey the room he has built, the restaurant he dreamed of, and revel for a moment in the glory of a fabulous opening night.

"If this restaurant were a woman," Bruce says softly, his eyes scanning across the room, his voice practically trembling, "I'd fuck her in the ass."

/By 1:30 in the morning, the place had finally quieted a little. One waiter had even gone home. Groups of revelers still dotted the room, sipping late-night cognacs, laughing, talking. But the music had grown mellow. Coltrane had replaced Sinatra, and the lights had dimmed even more.

What a night. More than 150 "covers," the word they use in the restaurant biz to describe people—more than 150 people had dinner here tonight. With only ninety-six seats, that means several tables turned over—not literally of course, that's just another term in the biz. Most of them were friends and acquaintances. Some of them were investors. All of them knew, somehow, that this was the first night in the history of The Falls.

The bar did massive business, too. Over the course of the night, hundreds of drinks were poured. Two dozen bottles of champagne were opened and poured. Fifty or sixty people crowded around the bar at any given moment. The tables by the bar presented their waitress with an almost impossible logjam every time she delivered food—yet somehow she managed, endearing herself even though people waited hours for their orders to arrive. Behind the bar, Gary and Rebecca, bartenders experienced at the task of keeping people happy and drunk, never stopped moving. Their clients, unlike most others in the place, got quick, painless service all night, and rewarded them with hundreds of dollars in tips.

The third bartender, Katherine, did not fare quite so well. Everything changed for Katherine around 10:30 P.M., in the absolute height of the rush, when she was observed clutching a bottle of Perrier-Jouët champagne in one hand and a wine corkscrew in the other, attempting to open it like a bottle of wine. Henry, done with his nap, went over to coach her, and gently explained that a champagne bottle works differently.

So much for Katherine.

In the kitchen, Manuel, the dishwasher, has before him a pile of dishes that no mere mortal could look at without pain. He faces them down and scrubs and sprays. The hardest-working man in show business, Bruce calls him. His kitchen colleagues—beaten from the long, long night of delays and misfires and mistakes—finally take a break and visit the bar themselves. Beers all around, the clinking of glass . . . never mind how bad it went. We all have jobs, the place is hot, and we all have much to celebrate, don't we?

Brian gets himself a glass of fine Chardonnay. Many things give him pleasure—a beer at lunch, a cognac in the heat of a dinner rush—but sometimes there is nothing like a fine white wine. It is 1:35 A.M. Time to take stock of the night, of The Falls and of the future. Time to talk to Bruce. They sit down together in the back of the restaurant, away from the buzz of conversation.

There is a necessary agenda for this. Tonight was a smash; but it was a disaster, too, slowed by a computer that no one could operate, a system that didn't work, a staff that couldn't function.

"For some reason, usually when a room gets full, it feels crowded and small," Bruce says. "This place has a nice feel. You gotta give those designers a lot of credit for the way they laid it out. It's got a straight line right around to the bar."

"It's nice," Brian says. He is drinking and dreaming. There are no laws against that. Bruce's words waft over him.

But that's all right. Bruce needs no audience. He is dreaming, too. "The bar is the centerpiece," he says. "It was four deep most of the night. What we should do tomorrow—tomorrow have brainstorming, a face-to-face conversation with the floor, really laying it out."

A meeting? Is that absolutely necessary? "Jonathan really knows what's going on," Brian says.

Bruce looks unconvinced. Yes, Jonathan was tonight's star waiter. Close to $200 in tips. But is he the man Bruce is looking for to lead the charge? Bruce is suspicious. He tends toward suspicion, and the fact that Jonathan is so good, well, that is certainly grounds for a raised eyebrow at least. Why did the guy leave his last job? It was a better restaurant, hardly a breeding ground for The Falls. And tonight, when the dishes piled high and the computer failed, Jonathan was the first to suggest that this elaborate system, the deal Bruce cut, was not going to work. Jonathan said it, and perhaps it was true. The Falls might be a hit, but the computer was a major flop.

"I wish he would not be that kind of guy 'cause I'd like to have some faith in him," Bruce says, "but I'm not quite as confident as everybody else."

"Let me put it this way. He sees what needs to be done," Brian says.

"Yeah . . . but one stupid comment he made . . . he wanted to put these fucking speckled stars on the table. The funny thing is, now, every time he gives me something that's really good, I say, Thank God it's not another star idea. And that's a nice thing to keep going on.

"Between us . . . Brian, I can't tell you how much I want to keep these people happy. Because I don't think—I think it's important, and I think the rewards from it are going to be gratifying . . . not just monetarily. I think to make the people happy on a continuous basis, without robbin' 'em, is a nightmare."

"It really is." Brian gulps down the last of his wine.

Bruce falls deep into his trance. He is high tonight; and when he is high, he thinks grand, global thoughts on the meaning of life in restaurants. "You're using people who are forty, or thereabouts. And it's that age group, that are all of a sudden realizing that there's a whole change in the 1990s, and their forties, I don't want to be treated like I used to, I don't want to go to all the same places, I don't want to be treated like a juvenile because I'm not young anymore, so why am I hanging on in these places? There's this whole thing going on, and I think they want to hear good music, they want to eat good food, they want to see some nice people, they don't want to be totally crowded at the tables."

Brian isn't exactly sure what Bruce is talking about.

"They're getting good food at a good price," he says.

"That's what I'm saying!"

"No doubt about it," Brian says.

"At 6:00 it was like . . . but then it was . . ."

"Oh boy . . ."

"But we knew it was gonna be rough," Bruce says.

"But it wasn't that bad."

"The waiters, some of the ones who were less experienced, didn't know what to do . . . like Jonathan told me . . . don't get too mad. We may need another computer . . ." Bruce gets up to refill his wineglass.

"A lot of people are good, but we need the key."

"That's Jonathan's attitude." Bruce cannot shake the subject of Jonathan. He will not halt his obsession. Not until Brian agrees. Jonathan is a threat. He must be eliminated. Not the computer. *Him*. "His attitude was, this system should work, once everybody gets into it. And there's another thing about it. I jerked this thing around . . . making whatever chiseling deal I could make, I did that . . ."

"If it was *his* cash would he be singing this song?" Brian sees the light.

"It shoulda been here two weeks ago. And I accept the blame for that. But . . . I got this thing in here for $1,600. They were talking thirty grand."

"I believe you."

"This is beyond a restaurant," Bruce says. "This is like being in the VIP room but getting fed, you know? It's true. It's true."

"You set out to do something, and you got it."

The two men pause and drink. The fruits of success; the nectar of heat.

"I don't think it's like a week from now, people are going to go, well, and it's going to die down. No," Brian says.

"No," Bruce agrees. "We're going to get better. See—we can't be . . . Nobody's going to wait around forty-five minutes ever again. So we know this. Now we have to offer something else. Change our attitude. This is what we do . . . at quarter of two, we say, it's been a long day, we close up early tonight. We'll close at 2:00."

Kimberly walks by. She has had a long day and a long night. But she is here, and as long as she is here, Bruce will not stop giving her instructions. "What you should do," he tells her, "is see if there's a waiter who wants to stay and do this. But I want to know who it is. I want to know who it is."

Bruce gestures at Lisa, the waitress who tended the tables near the bar. She is still carrying dishes back to be washed. "She was good. That fucking bar area—you know what? She never made so much tips in her life. So right off the bat—realized potential. I tell you, I couldn't be encouraged. I never expected this."

"I did," says Brian.

"A *Thursday night!*"

"Yeah," Brian says, "but a lot of people know about this place. They anticipated this place. They really did."

"Friends from all over," says Bruce.

"Terry called people."

"Our investment band!" Bruce says. "Our band of investors!"

"They're quite a clientele."

Bruce leans back against the banquette and rests his feet on a chair.

"The one thing I learned from all this was, you know, they got something for their money, but they also got something beyond that. If you've got a discretionary $20,000 to invest, discretionary—don't-give-a-fuck money—their accountant'll tell 'em things.

"But they don't have to look at the paper every day and see how their mutual fund is doing. They have wasted more than that money on many occasions. This is almost like home entertainment or a private club."

Brian nods. But he is thinking about his own spiritual investment.

After tonight, he knows it is going to pay off.

/Finally the night is done. As Bruce and Brian continue their conversation, the waiters and waitresses divide their tips. It has been a very good night.

Still, Jonathan cannot stop thinking. That computer is never going to work. Not unless we all get together and lick this thing, right? No rehearsal, no practice, no lessons . . . this is no way to start a restaurant. He must come forward and tell Bruce. We need another terminal, three are not enough, we will never get through a night like this again.

But Bruce already knows. He does not need to be told by Jonathan. How bad could they have been? Hundreds of people were here . . . thousands of dollars were made.

"When everyone knows it," Bruce says, "then it doesn't work, I promise to get another terminal."

"You have this weekend and you have next week," Jonathan says.

"And I want to say this," Bruce says. "I have to get some input from you guys. Here's the attitude that I'm telling the waiters tomorrow. Get in line or get out of the way. Because you're either going to adapt or you're gone."

"There's no room for it," Brian agrees. "But also we need lucidity in the kitchen so it's like—boom, this is what we're doing."

"Exactly," Bruce says. Jonathan is listening intently, as is Kimberly. "What I don't want to do is have waiters thinking that they—we can load this place up with fifteen terminals. But that asshole waiter still doesn't know how to punch it in, we're still not going to move."

Brian says, "When everybody's up to par, that's when you'll see . . ."

"Now's not the time to worry about the sell," Jonathan agrees. He doesn't want to start a fight tonight of all nights . . . this historic night. He merely wants to explain it to Bruce. "You had the most incredible night tonight. We were jamming. We asked too much of the waiters tonight, they were flipped out."

This is not Bruce's take. *No.* "Wait a minute, guys . . . this was a *total fucking surprise.* If you think I had any inkling . . . I swear . . . did I?" Bruce looks at Kimberly for support.

"He didn't," Kimberly says.

"My prediction was fifty to sixty people . . . and a lot of people at the bar for drinks . . . These kind of people . . . I wouldn't fucking bet my ranch on them coming back every night. The truth of the matter is, the place speaks for itself. It's gonna happen. Now we just gotta fulfill our share by getting this logistics stuff done. I will get freaked out at people once I know how the system's supposed to work. Tonight the professional waiters handled it the best they could, the other people got fucking mowed down."

"That's okay," Jonathan says. "Tonight is the place where you answer questions. That's it."

"We've got a lot to change tomorrow," Bruce says. "Micros has flipped out. Micros had not seen anything quite like this in a long time." He has planned a meeting for tomorrow with Becky, the woman from Micros, the company that sold The Falls its computer system. As part of its service tonight, she stood, incredulous, and watched as the untrained staff couldn't cope with the system.

"She said she never saw an opening night like this," Brian says.

"I just want to tell you . . . Let me tell you something . . . I went with Micros for one thing 'cause I like Micros, but my point is, they know that this is a real showplace for them to have their machines in. And they have to make it work. And they're gonna make it work with the least amount of things because they want to sell systems that work. They don't just want to sell terminals. Just selling terminals. They have two of their customers come in tonight and ask me. And the truth of the matter is, I blame myself for a lot of this, because I didn't fucking plunk down the money for the machinery so it was delivered two weeks ago. That's what I should have done, and I didn't. I procrastinated. And I jerked it around. But now, this is it. Let's make it work."

"I think you're right about that," Jonathan says. "Because the waiters are generally prepared."

"I accept that. That's why I wasn't all over everybody tonight. I'm not freaked out. I've paid. I came from Oklahoma, I've been to the fair, and I understand exactly what I have to do, now tomorrow's the carnival. But up until now—the computer thing has to be fine-tuned."

Terry Quinn has joined the conversation. He has pulled up a chair and has his own assessment. "Most of the people here understood that it was the first night," he says. "No need to apologize."

Bruce spreads his arms and flashes a smile. "Look at this fucking place. This is a great place!"

"Obviously," says Brian.

Bruce takes another sip of his drink. It is now after 2:00 in the morning. He is surrounded by the core group that created The Falls— Terry, Brian and Kimberly—and he is flushed with color. The red in his shirt brings out the fire in his eyes.

"We're gonna make it work," Bruce says.

/The lead story in the next morning's *Times,* a three-deck headline over two columns, read, WORLD DRUG CROP UP SHARPLY IN 1989 DESPITE U.S. EFFORT.

In the Weekend section appeared Bryan Miller's weekly restaurant review. This week he gave two stars to La Caravelle, a West 55th Street French restaurant that has seen happier days. "It would be premature to say La Caravelle is on the way to recapturing its former glory," he concluded. "At the same time, it seems to have postponed a trip to that big banquette in the sky."

He also reported the openings of two restaurants: Trieze, an American-Mediterranean restaurant on East 13th Street, and Jackalope, with Southwestern cuisine, on East 20th. The opening of The Falls was not mentioned.

IF YOU SERVE GUACAMOLE FOR

FREE THEY WILL COME

THIRTEEN

Everybody hoped that Friday night would be a repeat of Thursday. There was every reason to suspect that it would be. The reservations book—a large red-and-black hardbound volume titled simply 1990 STANDARD DAILY JOURNAL, with a full diary page devoted to each day, divided one dull February afternoon into half-hour time blocks by Philippe Dumont—held eighty reservations. Last night's crowd exceeded bookings by at least three- to fourfold, and there was no reason to think tonight would be any less wild.

Bruce has chosen, at the last minute, not to open for Friday lunch. This rankles the kitchen slightly, since Brian had ordered enough food to cover lunches and brunches as well as dinners. But Bruce, keen observer that he is of human nature, knows that his staff cannot and probably *would* not cope with the added burden of lunch. Plus everyone was up awfully late the night before, remember; who needs to come into work at 11:00 in the morning? More to the point: Who wants to?

So Bruce has relieved his kitchen and wait staff of the burden of lunch. This presumably will make tonight move more smoothly. It is going to be a Friday night crowd. Sure, last night was huge, but tonight could be colossal. Word is out. That's how it works in the restaurant biz. Bruce believes in the power of the word.

The staff—buoyed by the bonanza of opening night—has come to the party with added enthusiasm tonight. This one will be a winner. We know what our mistakes were, we will not repeat them. Practice makes perfect, right? Jonathan is telling himself that as he sits in the twilight neon glow, folding tonight's napkins and placing them carefully between two forks, a knife and a spoon. The computer is a tool to be mastered. The kitchen is a beast to be tamed.

Bruce wanders in around mid-afternoon. He is rested and ready. Whatever he may think of Jonathan, it is a comfort to see a young, bright man take charge. Someone has to. It is a large and unruly staff that cries out for leadership. That responsibility might have fallen to Philippe; but he is, quite simply, too cool to be in charge. You cannot have a boss whose idea of management style is to lean against the front desk and inhale. There had been some brief talk at one point of Henry moving out from behind the bar to run the room; but Bruce's suspicious mind got in the way. He does not trust Henry, for reasons he cannot articulate, and so he cannot give him the job. Besides, Henry feels most comfortable where he is, behind the bar. No one has any doubt about his skills at bottle management.

Jonathan has sensed this power vacuum. He knows that he can fill it. He will watch, and wait, and learn. He will light the candles and let them burn. He will glide across the room with plates and menus and bottles. The waitresses are good, yes; a few of them are beautiful. And Marcel—he has that Frenchness about him, that handsome Moroccan face. But Jonathan, this melancholy baby, is going to win. He will survive and prosper.

By 6:30, the dinner crowd has already begun to stream in. Last night is beginning to look pale by comparison. Parties of six crowd around tables for four. Waiters line up for the computer, and struggle with the codes. The bar is full; hands are waving in the air to get a bartender's attention. "Here we go again," says Bruce. He is more effervescent than a bottle of Taittinger's Brut. This is what a restaurant is supposed to be! People, food, drinks and cash . . . plenty of cash. The American Express machine still isn't ready.

By 9:00 P.M. the room has filled completely.

Three couples—trendy sophisticates from the Yupper West Side of Manhattan, a legendary restaurant wasteland, desperate in their search for quality cuisine in hip-hop surroundings—have donned their oversized jackets and miniskirts for the journey southward. Two cabs' worth of people have piled into The Falls and note immediately upon entering that they are not the only ones dressed for thrills. It is a leggy crowd, with women of stature at every table. "What is the gene pool in this place?" one of them wonders wittily. Happy trendy people with money enough to buy bottles with corks. You can hear them popping.

Marcel will be this group's waiter tonight. Smack in the middle of the room. Do his highly touted skills translate from his native French?

A bottle of wine is ordered. Marcel has suggested a 1983 Château Fombrauge Saint-Emilion for $26. The customers instead request a 1988 Brouilly for $19. They ask Marcel whether it will come slightly chilled, presuming that he, this classy French waiter, will surely know that slightly chilled is the proper way to serve a Brouilly. They are tragically mistaken. They are also mistaken when they expect the wine to be served promptly. It fails to arrive for ten minutes.

Appetizers are ordered. Marcel makes several suggestions of what to order. He likes to suggest the most expensive things. They are, as it happens, what is ordered—the $8 carpaccio, the $6.50 peppered smoked salmon, the $7 warm goat cheese salad, like that. Never mind money. These people are here to have fun.

Unfortunately, they are also here to have food. This is going to be a problem. After forty-five minutes, their appetizers have yet to arrive. Marcel has instead brought them two more baskets of bread and another bottle of wine. This meal is beginning to resemble not so much a restaurant dinner as an afternoon picnic in the Luxembourg Gardens in Paris. A loaf of bread, a jug of wine . . .

When some annoyance is expressed, Marcel goes in search of an explanation, and comes back a few moments later with this one, you couldn't make this up: Your appetizers, he tells the half dozen now-tipsy customers, were inadvertently brought to another table, and *those* customers, also having waited endlessly for *their* appetizers, decided to not say anything and eat *your* appetizers. So now, he says, I have reordered your appetizers, they will be here any second, and I have also brought you a bottle of wine on the house!

At 10:15 P.M., seventy-five minutes after entering the restaurant, food is finally being served to these hungry patrons. They eat it. They enjoy it. They are finally able to adjust the topic of dinner conversation away from their hunger, their lack of service and their general annoyance with The Falls. However, they have eaten so much bread, and now the appetizers . . . they're *full!*

This does not bode well for their attitude toward the main course, which arrives at precisely two hours and ten minutes into the evening. Midnight is fast approaching. The three couples are now officially drunk.

"I am so sorry . . ." Marcel is attempting to clear his name. The group of six forgives him, pays their check and goes across the street to a disco. Across the restaurant, the stories are the same. The apologies are the same. The problems are the same. No food. No service. No fun. Oh sure—it *looks* like fun; from where Bruce is spending most of the night, at the end of the bar near the lights and the music, the room has its familiar glow. Plates do seem to be moving, and customers remain seated with forks and knives in their hands. What the hell can Bruce do, anyway? Cook it all himself?

It is Friday night. Everyone wants to be happy. Bruce is not going to let a few little slipups get in the way of his glorious, wonderful success.

They will come back. They will *all* come back.

Won't they?

/What does it take to open a restaurant? There are many theories about this, of course. If one is searching for a literal answer, here are the dry goods on hand, based on an inventory taken at The Falls that Friday morning:

50 pounds salt
Kosher salt
1/2 case Kikkoman soy sauce
1 case red wine vinegar
1/2 case balsamic vinegar
1/2 case Spanish cherry vinegar
1 case cheap olive oil
1/2 case extra virgin olive oil
1/2 case walnut oil
2 gallons sesame oil
2 gallons Dijon mustard
noncholesterol corn oil
1/2 case capers
green olives with pits
Malaysian green peppercorns
1 kilo bag sun-dried tomatoes
water chestnuts
2 slabs semisweet chocolate (22 pounds)
pancake mix
bitters

1 case Lea & Perrins worcestershire sauce
1 case sugar packets
1 case Sweet 'n Low
1 case Rose's lime juice
1 case grenadine
1 case tomato juice
1 case pineapple juice
1 bottle Ocean Spray cranberry juice
1 case lemon juice

By Monday—just four days after opening night—The Falls is approaching complete chaos. Or is it past chaos and into some altered state of being? Two waiters have already quit. Another has been fired. Henry is in trouble. Brian is unhappy. Why is Bruce so . . . *serene?*

Valerie became the first victim of the miniskirt syndrome. Like most of her female colleagues, she tended toward extremely short, tight skirts—a combination of pressure from external forces to maintain a properly sexy image for The Falls, and a personal desire to stimulate large tips. It would be fair to say that a direct, inverse equation existed between tip size and skirt length, and that Falls waitresses were among the foremost exploiters of this phenomenon. But Valerie did not anticipate that in this classy, upscale place, a customer named Joey—referred to by everyone as a "mob guy" though never officially identified by his specific rank in any crime family—would actually grab her body.

But he did. And she quit. "I don't need to be grabbed," she explained.

Bruce and Joey know each other. Restaurant people know mob people. It is a fact of New York restaurant life, and to paraphrase David Mamet, it may mean nothing and it may not. What Bruce believes is this: Valerie overreacted. On Monday, after tensions have subsided slightly, Bruce is taking Joey's side.

"There's different ways to grab someone," Bruce says. "You can grab someone's arm, touching them. It's the waitress's responsibility to say to somebody, 'I'd appreciate it if you didn't grab me.' "

Well, it's true, Valerie neglected to say, "I'd appreciate it if you didn't grab me," to Joey. Instead, she quit. Too bad for her.

Lance also quit. Another waiter with a problem. Nobody's sorry to see him go. Now they're saying if he hadn't left he'd have been fired. A lot of people pointing knowingly at their nostrils. Finally Bruce comes right out and says it. "The guy had a huge coke problem," Bruce says. "You could see this guy's jaw moving all night."

And Tony has been fired. An attitude problem. That is worse than a coke problem, apparently. Tony had the temerity to insist upon keeping his own tips. From the start, he opposed the principle of pooling tips—an arrangement agreed to by all concerned the week before. Then, Tony called it Communism. Now he calls it the reason for his dismissal. There is some small measure of guilt—the guy had pitched in before the place opened, he wanted to work, he *cared*—but he didn't do what he was told.

And what about Henry? Four days and even he's on the ropes.

"Henry and I have a problem between us," Bruce says. "It's an attitude thing. I don't get what his problem is. I think he's pissed off that he did all the work and then these guys walk in here and make all the money from the bar tips. It's natural. We got to work out what his role will be here."

All is not well in the kitchen, either. Brian is not happy. He does not like putting the vegetables on the same plate with the main dishes. "I would have ordered bigger plates," he says. He is being polite. What he means is, I did not get into this business to be slopping mashed potatoes, I don't care *how* good they are, next to my carefully designed cuisine. No sir. At L'Acajou I delicately placed the vegetables on a separate plate. And it looked mighty good.

/There has been one other opening weekend casualty, by the way. The flower lady.

On opening day, Bruce paid an odd, dark woman named Rachel $160 to bring flowers to The Falls. She had come in the week before to sell her services, and Bruce thought she looked like a flower lady. She was. They were pretty. She arranged a large vase in the center of the bar, made even more dramatic by the large circular mirror behind. She also threw a few flowers into a pot on the desk by the door. There had been considerable oohing and aahing over the flowers throughout opening night, and much praise for her expert hand.

She has now returned on Monday with a new arrangement. This one displeases Bruce immensely. It consists of two short orange flowers and one long red one. Their varieties are of no consequence. Bruce is more concerned with the issue of quantity. What do you think? Rachel would like his opinion. On opening day he told her one thing; today he has told her another, or so she thinks, when his answer is to gesture brusquely at the three flowers and say, "That's ridiculous, right?"

No, she responds.

"I want a pretty selection of flowers," Bruce says, "and I don't want it to look like some kind of arrangement."

"You keep changing your mind all the time, though, Bruce," Rachel says. "I can't give you what you want."

Bruce screams, "I just want something *nice!*"

Rachel backs away.

Bruce tells Rachel to fill out the vase with more flowers.

Rachel says no.

Bruce tells Rachel he doesn't even like her vase.

Rachel says fine.

Bruce tells Rachel to figure something out. He will be in the basement awaiting her solution.

Rachel says okay.

Bruce goes to the basement muttering about how he'd like to fire her.

Rachel follows him there two minutes later, and says, "I quit."

Is this Bruce's management style? A pattern is beginning to emerge. He does not like to fire people. He prefers to make their lives miserable. He can do that very well. He can make life so miserable that you think, This is his restaurant, not mine, and therefore I must leave this horrible place and get on with my life.

/"I'll Take Manhattan" played on the sound system Monday night while it snowed. People don't like to eat out when it snows, apparently. Or is this just some kind of plausible deniability? There's no one here, that much is certain. "Will *anyone* come in?" a waitress asks.

This question could be applied to Bruce. He may or may not be coming in. The evening goes by smoothly enough without him, and when he finally walks in at 11:10 P.M., the night is basically over. It seems he has come to make sure the machine is oiled and smooth. This he can do by a brief glance before bedtime.

Bruce stands by the bar in the back. Okay, so there's nobody here. I'm not going to get upset about that, it's Day *Five* for chrissakes. But Bruce *is* going to get upset by the fact that—as it has just been explained to him by Gary at the bar—five cases of Volvic water are already gone. Twelve bottles to the case.

Volvic is not a fancy drink. It is, essentially, water, though it is sold for $2.50 a bottle to customers who cannot be truly happy unless they pay for a beverage of some kind. This includes recovering alcoholics, who like to have a bottle of *something* on the table. The irony is that

New York City happens to be blessed with an unparalleled local beverage, available for free, known as tap water. If only it came in a bottle! If only we could *pay* for it! Alas, beverage addicts must have something a little classier than tap water in their glass.

But sixty bottles of Volvic? It seems improbable. Even in 1990.

"We didn't sell sixty bottles of fucking Volvic!" Bruce bellows when he hears the report. It is day five of his beloved new restaurant, and he'll be damned if he's going to lose money on water sales. "If any of the staff goes near the bottled water," Bruce issues forth, loud enough for every staff member to hear, "I'll fucking fire them."

Meanwhile, down the bar, three men have just sat down for a drink. One Campari and soda, one diet Coke, one nonalcoholic beer. After a few minutes of semiprivate giggling and amused debate, one of them lifts the rather attractive Perrier-Jouët ashtray sitting on the bar in front of them, and puts it in his pocket.

"I'll take Manhattan . . ."

There's that song again. Is Bruce paying attention? The tape appears to be on a loop.

/"People gotta learn the amounts."

Bruce is lecturing Henry at the bar. It is now eight days into the venture, and he has pinpointed a problem: bartenders are not pouring drinks properly. They are giving customers too much to drink. Too much for too little, that is. It is here at the bar where the profits are supposed to roll in. Bruce is going to make sure that they do.

"People gotta learn the amounts," Bruce is saying. "If they don't they're outta here."

Henry's annoyance with Bruce is building steadily. Bruce refers to it as an "attitude problem." That may be; Henry definitely has an attitude about Bruce, and it is negative. That is the problem. Henry has come to believe that Bruce does not have what it takes to pull it off. He has seen restaurants come and go, mostly go; and he had believed Bruce could make this one work. But now Henry isn't so sure. He has become friendly with Brian Moores, and the two of them— comparing notes on the first week of business—have come to the conclusion that Bruce is mismanaging the place.

Brian has told Henry a rather tragic statistic. So far, he reports, The Falls's food cost is 50 percent of its revenues. In a successful restaurant, that percentage is supposed to be somewhere around 30 percent.

How could this happen? Two possibilities. One is that Brian is spending too much money on food. Let us not forget his famous fish fetish. Some of these wacky fish are pretty expensive. If you're not careful, you can find yourself spending more than you can afford. However, one key fact worth mentioning is that Brian *is* careful. It does not serve his interests to be spending too much on food. It is a surefire way to insure disaster. That is the last thing Brian wants. If anything, he'd like to keep food costs *way* down and guarantee quick profits. There's no percentage for Brian in spending The Falls to death. He needs the job.

The other possibility—the one considered most likely by those who've kept a close watch on Bruce and Terry this first week—is that they have been giving too much food away. "Comping" your friends is one guaranteed way to keep food revenues to a minimum. To comp is to give food away. It is a practice that is widely discouraged in the industry. It is not, however, a practice that has been discouraged at The Falls. And yet, in the opening days of the restaurant, no doubt feeling generous and expansive, Bruce and Terry have frequently given away food and drink. How much? Difficult to say, in that no one particularly wants to keep a close count of giveaways. One night in the first week, Henry guesses that Bruce and Terry gave away half of the meals served.

This is a peril not unknown to other restaurateurs. What do you do when your friends come in? Or Madonna? Or your investors? Or friends of your investors? Or Warren Beatty? At Campanile, a celebrity haunt in Los Angeles, a waitress remembers the owner telling her to give Warren Beatty's table free salads. Why should a restaurant give Warren Beatty a free salad? The thinking is that Beatty will remember that salad the next time he is flipping through the Rolodex for a restaurant. He will tell all his famous friends about the salad. He will call Jack Nicholson. *Hey Jack*, he will say, *go to Campanile, they'll give you a free salad*. And Jack will trundle on over to Campanile for his salad.

You see the problem.

Bruce is trying to do the right thing. But that kind spirit has its drawbacks. Other restaurant owners believe that by giving things away, you convey precisely the wrong idea to your most coveted customers—that they should not expect to pay. This is a dangerous precedent. You do not want people presuming that everything is free. Drew Nieporent, who runs the highly successful Tribeca Grill, has a strict policy about giveaways. He will give away Absolutely Nothing. "I charge everybody," Nieporent says. "I charge De Niro, I charge Madonna, I charge everybody. That way there's never any problem."

But nothing will deter Bruce or Terry from their policy of being nice guys.

And this will now include guacamole on the bar, beginning at 5:00 P.M. every day.

"If people know it's there," Bruce says, "they will come."

THE BIRTHDAY PARTY

FOURTEEN

To adequately describe the events of last night at The Falls—which, after being open a mere fourteen days, has now officially been host to an evening of complete moral depravity and degradation that will here be recounted in gruesome, titillating detail—one must begin by defining a few key terms. These are the 1990s, after all, and occasionally one finds oneself using words and phrases that may not necessarily be self-explanatory to a wider audience.

Phrases like Jet Whore.

A Jet Whore is defined as a woman who will sell her body to a man who can provide her with access to a private jet.

Is that clear?

A whore is a woman who will sell her body to a man for money. A Jet Whore has higher standards, at least in terms of altitude. She (there do not appear to be any male Jet Whores, perhaps because most private jets are owned by men) likes the idea of traveling long distances in the first-class surroundings of a private Boeing or Lear. She enjoys the expensive French champagnes and Beluga platters. She relishes the privacy. She thrills at the speeds. And she knows no greater pleasure than making passionate love at 35,000 feet in an aircraft without propellers.

It takes a trained professional eye to spot a Jet Whore on the ground. They do not cruise the corner of Hollywood and Vine, or even 57th Street and Fifth Avenue. Nor do they wander the hallways of airports and courtesy lounges. If you get right down to it, you don't even know they're Jet Whores—at least not for sure—until you get them in the sky. If they perform, then, yes, they are Jet Whores. If not, then they are women who will not be invited aboard again.

Somehow, for reasons we know not, Terry Quinn feels certain that at least a few of the women present at last night's debauchery were Jet Whores. It seems pointless to doubt him on this matter.

At least a few of the women in question were, specifically, guests of a man we will call Austin Cort, whose thirtieth birthday was ostensibly the focus of the evening. Perhaps guests is not the right word. They were, without question, participants. The party had been planned for days, and the reservations book noted that more than thirty people would be coming. (The actual number turned out to be more like eighty, not counting the chimpanzee.) Also down for dinner last night was our friend the High-Ranking City Official, who seems to have developed a quick and abiding affection for Bruce's new, hip-hop-happening joint.

Customers had already begun to figure out about the Beautiful Girl thing. You could pretty much count on quite a few beautiful girls at The Falls on almost any night, but for some inexplicable reason, on a Thursday night it was a virtual certainty. Perhaps this is part of the reason that last night, in addition to the frolicking partygoers, The Falls had a fair share of what can best (and most charitably) be described as Onlookers having dinner.

Brian Moores knew it was a birthday, so he had prepared a lovely, large version of his flourless chocolate cake. It always created a stir on birthdays. He had baked it in the afternoon. By 8:30, a few of the principal partiers began to show up, among them the guest of honor, Austin Cort, and his girlfriend, Becky. There was much to commend Becky to the Onlookers in the house tonight. Most particularly her breasts. While this may seem sexist, it should be considered that Becky would take it as a compliment. She loved her breasts, and last night she took particular pleasure in flaunting them to whoever looked their way.

Brian remembers Becky's breasts very well. At around 8:00, just as the festivities were getting under way, Becky went into the kitchen to check on her boyfriend's cake. To her it looked . . . flat.

"How about putting a pair of breasts on top of the cake?" Becky offered sweetly.

"A pair of breasts?" Brian felt certain he had never before been asked to put a pair of breasts on top of a cake.

"Oh *yes* . . . you can put them right on top."

After some amusing banter, Brian realized that Becky's suggestion was serious and that her boyfriend would very much like to see a pair of breasts on top of his birthday cake. Brian was no dummy. He could plainly observe that breasts were no doubt a major motif in Austin and Becky's relationship. So he reluctantly agreed, and it was decided that he would make them out of flan.

Mission accomplished, Becky did have one more thought on the subject.

"Maybe," she whispered, sidling up to Brian in full view of his dishwashers and cooks, "you'd like to use *my* breasts as a . . . you know . . . model."

Whereupon Becky lifted up her tight T-shirt to reveal, for Brian's personal enjoyment, two tanned, firm breasts, suitable for baking.

Examining them for a moment, Brian decided that while Becky's breasts were more than adequate for modeling the top of a birthday cake, it would probably be easier to work strictly from memory.

/By 9:00, the party was in full swing. Literally. A chimpanzee had been sent as a party favor, and it was being allowed to swing freely across the room. By this time the main dining room was packed. Most of the dinner guests were part of Cort's birthday crowd. Those that weren't either entered the spirit of the affair, or left. The High-Ranking City Official, not what anyone would call a live wire, took off at 9:00. But several others got into the party atmosphere and laughed as the chimp made its way from table to table.

Even Bruce, who later professed to despise the crowd, entered the spirit of the proceedings by skewing his musical choices toward a slightly younger audience. Gone were the Coltrane and Sinatra tapes. Tonight would be blues. Foot-tapping, honky-tonk blues. He cranked it up a little, too. The room was rocking.

For a couple of hours or so, the party climbed upward. People were having fun. Girls and boys together, you know? They jumped around, changed seats, leaned back, got down. Good bubbly has this effect. Takes the edge off. Smooths the rough spots. Fuck the food. We're fucked up.

The waiters coped. Yes, that would be the word. Jonathan had taken charge of the group, being the confident type, and with some helpful assistance from Kimberly managed to keep everyone happy. Thank God Brian had the whole meal figured out. Separate checks for eighty people . . . what a nightmare. Jonathan spent what seemed like hours racing back and forth between the service bar and the tables.

There seemed no end to their thirst.

/The bladder is a delicate instrument.

It works as follows: You drink, it gets full, you empty it, you fill it again.

Traditionally this process takes place in the privacy of a men's room. Men do have it a little easier, of course. They can empty their bladders without sitting down. Modern science has invented for this purpose a bizarre contraption known as a urinal. It enables men to simply unzip their zippers and do their business. This is why lines at ladies' rooms are so much longer. Men are presumably grateful for this biological advantage. It saves them a lot of wasted time.

Which is why it created such a stir when a guest at the Cort birthday party chose not to wait until entering the men's room before beginning the process.

At around 11:00, after the party had long since entered full swing, a couple of dinner guests—not part of the festivities, just plain old customers of The Falls—came down the stairs to use the bathroom. As they reached the bottom and were about to enter the men's room, they found themselves in the line of fire, so to speak, of a partygoer who could not control himself.

He was pissing on them.

"Jesus Christ!" one of them yelled. The man laughed and continued to urinate in their general direction.

Their screams of horror attracted enough attention that Kimberly heard it and came down. It was almost more than her demure, Southern personality could handle. "I don't believe it," she muttered. "God almighty." With the assistance of Bruce and a few other large men, the Urinator was finally removed from his position.

Sadly, this event typified the mood of the party at this hour. Everyone was pissed. It is a basic rule of partying that if you consume enough alcohol and little enough food, you will eventually become less and less capable of having a good time. An intensity came over the group that struck an outsider as somewhat less than enjoyable.

This motley mood carried over into the general atmosphere of The

Falls. Bruce mellowed the music. Terry wandered to other parts of the room. Henry, behind the bar, kept himself in good spirits only by trashing, in his inimitable style, the room, the party, the waiters, the restaurant and, of course, Bruce himself. And even to the most casual of observers, it was clear that some serious bad vibes were passing between Jonathan and Kimberly.

Which was strange, when you consider that for the last week or so, Jonathan and Kimberly have been locked in an intrarestaurant romance.

/It's not something either one of them has been bragging about. It just happened. Two young, attractive people who got together. Kimberly liked him right away. That sultry type really appealed to her. At least right now, anyway.

Now Kimberly and Jonathan were carrying on. It was nice. Everyone approved. They helped each other at work and consoled each other away from work. Her life was The Falls, his less so. But the common bond of their experience—having shared the grueling pressures of a restaurant opening, there's nothing like *that* to test the contours of a budding relationship—kept them together, for a few weeks anyway. No one had mistaken their feelings for love.

Though Kimberly did think he was cute.

At least she did—until around 10:00, right smack in the middle of the party in the middle of the restaurant in the middle of the night, which Jonathan chose as the perfect moment to complain to his new lady love that he didn't like the way things were going. No, Jonathan said. No, to be perfectly frank about it, things were going terribly.

And Kimberly, he went on, this is all your fault. You are quite simply not paying enough attention to me. And I don't like it.

This guy is serious. Real serious, Kimberly thought. *Too* serious. Out of his mind serious. He's getting on my nerves, this guy. She did not particularly want to become a part of Jonathan's new immediate family, no thank you.

And so she explained to him, as they took their fight into the wine room in the rear of the basement.

"You get up there and do your job," she hissed. "You're acting *so* unprofessional."

Jonathan furrowed his brow.

"I can't work here with you, Kimberly. I can't deal with this. I can't deal with being so close to you. I can't deal with this."

Before long the decibel level of their battle reached new pitches of despair as yet unheard of at The Falls. Through the walls of the wine room, people could hear it—back and forth, up and down, they hashed and hashed and hashed. It was no use. It was, like so much else in a restaurant, an issue of hot and cold. Jonathan wanted fire and passion, Kimberly gave him cold and ice.

She wanted no part of his emotions, nor to give freely of hers. As far as she was concerned, the relationship was over. "You'd better get back up there," she said.

He stormed out, hot and despondent.

She walked out, firm in her resolve.

Jonathan went upstairs to find Bruce. "Kimberly is making it impossible for me," he explained.

Bruce didn't care. He had more important matters on his mind, like the next tune to play.

"I quit," Jonathan said.

"Okay," Bruce replied. Sometimes you know when somebody's gone. Bruce knew it about Jonathan right around the day he started, and there seemed no need to act surprised.

Moments later Jonathan took off his apron and walked out of The Falls, never to return.

"It was the worst night of my life, that party," Kimberly recalled two months later, having lunch down the street from The Falls, at the very restaurant where Jonathan had worked. "It was so humiliating. It was a nightmare. I just quit going out." She took a sip of a glass of white wine as she searched her mind for just the right word to describe it. "It was . . . *creepy*," she said.

/"It was a nightmare. It was horrible."

No, this is not Jonathan's version of events that night. This is Bruce's, the next afternoon. But he is saying it with a bit of a smirk, an I-told-you-this-place-was-gonna-be-wild kind of attitude. And the bottom line is . . . the bottom line. The Falls came out ahead in the money department, right? So what's to complain? At the end of the nightmare, everything was paid for. Some guy pulled out an American Express Gold Card and paid for the entire fucking check! It was $4,000, according to Bruce. That sounds a little low—with eighty people, that's fifty bucks apiece—but sometimes you just gotta believe. And the tip came to $580. Which Marcel got, since Jonathan's midmeal departure forced Marcel into service, and since tip-pooling had been suspended.

Not everyone had a bad time. Like Terry Quinn, for instance. He enjoyed himself immensely, and believed that such evenings were good for The Falls, good for business and just plain good.

"It was fabulous, it was fun," Terry said. He was standing at the bar the next afternoon in a tight white T-shirt and jeans. After a moment of reflection, he added simply: "Beautiful girls."

/There is something else to be excited about today. Not yesterday's news. Today's.

Tom Cruise is coming to dinner. His agent has made a reservation for him on March 19, 1990. It is for nine people at 8:30 P.M. That's only four days away.

Tom Cruise!

"People are really starting to hear about us," Bruce says.

DANCES WITH DISHES

FIFTEEN

Brian has been dreaming again.

This time he's on a motorcycle in the French countryside. Not by himself. His companion is Guy Raoul. How's that for a French name? You don't invent a name like Guy Raoul in an American subconscious. Brian knows the name because Guy (pronounced GEEY) used to be his boss at a fun French bistro named, of course, Raoul's. The cramped, dark restaurant has faithfully (and successfully) been keeping SoHo customers in their bouillabaisse since the early 1970s and through the wild, restaurant-crazed 1980s.

Which is when Brian Moores worked there awhile.

Guy Raoul has been a mentor to young, aspiring French chefs for a long time now. They come, they cook, they leave . . . but they stay a member of his extended family. Brian did so by moving over to the kitchen at L'Acajou, which Guy Raoul also owns. But it is Raoul's where the signature remains. Brian drops references to Guy and his restaurant in conversation frequently; it is a proud reference, and when it comes you think immediately of pommes frites and foie gras and a feisty bottle of Côte Rôtie. Maybe two bottles if it's late enough and crowded enough. Raoul's is the kind of place you go to because it's crowded, not in spite of it. It is the kind of place you are still likely to find a young, good-looking couple having a few drinks at the bar, finding each other sexually attractive, and then escaping for a moment to the bathroom to have sex in between rounds.

Maybe it's that sort of behavior that prompts former chefs to have dreams about Guy Raoul.

In this dream, Brian is roaming the countryside with Guy. They are shopping. Every so often they stop at a store by the road to check ingredients. It is not entirely clear to Brian what is going on, but he feels certain that some cooking is in the distance. Perhaps a beautiful French kitchen, three Michelin stars sharing wall space with glistening, stainless steel pots and pans. This, after all, is Brian's fantasy when he is not dreaming. He sees himself, as most good chefs do, as a great chef. He imagines burners ablaze with the sauciest sauces to be found. And all of the world would find their way to his kitchens. (When you are a truly successful chef, you do not have a kitchen. You have kitchens.)

But Brian awakens to the fact that he is still in the United States of America, with merely one kitchen. Okay, so it's pretty big, and he runs it, and Guy Raoul is just around the corner in SoHo if Brian needs a missing spice. But it is not France, and there are no motorcycles, and Brian is still working at The Falls, and the dream is still a dream.

/How is the food at The Falls?

Sorry, Brian, but not everyone remembers the food at The Falls, because everyone is too busy looking at everything except the food, which is the only dish that isn't moving.

A careful study of all items on the menu reveals the following:

The food is good. The food is okay. The food is good for the price. The food is pretty good when you consider, but it could be better. The lamb chops are sublime. The chicken is not. But at least it's hot. The salads are green and full and there is plenty of dressing. The food is French, or is it continental? And what the hell *is* continental, anyway? Maybe it's American food. It's made in America, for Americans. If it were French, then the menu would be in French, n'est-ce pas? Although, when you pop your head in the kitchen and see Brian Moores hard at work, hands and hair flying in opposite directions, you believe that you are in a steaming, vibrant French kitchen somewhere in the heart of Burgundy, and that you will soon be served a sumptuous and flavorful nine-course feast with hearty wines and toast points and all that good French stuff.

Pass zee mashed potatoes, s'il vous plaît!

Inside that hundred-foot rectangular space at the rear of The Falls —through the swinging black door that one must pass en route to the bathrooms, with only a small window that reveals practically nothing of the goings-on backstage at The Falls—Brian rules a private domain. Most restaurant customers like that idea. They don't want to know what their food looks like . . . *before.* Customers shy away from an inadvertent peek into the inner sanctum. If they enter by accident, they let out a gulp of embarrassment before they turn on their heel. If they see plates flying out the pass-through area (the only real vista into the kitchen from outside), they dodge the food and avert their eyes. It is considered poor judgment to examine your food in its raw, unprepared form, unless it is sushi or breakfast cereal.

Still, it is a fun place. The only part of The Falls where people are not taking a respite from their lives by doing something else. The waiters and waitresses are here to more or less pass the time. But the half dozen men who staff The Falls's kitchen—yes, they are men, Bruce has no need for babes back here—are here to fulfill their life's mission. To cook! To stir! To bake a cake!

Even the dishwasher, Manuel, possesses a sense of devotion one finds lacking elsewhere. Perhaps his work ethic is because he works here illegally, as do so many dishwashers in New York, and is hoping, like his hundreds of dishwasher compatriots, that the next person through that swinging door isn't going to flash a badge. He scrubs each dish as though it were his last. He has no idea what sort of restaurant he works in, it might as well be Maxim's; all he knows is that they pay him in hard green currency, $150 a week, and that gets him a small piece of an apartment in Queens and enough money to send back to his family in Mexico, where his paltry American wages are a munificent sum.

Manuel's job is to stand right by the side exit that leads from the kitchen to the street. This puts him directly in front of the sink, which has above it a spray contraption that vaguely resembles a hand-held, stainless-steel Water Pik. To his left is a long steel countertop that waiters use to dump dirty plates, bowls, cups, silverware and half-eaten clumps of bread. They know that Manuel will dispose of such materials. Either he will scrape clean the plates into large garbage bins or he will rinse them off with his shower contraption. But he will then load everything into a large, top-loading dishwasher that The *Falls* leases for $85 a month.

Why rent a dishwasher? One might ask such a logical question. In

New York City there is, surprisingly, a logical answer. It seems that among the truly bizarre things New York City laws regulate is the temperature at which restaurant dishes must be washed. And that temperature—160 degrees—is so high that conventional dishwashers do not achieve such standards. Thus there is a huge business in dishwasher leasing. One of the by-products of such leasing, Bruce explains, is that you are offered the chance to buy special customized soaps from the leasing company for *more* than you would spend elsewhere.

Such a deal!

The machine works something like a normal home dishwasher, which focuses Manuel's efforts on the loading and unloading parts of the process. Somebody has to get all those plates clean, those glasses dry . . . it's one of the great miracles of the twentieth century that Manuel does not suffer from dishpan hands.

When Manuel completes a washing cycle, he must return the cleaned dishware to its proper storage location, approximately ten feet south and five feet up, on a shelf over the pass-through window. This is so that they will be an easy reach for the rest of Brian's backstage army. On a busy night, there will be only a few moments' rest for a plate on the shelf before someone throws a lamb chop or three on it and sends it back out for another trip to the dining room.

Once you move into the main arena, responsibilities become murkier. A dishwasher's title explains a lot; but can anyone really define the difference between a cook and a chef? At The Falls, one is likely to observe the chef tossing a salad, and a cook preparing an exotic fish recipe. Is the cook also a chef? Does the chef have to cook?

If you are glancing into a kitchen and want to find the chef, look for a tall, funny hat. Yes, this is true. Chefs like to wear tall, funny hats. They are called toques. Cooks don't get to wear tall, funny hats in a kitchen. They wear flat, two-cornered hats that suggest someone who is definitely not first in command. Perhaps it is the most revealing fact about chefs that, although they are usually fully grown adults, they have never gotten past a desire to wear tall, funny hats. You almost have to admire that about chefs.

On the afternoon of the opening night at The Falls, Brian Moores put on his tall, funny hat and paraded around the dining room a bit. His colleagues . . . the *cooks* . . . put on short hats and did a little less parading. By the end of opening night, though, Brian had put away his tall, funny hat and was working totally hatless. This is the other way to spot a chef. The chef is also the one person who is allowed to go hatless in his own kitchen.

The cooks are two young men named Larry Mebane and Patrick Gardener. They are black and have varying degrees of facial hair and Caribbean accents. Larry and Patrick are rarely referred to separately. Larry and Patrick used to work at Central Falls, and after it closed, their careers took a slight downturn. At the time Bruce was starting up The Falls, Larry and Patrick were working at an East Side hamburger joint. They weren't exactly sure they wanted to work with Bruce again, but they checked out The Falls (before it opened) and they liked the way it looked, so Bruce told Brian that he had these two cooks he wanted to hire, and Brian, being at all times a very nice guy, did exactly as Bruce asked. Larry and Patrick cook. They cook much the way ordinary people cook at home, only on a much larger scale. They use eighteen-inch spoons and yard-deep pots. They can stir a half dozen liquids at once. They follow Brian's directions as though he were Paul Bocuse, and they cook exactly the way he wants it. They make meat stock and soups and steaks and chops. They toss salads and chopped vegetables. They load the food and unload the food. They take the meat from the pot to the grill to the plate. They light the burners and watch the flames. They like to smile as they cook, and they enjoy listening to the Mets as they cook, and they like having an occasional sip of a beverage as they cook.

Joe also cooks. He does not smile quite as much as Larry and Patrick, perhaps because he spends a little more of his time chopping and less of it cooking. Joe is a short, intense man with a bushy brown moustache. If you greatly amuse Joe, you would know this because the sides of his mouth turn up ever so slightly in the direction of a smile. But most of the time Joe looks down, making certain that the sharp, long blade he uses to chop with doesn't remove a finger or a thumb. A cook needs all ten of his digits.

A cook sometimes needs a chef. This is where Brian enters the picture.

Brian rules. It is his decision each morning that guides the menu. What fish to order; what specials to feature; what soup to cook. He makes choices. It is not for nothing that he is called the executive chef.

"Today," he rattles to his men, "we'll do a veal chop." A sentence like that results in a chain reaction. Patrick and Larry and Joe must snap into action. When veal chops are the special, veals must be chopped. Stock must be stocked.

The grill, almost six feet high and black with a metal handle in the *middle*, must be lit to do its duty. Brian is very proud of his grill, bought in a deal before The Falls opened. It is, as he puts it, "a really hot grill." He means both figuratively and literally. Manufactured by a company called U.S. Range, it cost roughly $1,500 and is called a Radiant Grill. For a restaurant that serves so much fish, it had the definite plus of providing superior grill technique with no need for messy coals.

"It's a real beauty," Bruce says.

Every inch of space in the kitchen has been taken up by something —a bowl, a jar, a condiment or a spice. Underneath the pass-through window are sauces and dressings. This way the food can be dressed just prior to their delivery. There's a nice, long wooden surface for chopping and stirring and generally fixing up food. It is where the chef can make his final inspection; and Brian loves that part, frequently taking the opportunity to move one or two things around on the plate to make everything just a little prettier.

/From the kitchens of Brian Moores, directly to your table, comes this popular and very tasty rabbit dish, served as an appetizer at The Falls. (The squeamish amongst us may substitute chicken for rabbit.)

RABBIT SCALOPPINE

INGREDIENTS

4 boneless rabbit loins (or chicken breasts) pounded into scaloppine	2 tablespoons soy sauce
	3 tablespoons sesame oil
1/8 cup shiitake mushrooms	1/2 teaspoon minced ginger
1/8 cup chopped peanuts	1 teaspoon honey

Pound loins as thin as possible. Then dredge scaloppine in chopped peanuts. Pat firmly so peanuts stick to it. Heat sesame oil until it begins to sizzle in pan. Place scaloppine gently in oil and brown 30 seconds on either side.

Remove meat and reserve oil. Add shiitakes and ginger and cook 15 seconds. (Do not exceed the time limit, or risk complete failure.) Stir in soy sauce and honey. Pour sauce over scaloppine.

Serve immediately.

/The spirit of the kitchen is jovial. Larry and Patrick have a very good time, they've known each other for years and communicate between themselves in a way that suggests a powerful bond. Brian senses this. He likes them and treats them well, though he knows that he is a better chef than they are. It is possible that Brian resents having to hire them, though he has never said so. He is much too polite for that. It is also possible that they find Brian just a little too rarefied and fussy for their tastes—like do we *have* to have so much fish on the menu?—but they, too, are exceedingly polite and would never express such thoughts.

Perhaps the air in the kitchen is full of unexpressed thoughts, as it is often quiet except for the sounds of stirring or chopping or singing. The radio usually plays, and Brian will often sing along with a melody he knows. He is partial to what New York radio listeners think of as "classic" rock. That means the musician you are listening to is likely to be dead.

Sometimes they open the back door and let in the street sounds. On Vandam, this means the sound of cars, of motorcycles, or of homeless men and women rummaging through the garbage bins just outside the door.

The garbage of a restaurant is, in its own special way, a perfect microcosm of the restaurant itself. The very fact that it is there to be picked through—and not immediately removed by private haulers—suggests one distinction of The Falls. Before The Falls opened, when money was tight and important purchases still needed to be made, there was simply no money around to pay professional garbagemen to come and take away all the preopening crap—boxes, papers, old glassware, bags and bags of junk. It was not until a young woman, obviously poor and desperate for a few extra dollars, offered to remove all The Falls's trash for a mere ten bucks. Bruce went for the deal right away.

"She's going to take the bags and move them a block away, right near some other restaurant," Bruce offered definitively after handing her the ten, "and she'll get another ten from *that* restaurant to take it away from their door."

When a restaurant is up and running, it becomes necessary to develop a more formal relationship with refuse professionals. Bruce has retained the services of local haulers who set a rough cost of $250 a week to remove The Falls's garbage. That figure is based—*unfairly*, Bruce moans—by the yards of garbage produced by The Falls in its opening weeks of business. We shouldn't have to pay for our success, Bruce grumbles, we should only have to pay for our garbage.

At some restaurants, this involves financial dealings that are not entirely legal. "It is impossible to get your garbage taken away without dealing with some level of the Mafia," says one longtime New York restaurant owner wearily, the victim of too many hoodlums with out-stretched palms. But Bruce does not believe this is true. He will argue that if the garbage haulers in New York are mobsters, then they are so minor, so low-level, that they might as well be legitimate business-men.

"You pay them money, they take your garbage," Bruce says. "Does it really matter if they're crooks?"

REGARDING HENRY HAUCK

SIXTEEN

Henry Hauck quit today. It was coming, everyone knew that. Henry knew he'd been there too long already. But it is now the first day of spring, three weeks into the bullshit, and Henry simply could not take it anymore. He came in this afternoon and told Bruce, and Bruce said fine, no problem, you can leave tomorrow, and Henry said fine, no problem, and it seemed simple enough. Bruce had somebody else he wanted to hire anyway, an old bartender of his at Central Falls, and the timing was going to work out just great.

But beneath this simple solution lay a complex psychological tug-of-war that began when they met two months ago. Bruce and Henry were peers, don't forget; Bruce was forty-one years old, Henry was forty. Putting aside their stylistic differences, both men had certain similarities—most significant among them a powerful belief in their own tendency to be right. Both also knew what was necessary to make something work. It seemed quite plausible that if Henry had been the boss, Bruce would have been the one to leave.

But it was not going to be that way. Henry had his dreams, of course, like everyone; and owning a restaurant was among them. He imagined it now, in the cool breeze of freedom. His place would be out by the beach—perfect for tanning, Bruce would love that—and naturally

Brian would be the chef. They were friends before, back at L'Acajou where Henry also tended bar, but The Falls had cemented their bond. Brian spent many nights over the last two months on Henry's couch, some nights before the opening when Brian just didn't feel like making that ninety-minute trek to the old homestead, and the idea had come up many, many times in late-night confabs. Though their visions must have differed, they loved to dream aloud together.

"He was going through a fucking midlife crisis."

Bruce had his own explanation of matters the night after Henry quit.

"He's turning forty. He's sick of standing behind a bar pouring drinks. He just didn't have any small talk left. He'd come in and see all these young kids . . . to me it's different. I'm the owner, so to me they're like an army and I can command them. But to Henry they're just a bunch of young people he doesn't understand. He doesn't have any power. He's like a dinosaur."

To which Bruce added one further dimension.

"He couldn't date Kimberly," he said. "She's broken more than a few hearts around this place."

Henry did admit to having asked Kimberly out. He invited her to the dog show one day. She said no. I have a boyfriend, she explained, meaning Jonathan. "Let me know if there are any changes," he said. After that their relationship worsened considerably.

On the day he quit, Kimberly had reached, as she put it, "the end of my rope."

"Will you please help me bring up the ladder?" Kimberly said to Henry. "We need to change a light bulb."

"Kim," he said—knowing full well, of course, that nobody ever called this sweet Kimberly "Kim"—"Kim, you're not going to get much work out of me for the rest of today."

Kimberly was ready to respond—and as she did so, she calculated to herself that this next statement would pretty much be the last damn thing she ever said to Henry Hauck in her entire life. "Henry," she said, with as much anger as her demure personality could summon, "we've never gotten much work out of you."

/It comes as something of a surprise that a restaurant continues to operate smoothly even as its principals begin to depart. You might have thought differently. But bartenders, waiters, cooks . . . they are all replaceable. There is no such thing as someone uniquely qualified to the task of stirring a soup or pouring a drink. Particularly in 1990.

You need only sit by the front door and await the throngs of desperately unemployed. They will beg you for the chance. They will wear whatever you ask them to. They will take whatever money you feel like paying them.

Alan is part of the New Breed. He joined the staff of The Falls two weeks after it opened. He is a personal trainer, but not enough people want him to walk on their backs or massage their tenders or tendons or whatever. So now he is a waiter at The Falls. By the time Henry quits, Alan has established himself as practically a senior member of the staff. He has the look Bruce wants—blond, strong, handsome. The essential black wardrobe. He can carry plates and take orders and has even mastered the computer. Not all that quickly, mind you, but that's part of what enables him to fit in so perfectly at The Falls.

On the day Henry quits, Alan sees an opportunity for himself. Until now he has been making $10 a shift. Plus tips. This is standard pay. It's lower than average for a New York restaurant—some waiters make a base pay of $25 a shift or more—but The Falls is not average by any means. Alan, knowing this, requests a promotion. To what? he is asked. Head waiter . . . day manager . . . whatever you want to call it, he says. I would just like to be moved up a notch. It seems only fair. After all, he thinks, I *am* one of the few at The Falls who is capable of handling the work. In a restaurant fairly plagued with service problems, Alan believes correctly that he is a paragon of talent.

Bruce agrees. He promotes Alan to day manager. And his salary will go up. Instead of making $10 a shift, he will now make $15. This works out fine for a few weeks, until he quits.

The service problem continues unabated. Customers habitually wait too long for their tables, their wine, their food . . . nothing seems to be working right. The turnover rate has been nothing short of astonishing. Brian Moores has taken to counting the number of waiters so far employed by The Falls. At this point the number is too high, yes, but still within the realm of the possible at a new, evolving restaurant. He swears he will be patient, but for him it is a particular strain. No matter how effectively the kitchen is run, it is the waiters upon whom he must depend. And if they fail, the fault will be placed at his feet by the customers. He knows that waiters can talk their way out of a problem. He simply does not have the time or inclination to do so himself. There have been times he has seen a dinner order rest on the shelf for five minutes or longer, waiting for a waiter to pick it up; and there have even been times where he has grown so damned impatient that he has carried the orders to the table *himself.*

The chef himself! *Sacrebleu!*

What is going wrong?

Some people think it is Philippe. Amazingly enough, he remains at his post as host. This involves standing at the door and awaiting the arrival of his friends so that he may kiss them gallantly and assign them the finest tables. Technically, this also puts him in charge of the service staff, even though his form of service is, to use an appropriate phrase from his native tongue, laissez-faire at best. There are those who predicted that Philippe would be long gone by this point. Bruce was among them. He is pleasantly surprised to learn that he was wrong.

Philippe has been known to listen carefully, it is true; when you speak, he looks directly into your eyes and watches every inflection; he is patient, he is kind, he is soft.

Bruce observes the little details and recounts them endlessly, happily, like this one:

"Last week, on Saturday," Bruce remembers, "Philippe was getting all upset about the way things were going, so I said to him, 'Philippe, it's Saturday night in New York City.' So tonight I'm listening to him talk to a customer who's complaining about his reservation, says he asked for a specific table and he's mad that he's not getting it. Philippe says to him, 'Come on . . . it's Saturday night in New York City.' "

Is it not this very quality that so endears Philippe to Bruce? After all, how many employees of The Falls listen so intently to him, remember what he says and repeat it verbatim to customers?

Tonight the restaurant is packed solid. The heat from the kitchen remains high. Brian continues to watch his dishes pile up and cool down. Philippe is at the door and, as usual when that is the case, people are being kept waiting at the bar for close to an hour, with reservations, and no free drinks, nothing. These are, of course, people Philippe does not know personally. Or, if he does know them, he knows that he need not care about their happiness or well-being. He believes passionately in the principles of a hot restaurant, namely: People will wait.

At one point Philippe offers a table to a friend who has just walked in, as literally dozens of patient parties with reservations wait at the bar. Another part-time hostess, hired to handle busy nights, complains to Philippe that he is being *unfair*. Either this word doesn't translate properly into French, or Philippe doesn't care, or both. Probably both.

"I can't work with you if you don't let me do things my way," Philippe tells her calmly as he takes his friends to their table.

Yes, Philippe has his own special way of doing things. It is also the French way. Americans just do not seem to understand.

. . .

/Soon after Henry's resignation, Kimberly Jones makes her decision to leave.

Ever since The Falls opened Kimberly has plotted her departure. She has determined that she would like to be a part of show business. Her position at The Falls has given her many contacts in this field. And so, after a TV producer she has gotten to know offers to make some introductions around Hollywood, she feels that she can gracefully announce her exit and be done with The Falls for good.

Kimberly felt odd about quitting; for a while there she had come to think of Bruce as fatherly, and at least she was grateful for the chance to meet the people who could get her into something better. But she knew that she had to leave. There was no future for her at The Falls. Or, Kimberly firmly believed, for any women at all.

"What is so ironic is that every female waitress there has quit or been fired," Kimberly said a few days after she'd stopped working at The Falls. "It's all males now. It's an all-male place now.

"I remember Bruce said once, 'Her butt's too big to hire her.' I said, 'You want a model, then you pay her $6 million a year.' I was furious. No one's gonna stay if they always feel their job is in jeopardy. They'll just come in and fire someone at the drop of a hat. I had a real problem with that. No notice. 'There's no need. Go away. We don't need you.' Marcel has gotten away with fifty, sixty, seventy times more than anybody else. I can think of fifty incidents that anyone else would have been fired . . . it's not fair. He's Philippe's buddy. My best friend got canned. She looked at Philippe and said, 'You're a chauvinist and this place is fucked.' "

One May morning Kimberly got in a car and drove to Hollywood.

By June, Kimberly had gotten herself a job right in the heart of show business.

It was perfect, too. The people who produce the CBS series *Evening Shade*, the one that stars Burt Reynolds, took an immediate liking to this capable young woman from Arkansas, which just happens to be exactly where the show takes place.

"I DON'T WANT TO BE A

BOWL-BRIGGER"

SEVENTEEN

One month and seven days into the life of The Falls, we now have:

A packed room every night . . . a catastrophic service situation . . . a French laissez-faire personality managing the floor on busy nights . . . and an owner who is happiest ignoring both and fiddling with the dials on the stereo system, his back facing the extremely hot restaurant he has created.

High time for a staff meeting.

It begins at 5:00—a half hour later than scheduled, as usual—on a Saturday afternoon in early April. It is the first staff meeting in several weeks, and the agenda is expected to be the horrific low level of service that has become The Falls's trademark. People now joke about it regularly. "You can get a fork at The Falls, and you can get a knife," says one heavy-spending customer who has eaten here several nights since the opening, "but do not expect to get both a fork *and* a knife at the same time."

The waiters wander in, one at a time, as usual looking rather sharp. Things are bad enough, they don't want to get fired for their looks. They stop at the bar for a soda, smoke a cigarette, chat amiably with each other. They know that things are going badly, any idiot can see that. They are acutely aware that business is good and service is bad and that means only one thing. They are in trouble. But they see that Bruce is not here—only Philippe, and his friend Marcel, the waiter who has anointed himself head waiter in the absence of any other authority—so they suspect this meeting will go better than ones before, there will be no loss of temper, no swearing, no yelling, just a stern lecture about how we all have to pitch in and do better. Philippe will no doubt moan and groan about how no one is as good a waiter as his dear, dear friend, Marcel, who is nobody else's friend at The Falls, by the way, because he hogs tables and tips. Even Leonard—a young, handsome and exceedingly friendly black waiter whom everyone likes and who has taken to calling Bruce "Dr. Huxtable," after Bill Cosby's character on Thursday nights, for no apparent reason— even Leonard does not appear to be overly fond of the French contingent that has taken over The Falls.

None of the dozen waiters and waitresses now sitting at the back banquettes at The Falls, smoking, drinking and slouching, know or care particularly that Philippe has his own private agenda for today. The late-afternoon light shines through the blinds, and it casts a beautiful amber glow over everyone. It deceptively blocks out the cold air that chills the city today, and it mellows them. Tonight will be busy, but we will handle it. Yes we will.

Philippe, in a large, handsome sport jacket, T-shirt, black pants and black shoes, is not warmed by the glow. He does not believe in tonight, or the staff, or good luck. He is going to give a speech, and it is going to rival Castro and Gorbachev for length and repetition, and it is even going to have a theme so prevalent, so pervasive, that it should have a title, and so it will hereby be given one, then excerpted here at length. It is transcribed in the original staccato, almost pidgin English spoken by Philippe—who, although fluent in the language, still manages to drop articles and plurals, particularly under stress.

Today, he is under stress.

The "I Don't Want to Be a Bowl-Brigger" Speech
Philippe Dumont, April 7, 1990

"I called a staff meeting for 4:30. No one was here. No one. If you cannot be here, that's it. If you have a little respect for your job, show up on time. First of all, it's not professional behavior. That's one point. You're all here making money. There's no reason . . .

"The blame goes from one to the other. The busboys and waiters and the kitchen—nobody takes it as serious business. You come here, it's your job, but it should be much more than that. I will tell you what I think is good to do as far as customer relations. I also want to break good news, which is that we have put an ad in the paper to find professional waiters. The reason why we do that is we need professionals. People who have job here because they want to be an actress or a model or mother, or find something, if they want to be waiter or waitress, if that's what they want to do, professional—that's it. I have already two.

"The waiters we have show up when they feel like it, very casual behavior, that's why we need two more. You need four people who really move, who work, not chat around, smoke a cigarette. I don't want be like Bruce at the other side of the bar—just a guard dog. Who gives you no slack, no break, not one minute. And that's maybe the only way to work. That's what everybody say to me. And if I get the blame from you or her or him, I'm not fair, already it's my responsibility. Maybe somebody needs to be like this. I thought it would be a different way . . . New York and Paris . . . certain people face their responsibilities . . . most of them are really too casual. I might be the person. I don't know. I'm just trying to preserve your jobs. I don't have to preserve mine. Even if I don't keep work, somebody else will. The relationship you have with the next person . . . my way of doing it . . . doesn't seem like it's working. And that's true. So I put some power in Marcel, who I trust, first, my friend for many years. He says he has been a waiter for a long time, that's why he doesn't want to bus his own tables.

"I say, Marcel, you make money for the house, for yourself, and you have runners to run your food, and a busboy, and you go to many fancy restaurants in New York, and the waiter is well dressed, and he sells you wine, he sells you appetizer, he sells you dessert, but does not have to, and if he does, he does. And if he shows you that he can do it by himself, he will.

"I'm just telling you that I don't feel that I'm getting professional. First of all we're running an ad for professionals. Second of all, I hired a manager at night to watch the bar, watch you, and make sure that's everything's smoothly done. It's supposed to be in your hands. I cannot bust your ass all night. You have to take your job and do it as a job, show up for work, run, move, do what you know how to do. I don't question that you know what to do. Or you know what to do. I don't question that. I just question how much you want to do it. For the $60 or $80 or $100 you make a night. And this question I cannot answer with you.

"And what I am telling you today is that if you're still behaving the same way you're not going to be keeping your jobs—no chance. And that's the way it is, and gonna be, and don't tell me, 'Oh, I didn't know.'

"Today you know. No more nice guy, no more this, no more that.

"You come here on time, you do your work. You come in at 5:00, then at 5:30 you're ready, you have a cigarette. If you're arriving here at 5:00, or 5:15 . . . if you are five minutes late, it's out of the door, goodbye, see you next time. You have been warned.

"I've never really been very tough on you. I've tried to be nice to get everything working. You want to work, you want the responsibility, you have it, you face it. You don't face it, somebody else will—I promise you. Next week whoever doesn't have professional behavior toward his work—not eating, not smoking, not talking, not having a good time—but working. If you have a good time working, that's where your good time is. That's where your money is. That's where my money is.

"So the only good time you can allow yourself in this place is not with me or with Leonard, who is a great guy, or Marcel, or whoever, it's with the people you serve. If you're not better than the next one, the next one's gonna take your job, there's no question. Absolutely not.

"Bruce didn't come today because he didn't want to tell you all these fucking things. He had a list like this—he'll just shut up. That's his thing and I understand. He's the nice guy . . . now I'm going to ask Marcel to take a little more responsibility. That's the way it is. Marcel leaves after all of you every day, and as far as money, he's doing pretty good.

"Everybody else is telling me it's my fault. I should be a son of a bitch."

/He turns, finally. It has been a twenty-minute nonstop barrage of insult and hostility. The waiters have been practically motionless. Given the content so far, they fear that a false move or gesture might cost them their jobs. It is painfully obvious that Philippe is on a rampage that has little to do with anything that has happened in The Falls during the last thirty-seven days.

Philippe lights another cigarette. He has been chain-smoking throughout this speech. Marlboros, as usual. He takes a deep inhale of smoke, then swings an arm around to point toward the kitchen.

"This is the nicest kitchen I've ever seen in a restaurant. Ever. It's usually never like that. Usually those guys want to bust your *bowls* just because you have a better position than they do. Just because you have a better job than they do. Just because you have a better money than they do. Usually the ambience between the backstage and the front stage is not like that whatsoever. So you have already this advantage which is fantastic.

"Then, instead of having a bowl-brigger to bust your ass all night long, saying, 'Do this, do that, be like this, don't drink, don't put your hands in your pockets, put the basket there,' you don't even have that guy. And that's probably my decision. I'm not here to bust your *bowls*. I'm hoping to relegate this kind of work to somebody who knows how to do it. That likes to do it. Plenty of guys would be very happy to bust your *bowls* all night. I'll find those guys every day in New York.

"I won't speak for Bruce, Bruce is not here, he probably had other things to do . . . I have nothing to say about that. If he had anything to say he would be here, he's still the boss over all of us. He would use different words. I'm telling you the same thing a different way.

"You are responsible. You have the power of choice. You choose. You show up on time. You wait for whoever's in charge to let you go when you finish working. Not when you *think* you finish, because you don't have any more tables. That's not what it is. I told you what I want to happen. Get your shit together. I have six waiters today—it's going to be five, and I believe four.

"My job is not in jeopardy. Yours might be if you don't take it more seriously. If you don't help each other, that's your shit. One of you is going to go. I don't know which one, we are going to replace you until we find whoever wants this job.

"I don't want to be a bowl-brigger."

What is he saying? What the hell is a *bowl-brigger*?

Wait . . . it must be that damn accent of his. He must be saying something else. Bowl-brigger, bowl-brigger. What? Of course!

Ball-breaker! I don't want to be a *ball-breaker!*

"About the French speaking. I know it bothers a lot of you. I understand. It's unusual. The fact that Marcel and I speak French . . . So there is no confusion, Marcel is a friend, he has responsibilities toward me.

"As far as money goes, we all have to make money. Marcel is the one that makes the most money for us, and probably for himself. That's why Marcel is respected and wanted. The extra attention—he is focused in his job and it works. That's the job. The job is to please the customer, to kiss them goodbye, to be happy. You are the in-between. That's what you are. If you don't realize that you don't belong as a waiter at all. Not only to be good, but to be gentle and willing and . . .

"If I were going to be waiter today I would follow Marcel for one week and Leonard for one week. Leonard because he's very smart and very nice, and Marcel because he sells them everything. If there's four pieces of fish left, and four people who want to eat chicken, they're going to eat fish because he's gonna sell it to them."

/At this point Philippe has been speaking for more than half an hour without interruption. The waiters are, to put it mildly, shocked. They had expected to be chewed out, but they had not anticipated a stream-of-consciousness diatribe from a man who, in the five weeks since The Falls's birth, none of them had ever seen carry so much as a plate. To them, Philippe was something of a joke. His job was to greet people at the door, but invariably he would become so distracted by the presence of his friends that he would join them at their tables—very good tables, the ones he'd parceled out—and leave the front door unattended. Frequently, waiters would see couples or groups standing by the door for two minutes or more, waiting for someone to seat them. Sometimes a helpful waiter or waitress would take it upon themselves to take care of them; other times, people would simply be left standing.

And *this* is the man doing the lecturing! And to make matters worse, he isn't even done. Now he wants to turn over the podium to Marcel, his friend, the exalted waiter who is being held up as a paragon of talent and virtue, the waiter who on opening weekend kept people waiting ninety minutes for their appetizers.

Marcel, too, has a bit of trouble with English. But like Philippe, this barrier does not prevent him from long-winded oratory. He has his own list of complaints. Never mind that Marcel is in no way superior in rank to any of those now forced by Philippe to listen.

"The bar—stop screaming at Gary," Marcel begins, referring to the good-natured forty-two-year-old bartender who has been at The Falls since opening night. "I'm the one who's screaming more. Gary is going to be mad and not giving you anything anymore. Or you are going to be waiting like crazy. That's because he's a professional. Just wait, ask him please or whatever.

"Ask for the kitchen if they have something to sell. Like special. What they want to sell first, what they want to put out.

"The menu is still staying on the table too long. I don't want to say any names, but twenty minutes on the table is really long. Really, really, really long for a table. The computer—85 percent of the people don't sell drinks before dinner, or after-dinner drinks. And wine or champagne, whatever. What Philippe told you is not what he's really thinking, it's what all the others are pushing. We are only a number on a machine.

"Empty the plates. When we need fork or knife or glasses you cannot give it to us for one reason. He have a full piece of shit—it's like this. It's not helping him at all. I'm telling you, this guy"—he is referring here to Manuel the dishwasher—"is gonna leave in days. He's make $20, $30 a night. He's starting at 4:00 and finishing at 4:00 in the morning. Think about that—$30.

"Bruce told me, too, let's stay more with the customer. Everybody knows some of the customers. Don't be jealous if someone comes to talk to your customer on your station. Just trust me to your customer and I trust you to mine, and that can help everybody. For five years, six years, or nine years I've been working in New York, I always have the same customers, that's my connection, let's just . . . don't . . . I don't want to . . .

"This place has to be like a family," Marcel is saying. "Not even like a team. A team is a family. But a family is a family. It's better than a team. Stronger. And we all on this ship together."

Questions from the floor are now being solicited. Why are we being forced to listen to this guy? That is the prevalent question at the moment.

Without any questions, Philippe takes back the floor.

"Bruce is most important," he says. Another Marlboro is lit. "There is no question. Whatever he has to say—he's gonna have his say. The less bullshit you pull to him, the less you gonna get back."

Marcel interjects. "I'm gonna have my business soon, you know. That's my life. You think I'm gonna fight with nine people I know? I know this guy"—gesturing at Philippe—"for fifteen years, Bruce for twelve years, all the others for ten, six . . . you think I'm gonna fight with nine connections, on this business, nine strong connections?

"I know Bruce for twelve years, I've been partying with him in the Caribbean, you think I'm gonna fight with those guys, says, Fuck you, guys, I don't want you, I don't like you? Impossible. That's my business. Even for you, if you like acting, dance, whatever, perhaps you're gonna need those nine people to come visit you. That's what I'm thinking about."

Perhaps Philippe senses the bullshit quotient in the room, for he takes back the floor. "What Bruce wants from you is professional attitude, not bullshit," he says. "I don't care what you do, what he does. Show me that you can do it, that you don't need anybody else telling you what to do. Instead of hanging around, do it. On Saturday night, people need more attention. They have only two nights a week. That's where we have to be super, so they have a great weekend. 'Oh, we had a great time last weekend at the Falls.' 'Oh, the music is nice, the ambience is nice, good food . . .' This is stage. The audience is the customer. You present a good show, they'll come back to you, sure. If you don't they won't. It's time now, we don't have the excuse of the opening. The computer this, the computer that, okay. You got the computer. A five-year-old kid could get that computer.

"This is over.

"My fault is that I gave you guys more responsible than you are. This is my mistake. You are responsible. You show up on time. If you don't, I promise you, I will have a floor manager who is a fucking pain in the ass, who will fucking brig your *bowls* and fire you on the first occasion and put somebody else in. And that's gonna happen. If we don't change . . .

"I don't want to brig your bowls."

At last Philippe has come to the end of his remarks.

They have inspired the staff on duty for tonight to cover their groins.

LADY D'ARBANVILLE AND THE

BANANA CREAM TART

EIGHTEEN

Patti is pregnant!

Terry Quinn is positively ecstatic. Which for him means a slight upward curl at the outer edges of his mouth. The man obviously loves the whole idea of children. You tend to feel that way when you are one of thirteen children yourself. And let's not forget he's got two of his own already, and he's barely thirty years old. That's what we call, in baby-boom lingo, a countertrend. You don't find many hip young New York nightclub owners with two kids at home and another on the way. It's too bad, really, since most of them would be pretty damn good at getting up for those late-night feedings, and they're used to people crying till they get what they want.

Patti loves children, too. She's got her own boy, Jesse, from a previous relationship with another popular, handsome man named Don Johnson. Neither this Johnson fellow—once especially famous as the star of *Miami Vice*, now somewhat less so as the husband of Melanie Griffith—nor Terry Quinn has bothered with the societal convention of marriage in his relationship with Patti. And for Patti, a lovely, caring woman whose appeal is immediately apparent to anyone, this has not seemed to matter. To all outward appearances, she seems hopelessly in love with Terry, thrilled to be carrying his child, and happy to be jetting back and forth between her beach house in Santa Monica and his two-bedroom walk-up on West 14th Street in Greenwich Village.

Patti grew up in New York, the daughter of a Village painter, in the wild early 1960s—and her free-spirit personality served her well in her pursuit of men and modeling jobs. She became known as a rock star girlfriend, Warhol actress, and Max's Kansas City regular. Cat Stevens wrote a song for her called "Lady D'Arbanville." Terry once asked Patti if she'd ever met the Beatles.

"Yes," she replied, and then added for a laugh, "individually."

Before long, as most models do, she aspired to acting. Armed with connections and talent, she found herself in movie after movie, first bit parts, then major roles. She was always working and successful. She moved to Los Angeles, and by the early 1980s, before he'd reached full-throttle celebrity, Don Johnson became her regular steady boyfriend. In 1981 she had reached a level of relative fame, co-starring with Chevy Chase in *Modern Problems*. The movie came out right around the time *Miami Vice* took off, meaning that Don and Patti were most definitely a Celebrity Couple. Unfortunately, Don became the bigger star of the two—and of the sex symbol variety, leading tabloid-mongers to speculate endlessly about his status. Inevitably—or so it seemed, anyway—Don and Patti split up, with Patti retaining custody of their son and their home.

Patti became enamored of Terry in 1989. By then Terry had been thoroughly exposed to a wide variety of young starlets and was ready for someone a little more . . . adult. Mature. Sophisticated. Gone were the days when Julia Roberts would send Terry deeply meaningful love poems scrawled on postcards from the backseats of cabs. (Julia met Terry backstage at a performance of her brother's play *Burn This* in 1988, back before anything, it seemed, and it was love, true love, for at least a week.) Gone were the nights when beautiful starlets would share passionate glances with Terry across a dark bar at Peggy Sue's, hoping to be the last one there when he wiped it clean.

Here was Patti D'Arbanville, a strong, independent woman who loved Terry and whom Terry loved.

And now she is pregnant. She'll have the baby in Los Angeles, and Terry will go out there to be with her.

The baby is due on October 30.

It will be easy for Terry to remember that date. It's also his thirtieth birthday.

• • •

/While Terry is spreading his good fortune up and down the bar on a Monday night in early April, Bruce is adjusting the collar on his silver polo shirt. He's dressed up a little tonight, no good reason, just felt like it. Monday nights are a little slow, so why not jazz the place up a little? He's wearing an expensive black sport jacket and it must be admitted that under the right conditions—and the right lighting, which Bruce has made certain of at The Falls—Bruce can look pretty decent. As he pulls himself together, he examines the dining room at 8:00 and pronounces it a good night, even though it is early, and even though there are only six people having dinner. Six people isn't nearly enough, of course, but he has a point. The room is quiet, comfortable, the music is bouncing perfectly off the walls, not too boisterous, the food is coming out just right, the service is clicking . . . so what if there's only six people here tonight?

"This is the way I'd like a restaurant to be if *I* were on a date," Bruce says, and you know exactly what he means. Does anyone really *prefer* a packed, noisy mob scene to something small, intimate and alluring? Well, maybe Terry Quinn . . . maybe movie stars and models and those otherwise entitled to nice tables . . . but not the vast silent majority of restaurant-goers, the ones who get automatically dragged to the row of cramped deuces (a "deuce" is restaurant parlance for a table for two) and watch wistfully as large, empty tables stay empty in the vain hope that a celebrity might wander by.

Which, to everyone's overwhelming surprise, one has.

"Isn't that John Waters?" Terry has walked over to consult Bruce on this matter. He has noticed a man at one end of the bar, right by the front door, who looks suspiciously like the extremely bizarre director of extremely bizarre movies like *Polyester*, which was the first (and last) movie to have ever been released with its own accompanying scratch-and-sniff card. In recent years Waters's movies (*Hairspray* and *Cry-Baby*) have grown more mainstream. However, Waters has maintained the physical appearance of a cult director. He looks very weird, with a pencil-thin moustache, gaunt face, receding hairline, intense eyes and whiter-than-white skin.

If you saw someone who looked exactly like John Waters, wouldn't it probably *be* John Waters, because who the hell would want to look like him otherwise?

"Yeah, it *is*." Bruce is equally amazed.

"I wonder what he's doing here?" Terry asks. Actually, it it fairly obvious that Waters is having a drink. He is sitting between two women and talking in an animated fashion. There is a glass of something that appears to be wine in front of him.

"Did you invite him?" Bruce asks.

"Nah, I don't even know him . . ." Terry is confused. "I don't get it."

"What?"

"Did he just come in here? I wonder if he heard about the place from someone. Maybe he's meeting someone here." Terry pauses to think about who he knows who knows John Waters. He has many, many connections floating around in his brain; however, this one he cannot place. "I don't know, I just can't figure it out."

Someone nearby suggests that perhaps Waters has wandered into The Falls of his own accord.

"I guess that's *possible*," Terry says. "But I think somebody would have told me. I would have heard about it somewhere."

"What's he done lately?" Bruce asks.

"He did that Johnny Depp movie." Terry often thinks of movies in terms of stars instead of titles. Johnny Depp was the star of *Cry-Baby*.

"Maybe he's in town to do that. You know. Something related to that. Maybe . . ." What is Bruce trying to say? You almost expect that he will suggest some kind of publicity angle for this unexpected visit, a way to exploit this good fortune. But what? Nothing comes to mind, and his sentence is left unfinished.

So is John Waters's drink, by the way. He just left.

/He is not De Niro.

That is what the bartender is telling Terry tonight, and he's laughing, he thinks it's a joke, which perhaps it is, but he's saying it over and over again, laughing: You are not De Niro.

Not that anyone really knows who De Niro is.

But in recent days a new restaurant has opened, not too far from The Falls, and there is a widespread belief, among those who have supreme faith in gossip columns, that De Niro is there. It is called the Tribeca Grill, and it is crowded with people, famous and handsome and beautiful and dull and hungry and thirsty and hot and cold.

Terry is not De Niro. By the way, there is every chance in the world that Terry is superior to De Niro in all ways. However, in the way of actually being De Niro, he fails.

.   .   .

/As the evening grows more crowded—could word have spread so quickly throughout New York that The Falls is now John Waters's sometimes watering hole?—Bruce grows more excited. This is what usually happens. Something will occur to him. Ideas will germinate and spread. He will summon someone. Instructions will be given. He finds the prospect of new people genuinely thrilling. It triggers the part of his brain where new concepts are born.

Tonight the concept is banana cream tart.

It is hard to scientifically determine the process by which this concept was first hatched. Perhaps he was somewhere in the vicinity of sunlight, natural or otherwise. Bruce claims that he gets a lot of his best ideas in the sun. Now he has this idea for a new dessert, and he must share this culinary breakthrough with Brian.

Bruce goes to the kitchen, where Brian is busily chopping and slicing, and retrieves his chef. This is not difficult. Brian always loves a reason to exit the kitchen and wander over to the bar for a break. It need not be a good reason. So Brian diligently follows Bruce and eagerly awaits his boss's newest brainstorm.

Bruce gets straight to the point. "I've got a *great* new dessert idea," he says. "Banana cream tart!"

"Banana cream *tart?*" Brian asks. "What exactly *is* that, Bruce?"

"It would be like a banana cream pie," Bruce explains, allowing his hands to form an imaginary tart-like circle, "which is everybody's favorite dessert"—oh *really!*—"only we'd make it into a tart, so it'd be smaller and healthier."

Brian has no response to this except to roll his eyes, which he can do subtly yet with expert precision.

After a long pause, he finally mutters, "I guess I can make that."

After some polite discussion of ingredients—it's never enough for Bruce to offer the bare bones of a suggestion, he likes to hammer out specifics, as long as he's in the mood—Brian talks himself into making a banana cream tart. He isn't happy about it, it's not what he wants to do, but he is, after all, a very nice guy who likes to make people around him as happy as possible. Yes, he will grouse and moan when you get him off by himself, and no doubt we will hear again about this tragically stupid new dessert Bruce has suggested, but for tonight he will merely roll his eyes and return to the kitchen.

Bruce watches him go.

"He's upset because somebody ordered the mashed potatoes for dessert," Bruce says.

. . .

/Brunch is dead.

For three successive Sundays in March, Bruce tried to generate the kind of Happening Brunch he had so successfully executed at Central Falls. But he failed. This past Sunday about eight people showed up. One investor brought his family down, they were in New York visiting, and someone else brought in Elaine Kaufman, the famous, eponymous restaurateur.

Everyone in New York knows Elaine's. However, not everyone in New York goes to Elaine's. In fact, most New Yorkers probably avoid Elaine's for one of two reasons: Either they believe they are not famous enough to get a table there, or they have heard about the food. Elaine's is almost as famous for bad food as it is for its celebrity clientele, many of whom love to complain privately about the food at Elaine's, but who love to add that the food is not really the point. Woody Allen is the celebrity most commonly associated with Elaine's; the restaurant reputedly keeps a particular table clear for him every night, in case he decides to show up. He usually doesn't. After two decades of steady restaurant going, Allen finally figured out that there were other places in town to get a plate of pasta.

But to someone like Bruce Goldstein, Elaine is a legend. She has proven well her ability to get famous people through her door, night after night, year after year. She has done this primarily by being nice to her friends. If you are her friend, she might join you briefly for coffee. Some people believe that she carries in her head an intricate chart of power in New York, and seats people accordingly. Others argue that she has a powerful sense of loyalty and rewards that above all else.

Which is it? And why does anyone care?

But Elaine Kaufman is having brunch at The Falls, and it's a big event. Eggs and pancakes—and oh yes, coffee out of those little black things Bruce bought on the Bowery that nobody else wanted. Nobody else turned out to be right. They are about to become officially obsolete. By some bizarre coincidence, Elaine Kaufman is bearing witness to the final Falls brunch, and by no coincidence at all, has a very nice table.

Brunch is a difficult concept to execute, probably one of the most difficult in the restaurant business. People do not plan ahead for brunch. They do not make brunch reservations a week in advance. Nor do they necessarily know what time they would like to eat brunch.

All they usually know is that they would like very much to have coffee, perhaps a Bloody Mary or mimosa, and possibly eggs covered in hollandaise sauce. Why Americans only eat hollandaise sauce on their eggs at brunch, and not at any other time, is an interesting question for which there is no good answer available.

Why people do not eat brunch at The Falls is an easier question to answer. In fact, it is painfully simple. When you want brunch, you want it *now*. You do not want to take a cab to brunch. This is more hassle than should be necessary for a meal dominated by dairy products. You want to walk past a restaurant and say, *Hey*, I'd like to eat brunch *there*, which is why Central Falls had such a successful brunch. Its location on a broad pedestrian promenade, the kind of street where so many brunchgoers would congregate and work up appetites, served to attract long lines and steady business. It gave Bruce confidence, perhaps too much; he believed without any hesitance that he could re-create that scene, down to the classical combo he planned to introduce, at the corner of Varick and Vandam—where the only pedestrians on a Sunday afternoon tend to be people who are hopelessly lost.

Finally, tonight, Bruce has conceded this fact.

"I killed brunch," Bruce says sadly. "There's just no street traffic, it's almost summer, it just wasn't going to work." There is a sad, lonely pause that follows this explanation, then this elaboration: "Plus it was killing us to close late Saturday night," he explains, "and then be in here Sunday at noon." That sounds eerily like an excuse for something that simply wasn't going to work anyway.

With the death of brunch, Bruce is facing—for the first time in the thirty-three days The Falls has been open—the prospect of problems. Not *big* problems, you understand. Nothing that can't be fixed by firing someone, or changing things around, or altering expectations just a little. But . . . you know . . . problems. Little things that aren't working out according to plan. Tiny matters of business that suggest to Bruce that his scenario of success may not be quite as he imagined.

The problems grow darker and deeper. He mulls. He broods. He changes the music on the stereo. The songs are getting sadder. Yes, there he is . . . Sinatra. "In the Wee Small Hours of the Morning" fills the room. Certainly the customers aren't. It is a Monday night, and you know about Monday nights, right? Nobody goes out on Monday nights.

Bruce is recalling an episode that troubles him. Alec Baldwin—how many handsome hunks can one restaurant stand?—came in last week.

Bruce and Terry were both at the bar. He came with a pal named Doug something. A producer, maybe *the* producer, of *Prelude to a Kiss*, the off-Broadway show that Baldwin is starring in briefly between Major Motion Pictures. Alec and Doug and a bunch of other people, maybe six or eight, came in for a bite. Bruce remembers little about the group except that they did not pay their check. Not a penny.

"Terry comped them," Bruce says. But tonight, as Bruce sees for the first time that business is not quite as gung ho as once hoped, Bruce openly questions the comping concept.

"Terry has to learn that you don't do that," Bruce says, coming to a realization reached by others nearly a month ago. "Maybe you give them an after-dinner drink, or maybe dessert, but you don't give the whole thing away. It actually *discourages* business in the long run. Because the person says to himself, 'I don't want to go to The Falls 'cause I don't know what to do. Am I supposed to pay, or not?'" This is a thought that perhaps ought to be expressed aloud to Terry; but as he walks over to where Bruce is standing and waxing, Bruce drops the topic. He does not want conflict, will not lecture his partner on how to do business. And maybe, who knows, Alec Baldwin *will* come back to The Falls, and Bruce will have been wrong, and we'll be damn lucky to have a big-name celebrity in our midst on a regular basis!

Anyway, this is not what Terry wants to talk about. He has an amusing story to tell Bruce and it is top priority. It involves the man who is currently sitting at the Primo Table, a man unknown to Bruce, and known to Terry only as Arnold. He has been allowed to sit at the Primo Table because he is, as Terry now puts it, "a partner of somebody at Ford Models," which means that he knows somebody who knows somebody who knows somebody. And that somebody—who it is no one seems to know—has arranged for this Arnold fellow to sit at the Primo Table at The Falls, because he is celebrating. No, make that *bragging*. He has just told Terry that he has invested $95,000 in a new nightclub, opening this Thursday night. The club is going to be called Powerhouse.

"He's never going to see that money again," Bruce laughs.

But what if the place is a big success? Why then would Arnold and his ninety-five grand be permanently parted? Terry is asked to explain.

"*Especially* if the place is a big success," Terry says with utmost clarity. "If they're making money, the last thing in the world they're going to want to do is to give this schmuck back his ninety-five thousand."

Bruce is nodding furiously.

"*Never* invest in a total cash business," Bruce says. "There are no records, nobody knows what's going on, the money's constantly flying in and out. And it's suckers like that who'll give away their money and make a place like that possible."

Oh. Okay.

Notwithstanding this pessimism, Terry gives Arnold a free drink.

Patti's pregnant, remember?

CRIME AND PUNISHMENT

NINETEEN

There were at least two surreptitiously observed scenarios that got Billy, the bartender, fired this morning for stealing.

The bar-is-closed, here's-your-drink-anyway scenario:

A guy comes in for a drink. The bar is closed. The register is closed. The money is put away. The guy says, "Look, give me a drink." He puts a $10 bill on the bar. Billy gives him the drink. He takes the ten spot. Stuffs it into his pocket.

The free-drink, big-tip scenario:

Two people come in. Together. One is a bartender somewhere else. One isn't. They order some drinks. One of the guys—the one who was, as Bruce put it later, "not a bartender, not related to the place in any way, shape or form"—says, "Oh, how much do I owe you?" And Billy says, "Oh, I'll take care of it." So the guy leaves him a $20 bill and he walks out the door and he pockets the money.

Both scenarios are observed by an outside detective agency hired by Bruce to monitor the bar. Bruce has suspected that someone behind the bar, possibly Billy, was stealing. He had no concrete evidence for this. Nevertheless, he believed it was true, and he went ahead and hired these outside detectives—called "spotters"—to come by and check out the scene. Their report identified Billy as a crook, and Bruce had no choice. He called his manager, Michael Fitzpatrick, and told him to call Billy and fire him.

"You have to look at stealing in different ways," Bruce says moments after setting his dismissal in motion. He is anxious to justify an action that he knows might make him look like the Big Bad Boss. He has fired plenty of people already, but this is one of the first to be fired for cause. So he figures there'd better be one, and it probably better be good.

"Either it's just totally criminal, which I don't think in this case it is, it's neglect, or lack of caring, or greedy. I think it just comes down to greed in a certain way. Whether it's criminal or not I'm not even interested in. Unless someone's actually stealing. But you have aspects of it like—someone comes in, you buy them a drink, it's busy—and the two people you've bought a drink for are sitting at my barstools for an hour or two, they haven't paid for a goddamn thing and they leave you [the bartender] a $20 tip.

"I would call that, in my book, *stealing.*" Bruce pauses to see how that plays. He has finally labeled Billy's behavior a felony. Is that what he meant to say? He will be cautious now. "If I had to go before a judge he might not consider it that." So what did he do exactly? "It's more of a house rule than anything else."

Hmmmm. Billy must have left his Falls house rulebook in his other pants.

The likelihood that a bartender is ripping off his employer is real. Ask any bartender you happen to meet. This is one of the few universal rules of restaurants. Bartenders in Calcutta are equally as capable of stealing money as bartenders in Boston. The desire for illicit income transcends cultural barriers. The opportunity to take it, without permission, is far more available at the bar than elsewhere in the restaurant. Remember, unlike waiters, a bartender has immediate access to both ends of the transaction—the commodity to be sold and the cash to be paid. He pours the booze and holds the cash. Bartenders describe numerous scenarios that allow quick, unauthorized access to money. They have the authority to give things away, and with that comes the freedom to deal.

Yes that's right. It's not stealing. It's dealing.

You deal in courtesy at the bar. This is what people are paying for. It's cheaper to drink at home. But at a bar, you will have a napkin placed in front of you. A bartender will ask how you are. He will inquire as to your health and your opinion of the weather. He will introduce you to others at the bar. He will keep a watchful eye on your glass. He will make certain you will not go thirsty. What a guy, huh? You pay handsomely for these services, of course. Do not forget that a bar is where the profits are. A restaurant will sell you twenty-five cents' worth of vodka for $4. That's a hell of a lot for a napkin.

/And how about those tips! We're talking three figures a night, or at least high twos. Doesn't matter what the food prices are. A bartender commands a healthy percentage of his tab in tips. Far more than the average waiter. You buy two beers for four bucks, you'll leave him five. You get two vodkas for eight bucks, you'll leave one or two more. Maybe you'll pay with a twenty and forget your change. Either way, the bartender's getting a nice piece of coin for his work, easy enough to fill a glass with ice and pour out some booze, right? A little washing, a little wiping, big deal. It's a highly coveted job, and nobody's in it for the connections.

The job is so loose, so casual, that the line between good service and theft is tough to define. Let's say there's a guy who's settled in his barstool for the night. He has one, two, three drinks. Most bartenders have a policy: After drink number three, the next one is free. Drinkers know this. They have been known to say to their bartender: "Let me have my second free drink now"—after the first one—"and *then* I will buy my next three." A good bartender will make him wait. Get the money up front.

But there is incentive for the bartender to give away his product. It will invariably translate into a larger tip. So what a bartender is really stealing is booze. By giving you a free drink, he is robbing his employer of the opportunity to make more money, and giving it to himself. Nebulous, yet significant—if only because there is so much money to be made on booze that a restaurant will be that much the poorer if a disproportionate amount of it ends up in a bartender's pocket.

And that is precisely what happens. Not all the time . . . but enough.

Like the guy who comes in one night and has two drinks and then says to Billy, "I didn't give you the money. I didn't pay you."

You did, he says. I thought you did.

Nope.

"Thank you for being so honest," he says sweetly. He rewards him for his honesty with two rounds of free drinks. He rewards the bartender with a big tip.

Is that stealing?

T   H   E   F   A   L   L   S

SPARKLING/CHAMPAGNE
Domaine Chandon Brut	$24.
Schramsberg Blanc de Noirs 1983	$38.
Perrier Jouet Brut Champagne	$36.
Taittinger Brut Champagne	$44.
Veuve-Clicquot Yellow Label Brut Champagne	$55.
Roederer Brut Rose Champagne	$75.
Dom Perignon Brut 1982	$100.
Taittinger Comte de Champagne Rose Brut 1982	$125.

WHITE
Ferrari-Carano Fume Blanc 1988	$19.
Cakebread Sauvignon Blanc 1988	$23.
Innisfree Napa Chardonnay 1988	$18.
Clos du Val Joli Val Chardonnay 1988	$22.
Freemark Abbey Chardonnay 1988	$25.
Acacia Carneros Chardonnay 1988	$30.
Domaine Fief Guerin Muscadet 1986	$14.
Maufoux Sancerre 1988	$24.
Louis Michel Chablis 1988	$28.
Olivier LeFlaive Puligny-Montrachet 1986	$47.
Villa Marchesini Pinot Grigio 1986	$14.

ROSE
Pedroncelli White Zinfandel 1988	$14.
L"Estandon Rose 1988	$16.
Domaine Ott Chateau de Selle Rose 1988	$32.

RED
Kendall Jackson Mendocino Zinfandel 1987	$18.
Carneros Creek Fleur de Carneros Pinot Noir 1988	$20.
Ridge Marlot 1986	$23.
Seghesio Cabernet Sauvignon 1986	$17.
Spring Mountain Cabernet Sauvignon 1984	$25.
Heitz Cellars Cabernet Sauvignon 1984	$31.
Bedin Brouilly La Chapelle du Mont 1988	$19.
Louis Jadot Beaune Bressandes 1983	$39.
Paul Jaboulet Gigondas 1985	$21.
Chateau Touteran Haut-Medoc 1981	$18.
Chateau Fombrauge St. Emilion 1983	$26.
Vallana Spanna del Piemonte 1979	$22.

PORTO
Sandeman Founders Reserve Porto	Glass	$5.
Dow True Vintage Porto 1975	Glass	$12.
Fonseca True Vintage Porto 1975	Glass	$15.

"Oh," Bruce says, "they have these little games they play."

The game is hard to play when the Boss knows all the little angles.

Bruce loves the game. To him it is a spectator sport, except that it's fixed. Bruce always wins. He watches and waits. He decides who wins and who loses. He is ready for any gambit, any trick. Don't forget: He has scoped out The Falls and chosen the bar as his preferred vantage point, his prime position. He has his favorite stool and he isn't using it to read the paper. Watch those eyes pan and scan.

Bartenders have been stealing ever since the invention of cash. Stories are told of bartenders with identical cash registers in their apartments, printing out replacement tapes; of bartenders bringing their own bottles of booze into the bar; of bartenders keeping coins near the register to remind them of how much extra cash they can take from the register at the end of the night—a nickel meaning $5, a dime meaning $10, you get the picture.

So Michael Fitzpatrick has called Billy and broken the news that he has been caught in the act. He was none too pleased. His immediate response was to say, No, it was another bartender, Frank. Not me. I'm not guilty. It was *him*.

To which Bruce responded with amusement, "Watch the bartender's credo go out the window. Now that one didn't get fired and the other did."

Poor Billy, out of a job, and why? Because he had done what all bartenders do, and maybe he didn't even do it; who knows? All he knows is he gave away a few too many drinks. It must have seemed so ironic to him, working in a restaurant where free food and drink have been the hallmarks of the last six weeks. Friends of Bruce, friends of Terry; come one, come all! Have a glass of champagne on The Falls! The only difference was that he got tipped. He had to earn his cash, and if it meant a free drink to his regulars—and boy, did he have regulars; five or ten a night, greeting him warmly by name—then so what?

Bruce sees it differently. He is smart enough to know that there are no chances to be taken in this business. Billy must go.

But Bruce is nervous. The Boss can't help it. Is it the firing of Billy? It cannot be the restaurant. He knows he has a hit on his hands. The crowds keep coming, and boy, are they beautiful. This is the kind of place that gets you thinking, Hey, why am I so short? How is it possible that so many women can be over six feet tall?

"I get a little scared when I see all these models and fashion people," Bruce says quietly. Is it the guilt that is causing him to be so reflective? "Because I know what a trendy crowd they are. Who knows with them? I never thought they were much . . . they're beautiful and they're wonderful and all that stuff and they make a nice appearance in the beginning. It reminds me of a guy who used to make fasteners for American Tourister and one day he woke up and said, 'If American Tourister throws me out, I'm out of business.' And he started to go get other accounts. That's what it is in this kind of business. It's nice to have that main thing in the beginning but you have to bolster it with hard-core clientele. People who come in. The people you don't notice."

/The next day, Bruce rehired Billy. He said he was no longer quite sure whether he'd done something wrong. He came back to work at The Falls that weekend.

/The man who really rehired him was the man who fired him. Michael Fitzpatrick. Or Michael Fitz, as he was known around The Falls.

Fitz doesn't look like a Fallsman. Short, stocky, a New York tough-guy voice and a short shock of black hair, he doesn't scare children but he doesn't make them coo, either. However, he does manage to manage. It is a job that desperately needed doing. He worked for Bruce at Central Falls, and then worked at a nightclub up Varick Street a couple of blocks, called S.O.B.'s, where money was made on volume.

Bruce hired him to replace Henry Hauck, and never came up with a reason to let him go. Is it because he is a man? Or because he is a lot smarter and more talented than he might seem at first glance? Maybe it's because Michael had worked the bar at Columbus.

So Michael is keeping his job for a while. It's a good place for him to hang out, make $600 a week, maybe more, and learn how to run a restaurant. See, Michael lives in Hell's Kitchen, and loves this restaurant around the corner called Robert's, and it is a personal dream of his to buy the place, or someplace at least, and open up a restaurant like Robert's, a quiet, dark piano joint with good food and burgers and beer. Robert's had opened in the early 1980s, and there it was, still open, still thriving after all this time.

FUCKING FRUITS AND

VEGETABLES

TWENTY

Dominick Calderazzo, commonly known as Mugsy, gets up for work at around half past ten at night. He leaves his apartment on Mulberry Street in Little Italy a few minutes after eleven.

Mugsy has been living in Little Italy all his life. He remembers when you could go to sleep at night with your apartment door wide open.

Now, like the rest of this suffering hellhole, *the old neighborhood has changed*. The Chinese have intruded on his turf. Little Italy is now Chinatown. The doors are locked. Nobody comes into Mugsy's bachelor pad without ringing the bell.

Mugsy's face is all angles. You could chop carrots on his jaw. He's got a swarthy complexion, and a tough-guy haircut. Somebody might call him handsome, but somebody else will probably disagree. His body appears to be in a perpetual crouch. But he's not going to hurt anyone. He's going to spend the night at the Hunts Point Market, where seven million residents of New York City get their Fruits and Vegetables. Sorry, make that their Fucking Fruits and Vegetables. That is what they are called at Hunts Point.

He will spend most of the time between midnight and 7:00 A.M. lifting boxes of Fucking Fruits and Vegetables into his truck. He has been doing this for nine years and expects to be doing it for at least

169

nine more years, which for Mugsy is somewhere in the vicinity of forever.

On the side of Mugsy's truck it says C&S PRODUCE. That is the company that has employed him for the last five years. "I used to work for another guy," he says, "but then C&S made me an offer and it was good so I took it."

Mugsy likes his truck, which is good because he ends up spending a couple of hours a night in it, looking for a good parking space at the loading dock at Hunts Point. During the day, after he's done making Fucking Fruit and Vegetable deliveries to fifteen different restaurants below 14th Street in Manhattan, he parks it right near his house. Inside the truck as he starts out for Hunts Point one clear summer night are the following items:

a radio with a speaker, which he loves

copies of two recent issues of *Rolling Stone*

a copy of last week's *New York Times Magazine*

one coffee regular

You gotta bring some magazines, Mugsy explains, because you're gonna spend some time sitting around.

Up from Little Italy, Mugsy heads his truck toward the Bronx. Hunts Point Market is located in a particularly dangerous and poverty-stricken area of the Bronx. "If you get a flat tire around there," Mugsy says, "you just keep driving. You don't stop. You don't wait." He barrels his truck past the decrepit buildings and projects along the route.

Outside the Hunts Point Market, young black hookers offer blow jobs for $5. They perform their services, then take the money and buy crack. Most of them are addicted to crack. Hunts Point is known for its hookers. Sex is the one commodity sold there that is always in season.

/At the gate, Mugsy flashes his ID card. He is not one of those ultra-friendly people who yak it up with everyone at the market.

Mugsy likes to get to work early because that way he won't have to worry so much about parking, the official Royal Pain of Hunts Point. Don't believe what anyone else tells you about Hunts Point. The big deal here isn't the produce, it's the parking. Everybody's fighting for a space on the loading dock. Oh, man. Big trucks from California, little trucks from Connecticut. It's all a horrible *nightmare*. Everybody's waiting, sometimes a couple hours, for a premium space. Mugsy once had to wait three hours for a space, which was a major drag because he likes to get another cup of coffee with a pal of his before starting work. Perfectly reasonable.

"Basically, you just kinda plant yourself near where you think somebody's gonna pull out," Mugsy says. "You watch him and maybe you go around and find out how long he's gonna be there. You keep track and then if you're lucky, and nobody else is there before you, it's your space."

But usually it isn't. So you go and get yourself a cup of coffee and sit in your truck. That's why Mugsy always makes sure to bring some magazines. He has a subscription to *Rolling Stone,* and he doesn't give a shit that the magazine isn't quite what it used to be.

Mugsy gets a space around 12:30. He has already gotten out of the truck a couple of times, mostly to see whether his boss, Johnny, has shown up yet. One of the reasons Mugsy likes his job is that it's not one of those deals where you've got your fucking boss hanging over your head all the time.

"Maybe I see Johnny for two or three hours," Mugsy says. "The rest of the time I'm just working."

The space he gets is what you might call a tight squeeze. He hops out, opens the back, pulls out his hand truck, and gets right to work. This involves going to all the stands and finding out what orders Johnny has placed, then getting the orders and loading them, and then hanging around and doing squat.

But Mugsy adds one step to the job, partially because he likes to, and partially because it's smart employee behavior. He checks the vegetables to make sure they're all right. This is rare and admirable behavior among the trucking staff at Hunts Point. It means that he pulls out a few handfuls of lettuce or grapes or whatever it is, and checks it over to make sure it's fresh, or whatever it's supposed to be. Green and firm appear to be the most popular characteristics of fruits and vegetables.

"That way I don't get complaints," he says, and he doesn't.

The job description includes heavy lifting. Until about 5:00 or so in the morning, Mugsy has to work pretty hard. He can stop every so often for a few minutes' break, but most of the time he has to keep moving.

He hauls his butt from store to store—a "store," at Hunts Point, meaning an enclosed office space in front of the large warehouses that store all the fruits and vegetables. Each store has its own display of whatever it is they sell. Invariably, the displayed food looks quite wonderful. Almost as invariably, the food in the warehouse looks like shit.

/Johnny Caggiano, the buyer for C&S Produce, spends the night sorting through the shit.

Johnny lives in the Bronx, about ten minutes' drive from Hunts Point. On the weekends he wears expensive suits and shoes. At work it's a different story. Sometimes he doesn't even bother to shave.

On this night Johnny is wearing a blue-and-white jacket, an open-collar blue sport shirt, jeans and large black leather shoes. This puts him somewhere in the mid range of fashion at Hunts Point. Occasionally you'll see somebody in a nice sweater or even a tie, but most of the five thousand men of Hunts Point wear clothes they can get dirty. There do not appear to be any women at Hunts Point, except those who work behind the counter at the coffee shop. At 6:00 in the morning, Johnny stops at said counter to order a knockwurst sandwich with mayonnaise on a hamburger bun (the words "make it two" do not come to mind in this instance) and a cup of coffee.

The most commonly used words at Hunts Point are FUCK and FUCKING. They are presented here in capital letters because that is how they are typically spoken.

"You FUCKING cocksucker, I need some FUCKING arugula and the FUCK I'm gonna pay $12 when I can get it for FUCKING $10 all over the FUCKING place."

"Then why don't you go do that, and FUCK you."

"You won't see me for FUCKING six months, you slimeball."

"FUCK you."

Most of the men conducting business at Hunts Point are white, and either Italian or Jewish. There is an unwritten rule against ethnic slurs being thrown into the mix of insults when it involves white ethnic people.

Blacks, however, do not get the same courtesy. One store owner, holding firm on a price on tomatoes as a black buyer tried to argue with him, had this final word of advice:

"You get the FUCK out of here, you FUCKING *orangutang!*"

Whereupon the white, Italian salesman beamed proudly at everyone who heard him, while the black buyer walked away, shaking his head.

Johnny is not the sort of guy to hurl ethnic insults. He has been at Hunts Point too long for that. He has spent five nights a week here for the last ten years. Every night he tries to walk the full three and a half miles of Hunts Point, checking the produce and prices of everything. Therefore he limits himself to generically hurled insults, which means that everyone he deals with is merely a fucking cocksucker.

He knows practically everyone, most of them well enough to walk into their small office, not bothering to say hello, and make a phone call on their only phone. Never mind if they need to use it.

He also prides himself on his habit of tearing apart well-packed boxes of fruit and vegetables that he has no intention whatsoever of buying. Often he'll pull apart a box's contents and eat whatever part he feels like.

"I like to taste the stuff," he explains, " 'cause everybody here is lying, including me, which probably means that they're trying to sell me some shit."

Johnny spends the night filling the orders from the seventy-five restaurants supplied by C&S Produce.

One of those restaurants is a new place on Varick Street, where he actually likes to *go* once in a while. For a drink. Often with Mugsy. For several drinks. Sometimes the owner, Bruce Goldstein, will buy them one, so why not go there? Johnny is a man who can have several drinks, usually Glenlivet, and still appear to be on his first. He leans up against the bar at this new place, called The Falls, and has several drinks.

GAEL FORCE

TWENTY-ONE

Last Saturday, during a mid-April weekend in the middle of The Falls's rocking second month, a party of four—two couples—came to The Falls for dinner at 8:30, under the name "Dr. Larson."

One of them wore what appeared to be a wig and floppy hat. Her girth reflected a large love of food.

By 8:45, everyone at The Falls felt certain that "Dr. Larson" was a pseudonym for Gael Greene, the restaurant critic for *New York* magazine. Greene has been reviewing restaurants at *New York* for more than two decades. It is often assumed that when a large woman in a floppy hat and wig enters your establishment, she is Gael Greene, and should therefore be treated better than other people. This was precisely what then transpired at The Falls. The staff moved into a full-scale offensive, offering this diner every courtesy in the most subtle manner they could conjure up.

Bruce stood watch from the bar. He was none too pleased. Angry thoughts blazed through his mind: Why the hell is a major restaurant critic coming in here on a Saturday night? We're packed, we're hot, we're new . . . give us a break, lady. This is not the way it's done, check the manual. He knew he was helpless, though. A critic will write what she will write. He had been slammed before, at Central Falls, by no less a countenance than Mimi Sheraton of *The New York Times*, who deemed it mediocre, which Bruce felt it was not. But he lived with it, and eventually thrived. Sometimes the review doesn't matter—like when you're on a busy street with a healthy neighborhood in a thriving economy.

But The Falls, on a dark, empty street surrounded by dark office buildings smack in the middle of a recession, needed a good review. So far there had been no sign of Bryan Miller, the *New York Times* critic, whom Brian Moores had been insisting he would recognize on sight. Miller had already passed over The Falls in a Weekend section piece on TriBeCa trendies in March. Was that because The Falls barely bordered TriBeCa? Because it wasn't trendy enough? Or because he'd never heard of it? Bruce didn't know. He'd hired Peter Himler in part to approach Miller with letters and phone calls! Why hadn't that worked? Why nothing?

Nothing, Bruce thought, except that stupid, vicious slam in *The New York Press*. That, too, blazed fierce through Bruce's mind as Gael Greene contemplated her menu and adjusted her floppy hat.

What the hell is *The New York Press*, anyway? That is something Bruce would desperately like to know. The facts don't quite explain it. He is aware that it comes out once a week and is available in free street boxes around Manhattan. He has flipped though it enough to know it is a motley assortment of columns and features with a highly personal orientation. The lead column, called "The Mugger," relishes in ad hominem anonymous attacks (including a few broadsides against this writer) and provides a chronicle of the writer's alcoholic excesses. Another of its regular weekly features is a restaurant review.

A couple of weeks ago, an advertising salesman for the *Press* tried unsuccessfully to get Bruce to buy an ad for The Falls to advertise in its pages. Now in early April, a highly unfavorable review appears in the *Press*.

Coincidence? Bruce thinks not.

While awaiting the more important reviews, Bruce could—and did—spend hours brooding over its content. Not to mention its horribly perfect headline: BROKEN HIP, and large-type boldfaced summary subheadline underneath, THE SERVICE IS THE SAME AS THE FOOD: TERRIBLE.

"Enough already with celebrity-owned restaurants," the review, by Ken Frydman, began. "If I'm looking for stars, I'll go to the Hayden Planetarium."

He went on to list the celebrity investors, and to note the fact that during his one visit to the restaurant on Friday night in early April, the only Falls principal on premises was Bruce Goldstein himself. He then recounted his nightmarish experience at trying to get served:

> "SORRY, WE'RE NOT SERVING the full dinner menu anymore," reports the hostess-with-the-leastest. "But you can order from the late-night supper menu."
>
> Funny, that comes as news to me: The reservations clerk had told me on the phone earlier that The Falls served its core dinner menu until midnight Sunday through Thursday and until 1 A.M. Fridays and Saturdays. And this was definitely one of those seven days.
>
> "Never mind her," interrupts a waiter, overriding the hostess. "Just follow me and you can have anything you want on the dinner menu."

The guy hasn't even sat down yet, and it's an unqualified slam!

> AS IT TURNS OUT, I'd have been better off with the late-night menu. . . . Our first two entree choices—boneless Atlantic char ($15) and the snapper special—had both been "86ed." In their place was the bass, which didn't really turn me on.
>
> So we turned to our second options. My extra large gulf shrimp grilled with white truffle oil ($17) was truly disappointing. Unimaginatively prepared, the over-grilled, butterflied shrimp were less than fresh and served with primitively-sliced vegetables. The least executive chef Brian Moores could have done was julienne them.
>
> And I thought I had problems with my meal. A professional recipe tester and menu developer, my sidekick sends back an undercooked, whole split baby chicken with fresh herb sauce ($14). Believe it or not, the pollo came back nearly as pink the second time.
>
> Most perplexing of all, however, is the dessert. Coconut flan ($5) is a tasty egg, caramel and milk custard with a heavy, somewhat rubbery texture that I nevertheless enjoy. But, instead of a sprinkling of raw, untoasted coconut flakes, the coconut should be toasted, baked and mixed in to absorb some of the batter's liquid.

"Oh well," he sums up bitterly, "at least we had a $36 bottle of Perrier-Jouët Brut champagne to keep us company. But by the time the waitress decided to pour it, the chilled bottle was covered with ice cubes from the frozen bucket. Now I know how Eskimos drink their bubbly."

He takes a swipe at all aspects of the service: "It would help," he says, "if a busboy bussed our table, now overflowing with dirty plates and unwanted glasses." But then, almost out of context with the rest of the review, he concludes with strangely kind words about the essential nature of The Falls and its purpose.

> IT'S EASY TO BE HIP at The Falls, whether you are or not. The jazz is hep, the pink and beige tone play off the black chairs, banquettes and formica tabletops, and the gorgeous cut-glass back bar mirror is accented beautifully by floral arrangements and futuristic light fixtures flashing in sync to the music.

It was the kind of review that makes you want to run out in front of oncoming traffic. Too bad there isn't any on Varick Street at night.

/But wait! Gael Greene is here and she is ordering. She has ordered the ravioli and the spring chicken. No wine. The order is rushed into the kitchen, and per Bruce's instructions and Brian's wishes, given priority treatment. "There isn't much you can really do to make an individual meal that much better than anyone else's," Brian has previously observed, speculating on what he would do when this day came. "Everything's basically dependent on the quality of the food that day, the way you prepare some of it in advance, the dressings, the sauces . . . it's the recipe that matters. It's the way you design the menu and the idea behind the food. If you're doing it right, then when somebody comes in and you're trying to give 'em a decent meal, you can do it without any special trouble."

Nevertheless, Brian is taking care. He is not going to fuck this up. After that *New York Press* debacle there will be no chances taken.

Wait . . . what is this? Gael and her companions have finished their main courses, and they have *asked for the check.*

No dessert?

Brian is heartbroken. How he loves his desserts!

Bruce is pissed. How he desperately wanted a rave!

It is not entirely clear, as "Dr. Larson" pays the check, whether the meal has been a disaster. It is possible that she is checking out a few places. Maybe she has movie tickets. A late show? You never know.

Brian is very sad, though. He is pretty sure it did not go well. He wears his sadness discreetly, but it is plain to see. Brian Moores was blessed with a face best suited to a smile. There is little room on it for depression and malaise. For the rest of the night, and on through the next day and even the next, the confusion lingers.

"She didn't like what she had," Brian says definitively the next evening. He is shuffling back and forth between burners and the oven. "First of all, why did she come in on a Saturday night when we're at our busiest? That's not fair. And plus she was clearly on her way someplace, in a hurry, almost determined to have a bad time."

But did she? Clearly it would be necessary to contact Gael Greene and, finally, determine independently what happened that night.

Here is Gael Greene's account of the evening. [*Author's note:* Gael Greene and I are colleagues who share room on the masthead of *New York* magazine but have never met. I contacted Greene by letter in March of 1990 to seek her help on this book, by allowing me to accompany her on a trip to The Falls, or, at the very least, a face-to-face interview. She did not permit either; rather, she gave one twenty-minute telephone interview of a mostly general nature, and one brief follow-up. She also specifically said that the only reason she ever visited The Falls was because of my letter. Sorry, Gael.]

"We went there on a Saturday night," Greene recalled in the conversation a few weeks later. "Two couples. It was packed—you could tell it was already hot, it had already been discovered. They gave us a table by the window. We ordered—a seafood and a pasta, I can't remember what we had, it was so terrible. We had to beg for water, we had to beg for bread, we had to beg for wine. The service was nonexistent. When the food came it was terrible. Horrible."

Come on, Gael, tell us what you really thought!

"I told my friends, 'Stop eating. We'll go somewhere else. You don't have to suffer.' So we got the check and we went to Man Ray [a recently reopened bistro nearby] and ordered appetizers and desserts."

This information was, of course, not available to the folks at The Falls. Although one has to give them credit for figuring it out.

/Poor Gael. She thought she was through with The Falls. But suddenly, it is four days later, Wednesday, and here she is in The Falls again!

It seems that among Gael's many friends in the restaurant business is a fellow whom we will call Fritz. Now, this Fritz—who has worked

in several top restaurants and brokers restaurant real estate deals—
had plans to take Gael to a gallery opening in SoHo on this particular
Wednesday night. And naturally, Fritz knew that dinner afterward
would be a part of the plan. Dinner afterward is always part of the
plan with Gael. So Fritz and Gael went to the opening, and afterward
Fritz said, "Let's go to The Falls."

Gael told Fritz she'd just been there and had a horrible meal. "I
want to go to the Tribeca Grill," she said, referring to the just-opened
De Niro joint nearby.

But Fritz was determined to get Gael to The Falls. The reason—
which, of course, he was not disclosing to Gael—was that Bruce and
Philippe were both friends of his. Fritz has a reputation for helping
out his restaurant pals by getting Gael to their door; Gael later admitted that she knew that about Fritz. But on this occasion the issue of
his connection to The Falls didn't come up. Instead, Fritz chose to lie
a little. "It's my birthday," he told Gael. "There's a party for me at
The Falls, so we *have* to go." It wasn't Fritz's birthday, but really, how
would Gael know that? Finally, after much cajoling, she agreed to a
return visit. For Fritz's sake.

This time—knowing that Fritz would no doubt succeed in steering
Gael back—Bruce had a little more time to plan things out. He had a
birthday party to plan, and nothing excites Bruce more than to plan.
He assembled a group of beautiful women and glamorous men. He
enlisted Alexandra, Philippe's beautiful girlfriend, and a few of her
model companions. They came in gloriously sexy miniskirts and
smoked deliciously foreign cigarettes. The men wore black and more
black. They smelled better than the food.

And this time Gael liked what she saw and what she ate.

She ordered corn on the cob as an appetizer and fettuccine as a
main course. "Very weird," Brian remarked. "Not very representative." For dessert, it was to be the flourless chocolate cake they all
shared. *Birthday* cake.

The room was hot. The music was hot. The crowd was hot.

Even the food was hot.

Bruce had the time of his life. He hovered in and out of the affair,
which lasted for more than three hours. Gael was in the thick of it.
Good wine, good food . . . what more could a critic want? And from all
outward appearances, Gael was having the time of her life. She smiled
and listened and talked and laughed. She cleaned her plate. Brian
noticed that. She became immersed in a conversation with Alexandra,
who neglected to inform Gael that she was dating one of the prin-

cipal employees of The Falls and was an investor herself. She told Gael that another guy at the dinner was her boyfriend. Gael liked her a lot and suggested they all have dinner one night. "Okay," Alexandra said, though she didn't quite know how that was going to work out.

"It was hilarious," Bruce said the next morning. "She had *no idea* she was being fooled."

Gael Greene's account of the evening differed slightly with The Falls's version.

"After that first meal, I thought I'd wait awhile. I told Richard Story [a senior editor at *New York*] it'd be good for his Hotline column. I decided if someone told me the food got better, I might go back.

"But then the next week I was invited to a birthday party and told it was going to be at The Falls. I said to my friend, 'Oh, you don't want to have your birthday there, it's *horrible!*' There was a cocktail party first at a gallery . . . then we went to The Falls.

"When we got there I thought right away that this was The Falls's idea to get me there. But this time the food was much better. The fish was properly flavored, the sauces were good, the dessert was quite wonderful. The food was good in a way it hadn't been the previous time.

"It reminded me a bit of J.S. VanDam in its moment—it had its own brief moment after it opened when it was *the* place to go and you couldn't get in. I would go back to The Falls if someone told me there'd been a big change—that there was a new chef or something. But it was not special at all, not a place I would have written about under normal circumstances, not really even a place I would have visited."

/Shortly afterward, Greene published a cover story in *New York* called "Cheaper Eats." Her thesis was that New York City restaurants, responding to the recession, were offering low prices in a new strategy to prosper. Among the restaurants prominently mentioned were the Tribeca Grill, by now an established hit, and the Broadway Grill, run by famed cookie man David Liederman inside a sleek new Broadway hotel. Thanks to the stunt engineered by Bruce and Philippe, The Falls also managed three paragraphs:

Forced to vacate its prime real estate on West Broadway, Central Falls became **The Falls,** in the spot where J.S. VanDam once simmered. With so many investors' hopes pinned to whether or not The Falls falls—Central Falls owner Bruce Goldstein, film director Alan Parker (Mississippi Burning), Terry Quinn (Peggy Sue's owner), Matt Dillon, and more, and more—the place could hold its own on the loyalty of friends alone.

Right now, it's already hot: full of leggy mannequins, artists and art dealers, downtown 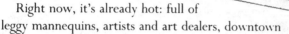 eccentrics, a woman in a silver garden-party hat, a man in a rose-pink pussycat bow, another with Maria Montez fingernails, and enough cigarette smoke from happily polluted French lungs that I feel I'm fighting a forest fire. Prices tread the line—dinner entrees $18 or under, the baby chicken just $14. But tonight, the staff is in a dither. We beg for water, plead for bread, pour our own wine, and find the food so sad that we ask for a check and race uptown for dinner.

Returning a few days later (none too eager), I find a bit more discipline in the dining room and more inspiration in the kitchen—deliciously glazed grouper, decent swordfish with savory black-bean-and-ginger sauce, and a rich chocolate-truffle cake that's hard to stop eating. But good food may not be the point here. And it's still early. I might put on a gas mask and come back to try again. ▬

It worked! All those crazy people . . . Bruce and Philippe (the French lung, of course) got them there. The leggy mannequins . . . that was them, too. No one will own up to the Maria Montez fingernails.

Could this be the break Bruce was looking for? Not that the place needed help at the moment—the crowds still swelled most nights, and there seemed no end to their procession. But Bruce knows how fickle people can be. He values the publicity he gets; each time The Falls's name reaches print, he believes it results in new customers, new business.

"I think people say to themselves, 'Where should we go to dinner tonight?' And they search their brain for the name of a place. You know, some place they've heard of, maybe they heard about a place on Page Six or *New York* magazine or Bryan Miller or wherever. If they haven't heard of it then they're not going to go there, right? So they say, 'There's that place I just read about . . . The Falls. Let's go there.' So they look up where it is and they go. They get a cab and they go. It's that recognition thing."

So to be included in "Cheaper Eats" is a victory for Bruce. It means that new hordes of trendies will wend their way to The Falls. It means that new crowds of hoi polloi will wait by the bar for a table as Philippe takes care of his own. It means that The Falls will be hip, hot and happening for as long as anyone can imagine. It is a fantasy come to life; a dream come true.

New York comes out every Monday, and appears in most subscribers' mailboxes when they return home from work Monday night. And for those who come into The Falls this week in search of cheap eats, Bruce has prepared a little surprise.

He has the idea for his surprise that Monday afternoon. Why don't we *raise* our prices? That way, he says, when the crowds pour in for their cheap eats, we'll hit 'em for a few extra bucks. Pretty smooth, huh?

He takes the menu and within an hour the prices of some entrées have been raised by as much as five dollars.

/Philippe has done his thing. Now he is ready to go do another thing.

With great fanfare Philippe has announced his engagement to the beautiful Alexandra. Perhaps the Gael Greene scam was the final push they needed.

But before they are able to be married, there is some work that Philippe must do. He must return to St. Bart's and supervise the construction of a swimming pool. In St. Bart's this is not so simple as it sounds. It is an island where the work ethic is somewhat less than Puritan, and so it is necessary to strictly monitor the work you are paying for. Philippe knows this.

"We will be renting out the house as a luxury rental," Philippe explains. "There will be someone there who will cook all of your meals and take complete care of you. It will cost several thousand dollars a month, but you will be treated like a king."

It sounds very nice, but first a swimming pool must be built. Even on St. Bart's, where visitors can swim in the bluest of waters, a swimming pool is absolutely necessary, and Philippe will not rest until one is built.

"This is it," Philippe says. "I think I am leaving here at the right time. I've done my job."

And so now Philippe will go to St. Bart's and build a pool and marry a woman and smoke many Marlboros and live the good life.

"He'll be back," Bruce says.

GIRLS, GIRLS, GIRLS!

TWENTY-TWO

Michael Fitzpatrick is staring into the eyes of a beautiful woman.

As manager of The Falls this is his job. You will not hear Michael moaning about it, either. He must interview prospective candidates for waitresses. Many of them are beautiful. Whether this is some form of natural selection taking place cannot be determined. Nevertheless it is true. Beautiful women seem to make their way to The Falls in record numbers, as customers and waitresses and revelers. Even the women who stop in to use the rest room are beautiful. The ad that ran in *The Village Voice* the first week in May, looking for new waiters and waitresses, made no mention of looks. Still, it seems to have worked out that way. A steady flow of tall blondes and green-eyed brunettes has made its way into The Falls, including the provocatively dressed young woman currently being queried by Michael.

The interview is going well. He is quite certain this woman will work out nicely. He shakes her hand warmly and tells her he will be in touch.

"Thanks," she says, flipping back her long blond hair. As she leaves, the eyes of everyone in the place—which, at this moment, includes Bruce and Terry and several other like-minded men—follow her out. They all admire her immense . . . qualifications.

At this precise moment, a woman in her fifties enters The Falls. She is not what The Falls management would consider to be attractive. She is frumpy and overweight and her long, ragged cloth coat is covered with political buttons. She approaches Michael and asks him for an application form. He hands her one, and after a few minutes at the bar, she has finished filling it out. She takes it to Michael, who is standing near the back of the bar.

"I'll read it," Michael says evenly, betraying no feelings at all about her appearance, "and call you if we want you to come in."

She starts to leave. But just as she gets to the door, she swings on her heels. Michael is all the way on the other side of the restaurant, but she is determined to get his attention.

She begins to scream.

"You don't want to interview me because you don't think I'm attractive. Isn't that it? You think I'm ugly. You said in the ad that you're interviewing people. When I handed you my application you were shaking hands with that younger woman, you interviewed her. You're a *very* boorish young man."

Suddenly all activity in The Falls has screeched to a halt. Terry and Bruce look up to see the woman making this enormous ruckus. They look at each other as though they are about to break into convulsive laughter. Michael, meanwhile, has kept a perfectly straight face. He approaches her, application in hand, in the hopes of calming her down.

"I told you that I'd read your application and that I'd call you, and that's exactly what I planned to do." Michael pauses for a moment. This is definitely *not* in the job description. "If you think I'm going to hire you *now* you're mistaken," Michael says.

Bruce and Terry and everyone left in the restaurant is amazed. Silent. Watching. Mesmerized.

The woman continues to yell. "I've worked all over. I worked at Max's Kansas City, I've worked in all the clubs, in the best jazz clubs. You're making a fucking mistake. I know what you people are like."

Michael cannot take it anymore. He has nothing left to say to calm her down. So he quietly, hopefully turns around and walks away. This woman has lost her audience; she may be intense, angry, but she appears not to be crazy enough to keep yelling without an audience. So she turns around and storms out of The Falls.

There is, at first, a long beat of stunned silence. Nobody knows what to say.

Finally Bruce breaks the silence. "Funny," says Bruce to Michael, "you don't look boorish."

There is, at this, hysterical laughter and applause. Terry and Bruce lead in the cheering. Michael has stood up for the values that make The Falls what it is: an elitist sexist institution that has no room for weird old ladies in ragged cloth coats.

/Let's face facts. The Falls is crowded primarily with three types of people: beautiful women, the kind of men who either date or hang around with beautiful women, and the kind of men who like to eat near beautiful women. It now seems abundantly clear, after two months of operation, that this is a formula for success in a restaurant. There is a magnet that draws beautiful women from one restaurant to another, and at the moment that magnet is buried somewhere beneath Varick and Vandam. It seems to be almost a statistical impossibility that so many beautiful women would come to one restaurant. And we are not talking about the same beautiful women every night, either. Sure, there are regulars—Ford models, Elite models, *Sports Illustrated* swimsuit models, aspiring models. They come because they have been expressly solicited and invited and, in many cases, paid for. But you will find that even the basic who-are-these-people crowd, the one that comes on Saturday night from areas outside Manhattan, is also pretty damn good-looking, even though they tend to wear ugly sweaters.

"Last Saturday night was *amaaaazing,*" Terry is saying. Terry Quinn is one of The Falls's foremost connoisseurs of beauty. Just watch his eyes dart around a room. It is five days later and he still can't get over it. What a crop of lookers! If only the Irish had a phrase like oy yoy yoy! "All twelves and fifteens and twenties," Terry says. [*Author's note:* The human body ratings scale traditionally ranges from one to ten.] "I've never seen so many beautiful girls in one place," he adds in a way that says, *believe* me.

Among the hundreds of restaurants that dot Manhattan, there are perhaps fifty that specialize in attracting the attractive. Somehow they need not advertise this skill. The information manages to permeate the collective consciousness of blond women all across town. They gravitate with ease to the newest, hottest, hippest joint, and stay there for as long as they reap the benefits: good tables, free drinks and . . . yes, there *is* a secret to all this . . . good lighting. This is the theater, and they are the stars.

To *The New York Press*, The Falls is responding as follows: Why go to the Hayden Planetarium when you can come here and see heavenly bodies?

Of course, it is not a simple matter of dimmer switches. There's only one of those, anyway. Calls have to be made, of course. It helps to know the right people. In the case of The Falls, the right people already had their finger in the pie—namely, Alexandra and Philippe. Her Victoria's Secret connections, coupled with his intimate friendships with the managers of Ford and Elite, virtually assured The Falls of as many models as it needed. Terry Quinn, whose connection to the modeling community is of a more personal nature, is able to bring in famous models as well.

He is particularly proud of having made a regular customer of Ashley Montana, or Ashley Richardson, or whatever the Ashley who was just on the cover of the *Sports Illustrated Swimsuit Issue* likes to be called. You know, the one with the particularly voluptuous figure that got everyone saying, hmmmm, I guess men are going for that kind of thing nowadays. Anyway, there is little argument that her name is Ashley and that she is generally considered to be quite beautiful and that she is a regular at The Falls.

She has, in fact, written a letter to Terry Quinn.

He is extremely proud of it. Documentation, at last, that beautiful women love The Falls!

Using a lovely block-printing style, Ashley bestows on The Falls its first rave review.

"In all my travels and the millions of restaurants I've been to," she reports ever-so-sweetly, "I've never come across a more efficient staff." And that's with *four* visits and *four* different waiters, mind you. No snap judgments here.

"The great food," she concludes with authority, "is an added plus."

So models really do go for the place. They think the service is good, which puts them in a distinct minority, but one imagines that the perspective of a *Sports Illustrated* Swimsuit Model is warped somewhat by special treatment.

Or maybe she just likes eating for free. Though Ashley and Paul may have paid for their meals, it is an undeniable fact that many of the models who come to The Falls eat for free, or at a discount. It is the stated policy of Falls management to fill the room with hot-looking babes, at whatever cost.

One day Bruce got a call from *Hard Copy*, the nationally syndicated TV show, informing him that they would like to shoot some film at The Falls. The topic of the piece was trendy celebrity restaurants—a topic made relevant in recent weeks not by The Falls, but by De Niro's *Tribeca Grill*. Still, The Falls made it to the list. Bruce knew what he had to do. He called one of the executives of Ford Models with an offer.

You send six of your most beautiful young things to The Falls, Bruce promised, and they will get anything and everything they want—for free. So, without much difficulty, the agency found what Bruce was looking for. How hard is it to find people to eat an all-expense-paid, all-you-can-gorge-and-swallow meal at one of New York's trendiest establishments?

The models dashed down at 8:00. They settled themselves in one by one, and incredibly, they all wore the same outfit: a short, tight black miniskirt. There were some variations in the length, and only four of the women went without hosiery of some kind, and only one of them had the temerity to wear a leather jacket over her low-cut top. But there they were, right smack in the middle at the center table Bruce had saved. All eyes were upon these gorgeous creatures as they ordered: Champagne! More champagne! Appetizers! Salads! Sirloins! Baby lamb chops! Desserts all around! Expensive red wines! Aged cognacs! There will be no check . . . there will be no tip. Bruce has taken care of everything, ladies. Never mind the $700 bill, it's all been paid for.

Just remember now: Smile for the camera.

The evening was a smash. The girls got smashed. Every neck in the room craned to see them fold and refold and unfold their fabulous legs.

There was only one slight problem.

Hard Copy showed up after they left.

"What are you supposed to do?" Bruce moans later. "It was the smart thing to do. And it paid off. We had a good crowd, a nice-looking crowd, that always helps."

True—but for how long? Nobody knows the answer to that question. There have been restaurants in New York that have been reliably inhabited by attractive women for years; but can anyone conclusively report that the physical appearance of their clientele is what keeps them alive? How many people—ordinary-looking people, that is, just the ones who don't scare small children—will continue to frequent restaurants simply because they know they will be surrounded by people better looking than them?

No one knows the answers to such questions. They are ridiculous questions, really. The Falls is hot at the moment; we know that. It has a good-looking crowd; we know that, too. We know what we see. We do not know what is coming. Or who is going.

We do know that Matt Dillon is coming. This has a lot to do with the general subject of girls, because girls love Matt Dillon. There is no arguing with the fact that he is what girls would call extremely cute.

He looks like Terry Quinn. To die for. He has been coming in nearly every day . . . finally! For the first two months, he was out of town. Shooting a movie. Now he is back, and it has all been very exciting, really. He orders the lamb chops, which are among the most reliable dishes on the menu. Sometimes he will also order the black bean soup. At the moment he is in town shooting scenes from his forthcoming thriller, *A Kiss Before Dying*. It is a remake of a 1956 hit of modest proportions, and Matt is playing the role originated by Robert Wagner. His co-star is the lovely Sean Young, who is famous for allegedly leaving a dead cat in front of James Woods's house.

Anyway, Matt is shooting all over town, and, as usual, hanging out all over the place. But as far as The Falls is concerned, he is eating only there, which is not true, but if you say it enough times, it sounds true, doesn't it?

"He comes in every day, or night, depending on where they're shooting," Bruce explains.

Really? Is that much black bean soup good for you?

"It's great," Bruce says. None of that John Waters shit. We *know* this guy. And not like that phony Tom Cruise reservation, either. Yeah, that's right. It turned out to be a prank. Nobody came, nobody called . . . probably some other restaurant playing a joke on us. That's what Bruce thinks. No, now we've got Matt, and that's good, 'cause we need a star, a *regular* star, one we can count on. Every day, or night, depending on where they're shooting.

"It's great," Bruce says. "There'll be two girls, they'll see Matt, and they'll call six other girls and *they'll* come in." Bruce loves it.

Terry doesn't. "The girls are ridiculous," Terry says. "They come up to him and say, 'I love your restaurant!' It's disgusting."

Damn right it is. It's not Matt's restaurant. It's *Terry's* restaurant. Matt may be a lot of things, but one thing he's not is Terry Quinn.

/It's really starting to get hot. No, not in the restaurant. In New York. It's the middle of May and it's hot *outside* The Falls.

Matt's movie is just about done. Tonight, in fact, is the final night of shooting. It is the seventeenth of May, and there is going to be a wrap party at The Falls. The cast, the crew, the girls, the boys . . . Brian is in the basement making platters of hors d'oeuvres. He seems a little nervous. Where is that bravado, that charisma, that confidence that makes a great chef? Perhaps it has something to do with toothpicks. No one likes working with toothpicks.

It is going to be a little tricky getting rid of the usual crowd tonight.

Michael Fitzpatrick is standing by the front door, in the vestibule, working on a plan. At 11:00 P.M., they officially stop letting people in. The party will begin momentarily. Terry Quinn and Patti D'Arbanville have arrived together. Terry is dressed in a very modish tuxedo-type outfit. It is not exactly a tuxedo—no tie—but it does have a ruffled shirt. He has a new haircut, to which he has added a healthy dab of mousse. Patti looks elegant and demure and pregnant.

/There are a couple of new waiters on duty tonight. This may or may not make things harder. You never know at The Falls. Eric quit the other day, and people now think things are going more smoothly than ever. Bruce, who used to extol Eric's prodigious gifts, now has some harsh words for his former employee.

"He's a thief," Bruce says. "He was fucking around with the American Express slips. He'd change the numbers and take the extra cash— change the tips. He'd make a one into a two. If the tip was $15 he'd make it $25. The thing is, he really wasn't that good a waiter—he was professional, but he wasn't all that great. As many people thought he was lousy as thought he was good."

Okay, Bruce . . . but a thief?

"He'd do it as much as he could get away with it," Bruce insists. "I predicted he'd be gone, didn't I? I knew the best way to get rid of him was to make it so he'd quit. We took away some of his tables, and he was pissed about it. He came to me and said, 'Bruce, I can't work this way, I need more tables, if I don't get them I'll have to quit.' So I said, 'I'm sorry to hear that. I'll miss you.'"

Bruce puts out his hand in a mock farewell gesture. "So he quit. He still owes me $500. I'll never see that. He moved into some apartment on 13th Street, it was $1,100 a month."

/The party will officially kick into high gear when Matt shows up. This is proven by the fact that Sean Young arrived by herself at 11:45 P.M., and the party did not begin. Perhaps this has to do with the fact that she is wearing a brown pantsuit. For a movie star, she seems to be having a great deal of difficulty scaring up a conversation. She spends a few minutes hovering around the food, and then wanders over to the bar. Matt finally shows up a few minutes past midnight. He is with his new girlfriend, Emma, who is blond and attractive. He moves graciously from table to table, proffering greetings. He is wearing a traditional black sport jacket, white shirt and a simple striped tie. It is an understated look, and if it has been cultivated it is difficult to tell.

The party lasts for a few hours. It involves a lot of mingling and chatting and drinking. It is, basically, a bunch of people standing around a restaurant. Restaurants are good for many things, but standing does not happen to be one of them. Some of them are famous, like Matt and Sean and Uma Thurman, who is also there. Uma is famous for, among other things, being June in *Henry & June*, and being sexy and talented in *Dangerous Liaisons*. Terry Quinn says he has known Uma for a while.

NON-SMOKING

PART TWO

MOE GREEN MEETS

OLIVER STONE

TWENTY-THREE

Here is a universal truth about hot restaurants.

They cannot be hot when it is hot outside. There is simply not enough room in the world for hot restaurants and hot weather to comfortably coexist. If you are desperate to find a new hot restaurant during the summer, you will have to settle for a place that opened in the spring. But let's face it, if you're looking for a hot restaurant in the summer, you're a loser, man. You're pathetic. Get with the program. Restaurants are new and hot in September or March. They're like magazines and cars and Broadway shows. They don't do well in the heat. They sweat. They get tired. They want to turn up the air conditioning and go to sleep early like the rest of us.

In New York matters are worsened by the existence of the Summer House. On a summer weekend in New York, if you are not at a summer house, you are considered to be lacking in some fundamental way. At the very least, you are lacking a summer house. But more likely, it means you are lacking money. You might protest that you just love the way New York empties out on summer weekends, and you get to have the city all to yourself . . . yeah, *right*. What fun is New York all to yourself? The whole point of New York is to have millions of people around. It doesn't work empty.

Neither does The Falls.

Gradually, and then suddenly . . . The Falls became empty. Not all the time. But some of the time. More of the time. Too much of the time. Sure, it's summer. That's it. People don't go to restaurants in the summer. They're saving their money for the Summer House. Big thick juicy sirloins aren't cheap, you know. A Weber grill costs three figures nowadays. And a summer rental will set you back upward of ten grand, and probably more if you want something halfway decent. Not to mention wine, and deck chairs, and champagne.

So restaurants are dying. Bruce has noticed this. You don't have to look very hard. People say a recession is coming, maybe it's here. Bruce knows there's definitely less money around. He wants more of it. The lamb chops will now be $23.

Fuck cheap eats. We need the cash!

Monday nights will now be West Indies Night or, alternatively, St. Bart's Night. Every Monday night. The food will be cheaper and presented thematically. Ribs, funky soups, Island music. ("St. Bart's night, like I could really get *that* into print," says publicist Peter Himler upon hearing the concept.)

Thursday nights there might be a celebrity bartender charity thing. Maybe an investor or two will don an apron and work behind the bar. ("Better," Himler says.)

Bruce will now be wearing new glasses. Perhaps this will help. "I'd been wearing the other pair for thirty years," he says. "I thought I'd try a new look." This new pair—trendy-looking, sort of square, sort of brown—make him look exactly like Moe Green in *The Godfather*. He gets a tremendous kick out of that particular observation. "People have been telling me that all the time," he says.

/Almost two months ago, a small change in The Falls's own physical appearance took place. Like his glasses, Bruce viewed it as a minor cosmetic alteration that would have no effect on business. Now, as summer approaches and customers do not, Bruce is beginning to change his view. Could the glasses be making things clearer somehow?

The change—a huge, imposing scaffolding that completely camouflaged the exterior of the restaurant—went up on the twentieth of April. The building's landlord explained that it was necessary because he was about to change the windows in the office building above The Falls. New York City laws required it, he said. So Bruce went along—what else could he do?—and made some mild protestations that his rent should go down, this wasn't fair, I object, and so on. "I'm trying to decide—do I hit up the landlord now for five more years on the lease? Or sit tight? I got them to raise it up an extra flight so that it's not right over the front. And they did a nice job of painting it—so it looks pretty good. We'll use more light on the inside."

The landlord, Richard Maltz, had his own defense for the scaffolding. It did not include any rent reductions for Bruce, though he sounded rather reasonable.

"Buildings are like people," Maltz says. "They die from the day they're born. So you have to do work on these buildings from time to time."

He goes on: "It's not anything I have a choice of. Because if I don't do the work the City of New York does two things. One, they fine me at a geometrically ascending rate, to the point where they own the building. Really, unbelievably high fines. And secondly they'll come in and do the work and it'll be garbage anyhow. We're talking about expensive work because it's all scaffold work."

He pauses for a moment. Maltz is looking for a way to define his relationship with Bruce. It is important that he keep it on good terms. "It's not anything that we're doing to Bruce," he says. "Being practical about it, we have a tenant there who we want to pay the rent. We made a deal with him. We liked him. We thought it made sense. And we said here, we're not going to get the last buck out of you. You're getting a pretty good rental deal. Which he was, and is. We want you to be well and be healthy and make a success out of it . . . It's not something that makes me happy and there's nothing I can do about it. If there were something I could do about it I would do it."

Maltz tends to spend a fair amount of free time in New York restaurants. Consequently he considers himself a bit of an expert on the business.

"From what I gather," Maltz says, "at night he's doing pretty well. I think his prices tend to be fairly high for this neighborhood. I think the economic atmosphere at the moment is not conducive to high-priced lunches. And he tends to be at the high end of the scale here."

Bruce would prefer to rationalize. He finds it much easier and more convenient than searching for any underlying explanations.

"This isn't the kind of place that gets a ton of walk-in business, anyway," he says. "People who come here are planning on coming here."

. . .

/But suddenly business is fading. The wild crowds of April and May have given way to slow, languorous nights in June when you would be likely to find only a handful of tables filled at The Falls. Monday nights have not taken off the way Bruce imagined; they all came the first night, when Philippe masterminded the debut by making it coincide with his departure for St. Bart's. More than 150 people at The Falls that night. But then the next Monday was slow, and the following Monday even slower. Peter Himler did turn out to be wrong about it, though; he managed to place a small item about St. Bart's Night on the Hotline page of *New York* magazine, right where Gael Greene thought it belonged.

Bruce needed to do something. How to get people in the doors?

The Doors!

Maybe we could get a wrap party for *The Doors!*

The Doors was Oliver Stone's new movie, now shooting in New York, based on the life of Jim Morrison and his legendary rock group. There were just a few New York sequences, but Stone had saved them for the end. Bruce knew somebody on the crew. Drinks were bought. Calls were made. A deal was cut. And suddenly, Bruce was lucky again. He was about to have the hottest night in the life of his new, hot restaurant. This would be the night to end all nights. Imagine . . . Oliver Stone, the cast, the crew, the stars . . . take that, De Niro! We will be on top yet!

/It is now June 19, 1990.

At 7:30 P.M., the Doors party is only hours away. Four rowdy guys, they look to be Wall Street types, crowd around a table near the bar. One is British, in a blue suit and yellow tie. The others are well-dressed Americans. They're all drinking Rolling Rocks. They order four bottles of wine, two red, two white. They pour white wine first and then pour red wine into the white-wine glasses, while there is still some white wine in them. They stir the mixture and drink it. To every woman who walks by their table, they say "Hey!" trying to get her attention. They order two bottles of Dom Perignon. They order lamb chops and buffalo burgers. They frequently abuse Julie, the waitress, who is cute, friendly and dressed in a short miniskirt. They make moves at her like they're going to grab her.

At one point they call Julie over by standing up and yelling, "Yo, bitch!" She has little choice but to respond. She wants a good tip.

Their check comes to $700.

At 9:00, three of them leave, just one of them stays behind, as though he is doing so to pay the check. After two more minutes, he too leaves. It turns out that they have walked out on their check, and left no tip. "I sure hope I don't have to pay for it," says Julie, practically in tears. "I think the one guy is a friend of one of the owners so somehow I think it's going to get taken care of."

At 8:30 P.M., Bruce explains the evening's scenario. At around 9:30 or 10:00, he says, "I've arranged to give free meals to twelve models. I called Elite this afternoon and arranged it. Then at around 12:30 we're going to have the wrap party for the Doors movie. Oliver Stone, all that. I arranged it this afternoon with the production manager, Clayton Townsend. They're paying $20 a head and we put together a special menu."

At 9:00 P.M., a busboy has accidentally gotten pepper in his eye. He spends twenty minutes in the bathroom trying to wash it out. Someone tells Bruce about it and he goes down to the bathroom. He then returns to the bar and announces, "He'll be okay. He just got pepper in his eye."

Tonight is also Celebrity Bartender Night. A television producer and a casting director have teamed up behind the bar. It quickly fills to a mob scene of young actors. One of them is here on the night before he leaves for the Bahamas for nine days. He quickly becomes enamored of Julie, the waitress.

"I don't want to sleep with her," he says, "I just want to sit across from her and talk to her about things, and occasionally touch her face."

He goes on: "I think a face is the most important thing about a woman, when you're talking physical characteristics. More important than breasts or legs. A great face is something special. It's what you wake up to the next morning, what you've got to look at."

At 10:00 P.M., five beautiful models enter and take a table in the middle of the restaurant. They know that their bodies make for excellent currency, they have been informed that their meals are free, and they proceed to order accordingly: champagne, appetizers, main courses, desserts. Meanwhile, people with reservations are made to wait at the bar; the bar tables are reserved for people eating dinner; and the Primo Table has been taken by Bob Colesberry, Falls investor and producer of *Billy Bathgate*. Brian Hamill, the photographer best known for his Woody Allen pictures, and for being the brother of Pete, the columnist, is also here. He usually hangs out at Columbus.

At 10:30 P.M., Bruce goes to the bathroom. "At home I go to the bathroom fifty times a day, but here I don't ever go," he says. "So this time I go in there and I see it's a complete mess, and I figure I gotta go get the dishwasher in here to clean it up. So who should come into the bathroom to hide? The dishwasher. That's where they go to take a break and hide for a little while. So I really surprised him, and told him he had to clean the place up, it was filthy."

At 11:00 P.M., Bruce is back at the musical controls. The room is packed solid now. All twelve models have arrived. Every table is full. The bar is jammed. No sign of celebrities yet. Bruce puts on "Love and Marriage," as sung by Frank Sinatra, a tune that is currently best known as the theme song for the television show *Married ... With Children*. It would seem to be an odd choice of music to anyone except regulars, who know that at such late-night moments, Bruce frequently turns to Sinatra.

At 11:15 P.M., Bruce is complaining that Nelson Mandela is having a benefit dinner tonight at the Tribeca Grill, for $2,500 a plate. "I woulda done it for $25 a plate," Bruce says.

At 11:30 P.M., Sean Young, Kevin Spacey and Woody Harrelson arrive. None of them are in the movie. But all of them are clients of a talent manager who is a friend of Terry Quinn, plus the Oliver Stone crowd, who have just called to say they'll be here early.

Woody Harrelson, an actor who plays a bartender on *Cheers*, goes to the bar to order drinks for himself and a pretty blonde in a red baseball cap. Woody is wearing a fancy dark blue sport jacket and light blue open-neck shirt. "I'll have a screwdriver," he tells the bartender, the aforementioned casting director, whom he knows. She says, "Am I doin' it right, Wood?" He seems uncomfortable with bartenders who play up to him. He takes a sip of her drink. "Not enough vodka," he says. She laughs.

At 12:15 A.M., three beautiful blondes come in with Chuck Pfeifer, who is a sometime actor, self-promoter who has befriended Oliver Stone.

At 12:30 A.M., the celebrities start to pour in. Oliver Stone. Val Kilmer, in blue jeans and blue sneakers, looking exactly like Jim Morrison. Kyle MacLachlan, who played FBI Agent Dale Cooper on *Twin Peaks*, is wearing a blue Twin Peaks–style suit. Meg Ryan is in a long black raincoat, presumably in character as Pamela Courson, Jim Morrison's girlfriend. Oliver Stone is wearing an expensive leather jacket, white shirt and black jeans. He is sitting with an extremely tall, beautiful dark-haired woman. Somebody else at the table says of the woman, "I met her on the Duran Duran tour a few years ago, she was Simon LeBon's girlfriend."

"THE DOORS"
AT
THE FALLS

ARUGULA & ASIAGO
SALAD

CHOICE OF:
GRILLED MAHI-MAHI
WITH BLACK BEAN & GINGER

BABY CHICKEN
WITH FRESH HERB SAUCE

CAPELLINI
WITH SEA SCALLOPS

BUFFALO BURGER
WITH FRENCH FRIES & HARVARTI

MANGO SORBET
OR
CHOCOLATE CAKE

At 12:45, Terry Quinn says, "Matt's gonna be pissed that he didn't come in tonight. Elaine Irwin was here." Elaine Irwin is a famous Elite model who has been linked with numerous movie stars. Doesn't *Matt* have a girlfriend? "Sort of." Wasn't Elaine Irwin dating Sean Penn recently? "Yeah." Pause. "Two years ago she didn't even know who Sean Penn was. I knew her. She was just a model. But since then she's figured out all about the movie business, who all the actors are."

At 1:00 A.M., Oliver Stone complains to Bruce that they didn't get the place to themselves. Bruce retorts, that's what you get at that price, you can't shut the place down at that price.

There's gonna be a phone call tomorrow, Bruce predicts a few minutes later.

At 1:15 A.M., Kyle MacLachlan waits three minutes at the bar before someone takes his drink order.

At 1:25 A.M., Julie the waitress looks around the room with awe. "This is the wildest it's been since I've been here," Julie says. "This place has been *dead*."

At 1:30 A.M., Val Kilmer leaves. Willem Dafoe, the star of Stone's *Platoon*, arrives.

By this time the room has basically been taken over by people here for the wrap party. A large buffet table has been set up against one wall. People are moving rapidly from table to table, chairs have been pulled over to form large circles. Finally Bruce's musical selections have taken an upbeat turn, although they occasionally flutter back to Sinatra and Coltrane.

A. Kitman Ho, Stone's co-producer, seems to enjoy rubbing the shoulders of the star and director. Occasionally he will whisper something into Stone's ear, and Stone will appear not to have heard it.

At 1:50 A.M., Kyle MacLachlan appears to be having an intense discussion with his girlfriend, Lara Flynn Boyle, who plays Donna the good girl on *Twin Peaks*. Of course, they may have been talking loudly just to be heard over the din.

At 2:20 A.M., Bruce decides to leave. As usual, his Mercedes is parked alongside the restaurant. He jumps in and drives away with no good-byes to anyone. He leaves behind a hard-core crowd of partygoers who do not notice that the music has suddenly become just a little less mellow.

No more Sinatra tonight.

Judging from the foot tapping and party downing that follows the change in music, one has to wonder whether other people—specifically, people who come to The Falls—like listening to Sinatra quite as much as Bruce does.

BRUCE, TERRY, AND THE THREE

ICELANDIC BLONDES

TWENTY-FOUR

Bruce just got back from Sag Harbor a couple hours ago. He likes to go there sometimes to visit friends who have summer houses out there, a three-hour drive (at least) from his apartment. Usually, if he is not someone's guest, he likes to stop by the American Hotel, which is considered an extremely tony joint among those who can afford to rent summer homes by the night. He is particularly fond of the bar and restaurant—but what's the point? He can't understand why anyone would run a restaurant in the Hamptons, which is the generic name for the area of which Sag Harbor is an integral part. He thinks seasonal is stupid.

Four good months, and then death.

He didn't end up staying very long, the sun wasn't very good, and again—what's the point? He saw none, and left. On the way back, as he drove leisurely down the Long Island Expressway toward New York City, the sun finally emerged from behind the clouds. Right, as it turned out, by the exit for Jones Beach. A fine coincidence, Bruce thought. So he exited the expressway and went to the beach for a few hours. He always keeps equipment in his car for a sunny day.

He finally *got back into town* on Monday night and went straight to the restaurant. That's where he is now. He has noticed that there are no more than ten people in the restaurant and this time he has a brand-new explanation.

"Summer is always weird," he is saying. That is not the explanation. It is merely a fact. "And then there's that Daylight Savings Thing." Ah yes . . . it's still light out! He's right about that. Generally speaking, people do not relish the thought of dinner in broad daylight, which is basically what it is at 8:00 in the evening these days. He has correctly diagnosed the problem this time. Unfortunately the matter is out of his hands.

"In France it's great," he says. "You can stay on the beach until 9:15 and then go out to dinner." Now the sun is good? It must be tough to be a man who relishes the day and wishes it were night! He goes on, musing, dreaming . . . "The sun's nice there . . . it's different . . . it feels stronger. It burns . . . but it doesn't give you a *deep* tan."

Bruce is never burned. He has achieved a lovely shade of brown that will never fade.

/"Business is basically always shitty here," says Julie, the waitress. "Nobody comes in. The people who do come in are lousy tippers." She is bitter because she can barely afford to pay her rent, her bills, or even her subway fare to work. She is angry because she has to take extra jobs tutoring three New York University students in French. She is frustrated because there is no place else to work, every restaurant in town seems to be suffering, and she does not know what to do.

Tonight she has decided she is going to confront Bruce. Not about the money. She is not quite ready to do that yet. No, tonight she is just going to mention something about Elvis Costello, whom she loves, and with any luck she will convince Bruce to add the British rocker to his playlist. Julie is not particularly enamored of Bruce's musical selections.

In fact, she thinks they suck.

However, she will not be saying this.

She walks over to the bar where Bruce is sitting, looking through his notebooks that list the contents of his many hundreds of cassettes.

"There are no Elvis Costello songs on your tapes. I love Elvis Costello. I've been listening to him since the eighth grade."

"There's one," Bruce says. "*Almost Blue*. I don't like Elvis Costello."

Julie doesn't like that answer. But more to the point, Bruce doesn't like Julie. He gives her a glare that definitely says, *Your days are numbered.*

Bruce has been sending that message at a rapid clip. As of today, Brian Moores has counted over forty departed employees at The Falls. He is not ready to declare it a record or anything. New restaurants tend to go through a lot of changes. But one can't help but think back to the opening days and weeks, when Bruce would explain the heavy turnover by saying, "This is natural for the first few weeks. If it happened like this all the time, it would be unnatural. But this is the beginning." Now it is summer, threatening to become a pattern. Bruce's explanation now is that Bruce is searching for magic. Bruce believes in magic, by the way.

Bruce waves his arm, as if holding a magic wand, in the direction of one of The Falls's newer employees, a handsome young man named Steven, who works behind the bar. He is a friendly fellow who has a smile for everyone. He is a dancer, this is something about himself he likes to share immediately, and it would be no secret to anyone since he has a dancer's lithe body and graceful movements. If you inquire further, as most customers do, you will discover that he has also worked at several different bars around the city; he likes to move around.

Unlike a lot of bartenders, Steven does not believe in the concept of regulars. He thinks they're cheap, and he'd much prefer to serve a drink to someone he didn't know, thinking, this one will be nice, not like the last one, or the next. That is how it is. A bartender lives in the moment, but waits for the next one.

"I worked at Curtain Up," he says. Curtain Up is a restaurant just where you'd think it was, in the theater district. It's an established institution with regulars. Steven never liked the regulars there. "They were always the worst tippers. They'd order the cheapest drink—three of them—because they knew it was the house policy to buy them the fourth drink, and *that's* when they'd order a Rémy."

Sometimes, he remembers, the regulars would be so obnoxious and annoying that they would come in and, upon discovering that someone was sitting on their barstool, become self-righteously indignant. "They would tell people to move," he says, his face darkening for just a moment, "because they were sitting in *their* seat." He shakes his head. The depression is mounting. The memories throw him temporarily off-kilter. He must remove this heavy weight from his chest. Regulars! Ugh! "They act as though they're talking about state secrets, talking so quietly," he says. "But they're never really talking about much of anything."

• • •

/"Sometimes it's too much," says Marco, a twenty-four-year-old waiter who began on Day One and has survived despite his cynicism. "I was thinking about that this Sunday, you know? I was working and I thought, maybe this is too much."

Or forty-two-year-old Gary, who has been behind the bar since opening night, and has no intention of leaving—he has poured drinks for so long he cannot even find the tunnel, let alone the light at the end:

"You get a job in a restaurant or a bar right after college because you can make more money doing this than just about anything else, starting out. It's really good money. And you figure, I'll just do this a little while and then I'll do something else. And then one or two years go by and you're still doing it. Then before long it's ten years and you're still behind the bar. Now it's not something you're doing on the way to something else. It's a *job*. And it's what you do. But I like it because when work is over you leave it there. You go out for some drinks or something and you forget about work. You don't go home and worry about what's happening at the restaurant. You can come in and be in a good mood, a hopeful mood, thinking everything will be just fine. And then somebody will leave a dirty bottle on the speed rack and it'll all be over. You'll be pissed off. Except what's the point of getting upset? You gotta just let that stuff go by."

Marco goes on: "The problem is that after work you go out drinking. And you're out really late so it kinda ruins your next day. I used to work in a nightclub for three or four years, and it was working from nine to four, and afterward you'd go out, and so you'd end up being out all night."

Then Gary: "This weekend I taught my kids how to make pancakes. They loved it. If they want to make pancakes for dinner I don't tell them they can't, I mean, why not?"

This goes over Bruce's head, or around it. If he heard these thoughts, *everyone* would be fired. Luckily he is not listening. He is talking about other things. He knows little about the pain of waiting. About the perils of the working man's daily grind he knows even less. To him it is all abstract, philosophical. "Gave Brian a day off," he says. "This isn't his kinda thing, the Caribbean food. What a personal life he's got. To go from the bachelor life to having three or four kids—I could *never* do that. I'd like *one*. One would be nice."

He thinks. He pushes up his glasses to rub his eyes.

"People like the glasses," he says. "I'm getting laid a lot more. Today I got sunglasses the same type. The place I went to get the frames is right by the Time Cafe so I went to take a look at it. I don't get it. It's nothing. The space is crammed, it's uncomfortable. I don't see what the fuss is." The Time Cafe is a hot new restaurant that is packed solid tonight and tomorrow night and every night. The Falls is not.

Bruce is upset. And so is Gary and so is Marco. There is something to be upset about. It has nothing to do with the price of wine in France. Too much money is going out. Not enough is coming in.

/The July Fourth weekend was dead. Bruce went away, and so did everyone else in New York City except a couple of waiters and busboys. "It was a devastating week," Bruce says afterward. "From now on I'm going to close holidays. We'd have been better off staying closed all week. Labor Day I'm going to close for six days."

On Monday the ninth of July Bruce returns with renewed determination and entrepreneurship. He will make things work. He will even make Monday nights work, damnit! He has chosen to try out live music to jazz up the lackluster St. Bart's Night concept.

So Bruce has retained the services of a friend named Bankie Banks, who is to the people of Anguilla what Bruce Springsteen is to the United States.

Unfortunately, though, The Falls is on Varick and Vandam, not Anguilla. Thus there are only about a dozen or so customers in the place, and most of them seem completely uninterested in the music. Most except Bruce. He is tapping his foot and swaying back and forth. He loves the deep, resonant tones of Bankie's voice. He admires the way it bounces off the back walls and reverberates in his soul. It reminds him of the days he spent in the Caribbean, and it feeds him like . . . like *food.* The set is quiet, gentle; a soft drumbeat and a simple electric piano back him up. The songs are barely distinguishable from one another, with the possible exception of one attempt at humor called "The Trump Scuttle." That one gets a few laughs from everyone . . . even Marco. Even Gary. And even Julie.

Otherwise, Julie is miserable tonight. This is not Elvis Costello night, after all. She is not terribly interested in the culture of the British West Indies. She is, on the other hand, terribly interested in money. She pays $200 a month in rent on an apartment she shares with her sister, and she can barely afford that, even with working full-time at The Falls and tutoring.

"Last week, after all the deductions, I made exactly $5.99 on my paycheck," Julie says. "I should be able to leave." She is saying that because there are barely any customers at The Falls, so why should there be all these waiters and waitresses? But what she really means is, *I should be able to leave.* I should be able to do something better with my life than this. I am young. I am not old. I have dreams and desires and ambitions. It is 1990 and I am living in the heart of all the excitement in America, that's right, New York City, and why do I need to be here at The Falls? Oh yeah. Money. Well, there isn't enough.

Bruce hears this. He has heard Julie before, moaning and complaining, and he feels that this is counterproductive. He does not like to have complainers around. So it turns out that her days have been numbered specifically, and this one is the number zero, or whatever you call the final day. She is now able to leave.

Because Bruce has just fired her.

/A few nights later, Bruce and Terry are sitting at the Primo Table.

Three tall Scandinavian women come into the bar. All of them are blond. All of them are tall.

"Are they good-looking?" Terry whispers in the direction of the bartender. One of the problems of the Primo Table is that from it you cannot see every babe at the bar.

"All right," he says. "So so."

Terry keeps one eye on them as he tells a little story.

"I blew off these two Icelandic chicks the other night," he says quietly. He loves stories like this. "They were in here. Really beautiful. I think they both wanted to fuck me. I had to say no. At the end of the night—I was at Peggy Sue's with them, the friend I was with had gone home already—I just looked at them, and thought . . . *naaah.*"

Bruce has little interest in such stories. He pays far more attention to the here and now. He leaves his seat to go make conversation with the bar babes.

"Real langoustines," he says as he gets up.

Moments later Bruce is sitting next to them and practicing the art of lively conversation. "You're going to have a terrific time here tonight," he says. "Just wait, go have dinner, you'll see."

Meanwhile, Terry is talking further about the tribulations of his love life. Some of it has been discussed publicly in the press. For example, in *New York Newsday* the other day there appeared the following item under the headline, "Peggy Sue Isn't Getting Married":

━━━━━━━━

Former firefighter and current club owner–restaurateur **Terry Quinn** (Peggy Sue's, The Falls) appears to be burning his bridges faster than he's building them . . . at least that's what his current flame, **Patti D'Arbanville,** says. Fourth of July festivities found 45 friends—including NYC Film Commish **Janey Keyes,** theatrical manager **Loree Rodkin,** producer **Barbara Ligiti** and actress **Dana Wheeler-Nicholson**—rallying around D'Arbanville, who's been burned. Seems Quinn told Patti, who's six months pregnant with his child, that despite all the love talk he isn't ready to make a commitment. "I'm so heartbroken, I can't believe this is happening," said D'Arbanville. Even though Quinn isn't standing by her, **Don Johnson** (her former love and father of her son, Jesse) is. When he and wife, **Melanie Griffith,** called Patti on the Fourth, Johnson said he'd stand by her no matter what. Where there's smoke there's fire. Stay tuned for the real pyrotechnics.

━━━━━━━━

Terry found the item deeply troubling. He says it was printed without checking, and that it was fueled by a dispute between him and a friend of the writer. "I like Patti a lot . . . I love her," he says. "I guess she hoped I'd be the one. But I just don't want to get married again. I have my sons. That's what you get married for. I don't know if I ever want to share that much of myself with somebody."

As Terry talks, he eats a bowl of conch. It is another St. Bart's night and this is becoming a regular fixture on the menu. However, tonight Terry is displeased. "I liked the older conch," he says. "This conch isn't as good. It's not bad, but the old conch is better."

HOW TO SAVE THE FALLS:

A ONE-ACT PLAY

TWENTY-FIVE

On the afternoon of July 18, three people are sitting down to find a way to rescue The Falls from the summer doldrums. Their ambition is to use the Labor Day return of all the weekend vacationers to revive the business that they believe was lost to the Hamptons and Fire Island and Connecticut. The conversation, which is taking place at the Primo Table, begins with three people: Bruce Goldstein, publicist Peter Himler and a longtime employee of Bruce's we will call Linda. She had worked at Central Falls and been instrumental in putting together celebrity art shows there—promotions that ended up getting Central Falls a great deal of press attention.

Now is the time to make that happen at The Falls.

The idea of this meeting is to come up with ideas—for parties, for promotions, for anything that will inject life into this dormant, decaying restaurant. The scaffolding still stands out front. The customers are still staying away. On a good night, a hundred or more people might come in, but the good nights are once every week or ten days. More likely is a night with thirty or forty customers, enough to pay the bills but not the piper. There are tax bills adding up. Payrolls to be met. Cash to be spent.

What follows is an edited transcript of the conversation these people are having as their ship begins to sink.

BRUCE: I got the idea. Maybe you can do a preproduction party for this Dustin Hoffman movie. I think they're gonna get rolling right around the twentieth [of September]. They're shooting in New York and then they're going to North Carolina.

LINDA: There was never an official opening party in March, when it opened, to let people know. Now September comes and September's a big month in New York, a lot of things happening, people should know—

BRUCE: Here's my gut feeling about that. I can't stand giving away things to assholes. I can't stand the people walking in this door who go from place to place and party to party looking for free things that I may never see again—and basically the night that we did open, even though it was totally unannounced, was one of the best nights we've had here. I don't think we gotta do that. I'd rather tie a series of three or four events over a two-week period that creates the fact that people should be here at least one of those nights over that period.

PETER: Okay, so rather than look at an opening party, that I think is contrived and kind of weird—unless all the principals are going to be here to do it, okay?—let's look at the kind of opportunities there are in the fall. Potential for Bob Colesberry's party . . . Preproduction on Dustin Hoffman. There's potential for Edie Baskin [Falls investor/*Saturday Night Live* art director] to do a post-*SNL* opening show wrap party.

BRUCE: When does their season start?

PETER: Season starts in the fall, right?

BRUCE: She's away for a month in Idaho.

PETER: Fine, so call her in Idaho.

BRUCE: I can do that.

PETER: In terms of giving away stuff to schmoozers, I'll give it to the cast of *SNL*.

BRUCE: They don't do that. Everybody pays for their own. After ten years or fifteen years or whatever they're doing they know better.

PETER: [movie director/Falls investor] Alan Parker?

BRUCE: Alan Parker forget about.

PETER: When does Colesberry's movie open?

BRUCE: Christmas.

PETER: *Come to the Paradise.*

BRUCE: (dictating to Linda) *Come* See *the Paradise.* Christmas opening. Preproduction party, Colesberry's movie.

PETER: What can Jeff do for us? Ross? [A friend of Bruce's who works with *SNL* producer Lorne Michaels.] Lorne Michaels is doing a lot of stuff now. See, you got to give a little to get some back.

BRUCE: We could probably have a party for these Kids in the Hall [a Lorne Michaels comedy troupe] when they're in town. Little thing. The other thing . . . Jimmy Buffett will be at Jones Beach August 6. Maybe we can have him over—

PETER: Dennis Conner. [America's Cup yachtsman, and friend of Bruce.]

BRUCE: Dennis Conner—what can he do? Is any people sponsoring him?

PETER: I think he's picked up Cadillac as a sponsor.

BRUCE: He hasn't got a champagne company yet?

PETER: No. Taittinger's is not going to sponsor him.

BRUCE: Taittinger could get a lot of rub-off by sponsoring a big event for him and—

PETER: Yeah, except he wants two and a half million dollars, Bruce. (Laughs.) What about Jimmy Buffett? Is that a possibility?

BRUCE: I gotta get hold of him. He's on the road now, but I saw him on Johnny Carson the other night so he must be in L.A. for at least a night or two, and then he'd be coming—he's here on August 6. I got to call Larry, his friend—

PETER: By the way, you know that thing *Punch*, they were in here? Well, we're in it. They gave us two stars. They say it's a great business value in terms of the cost and the quality. It's a thing where you call in and ask what kind of food you want and—it's like a call-in reservation service.

BRUCE: I want to get some book publishers—we want to at least notify book publishers, record companies—that we want to do book signing parties, we want to do publishing parties, we want to do record release parties . . . It's just letting them know that there's someone here to contact if they want to do that sort of stuff . . . The other thing we want to do is this concierge thing in all the hotels. I want to send out the menu to all the concierges in all the hotels. It was very successful in Central Falls. The concierge would send people down to the restaurant and we would buy them an after-dinner drink in the name of the hotel—and they would leave a generous tip and you'd give the concierge a free dinner.

PETER: Remember we translated the menus?

BRUCE: Yeah—let's do that again. We translated the menu into five languages—that's something that's gotta happen immediately. If you know any waitresses that want to make extra money, or any of the new girls . . . put 'em on the clock at $7 an hour, cash, this has got to happen soon.

PETER: Hey Bruce, are you friendly with the people across the street, *El Diario?* [New York's main Spanish-language daily paper.]

BRUCE: They come in . . . on Friday night they're all here. From the moment they get out at four o'clock on Friday till 2:00 in the morning.

(At this point, Michael Fitzpatrick joins the conversation, which turns to service matters.)

BRUCE: We have to realize that we gotta take the time—it's good for business to have pretty girls working here. What I'm suggesting is that even though we got rid of Julie, my feeling is I'm gonna live with an attractive girl until we have an attractive replacement. I'm not going to get rid of somebody just because we don't like her.

MICHAEL: Yeah, but we want the service, too—that's what we're working on building.

BRUCE: We should be able—between the maître d's in this place and Pam [another waitress] and the business being slow in the summertime, there's no excuse for the customer to receive bad service. Even if we get on a clunker waiter. 'Cause there should be enough people that should be scrutinizing the service.

PETER: How is the service?

BRUCE: Much better . . . I don't want to hire *anybody* anymore that isn't attractive. I don't want to hire anybody who doesn't fit into the image that we're trying to do. That's it. The statement is done. That's it guys, I don't want to do it anymore. This is very important from now on to be very selective.

(Lori, a waitress, has joined the conversation.)

LORI: A lot of people coming in for these big parties, they're sharing entrées. They're not ordering appetizers.

BRUCE: They book a table?

LORI: They sit there for three hours. They're not ordering appetizers. I had a party of twelve here the other day, nobody ordered appetizers.

BRUCE: I'll tell you how to handle that. When the reservation's taken you have to have a contact person. Someone has to call that contact person back when it's a large party and tell them, you understand you're booking a table at prime time, I just want to confirm—

this is a dinner party, correct? That's all you want to get across to them. That means everyone should be ordering entrées.

MICHAEL: If anyone wants to share we'll put a $2 extra plate charge.

PETER: You could do that with everybody.

BRUCE: What's a fair extra plate charge—$5?

MICHAEL: Two to three bucks.

BRUCE: The thing is, I'm telling you, the way to handle this is to contact the person who calls and let them set down the ground rules. And then when they get there say we talked about this on the phone and you said this wasn't gonna happen, here's what we have to do. Tell them it's a $15 minimum per person—$20 per person.

LORI: We're going to take anything right now.

BRUCE: This publisher thing is important to do.

PETER: What's with Madonna?

MICHAEL: What is that?

BRUCE: A five-foot nude picture of Madonna.

MICHAEL: That's going out on the—

BRUCE: To go right there. (Points to wall over kitchen.)

MICHAEL: Why would you want to do that?

BRUCE: I like to look at Madonna.

MICHAEL: Yeah, but that does not go in here.

BRUCE: Have you seen the picture? It's kinda arty. He's got a book coming out.

PETER: Is it a book of her, or is it a book of all kinds of different stuff?

BRUCE: It's a book of her. All her.

PETER: All her.

/The next night, Michael Fitzpatrick brings in a new waiter.

He is in his mid-thirties, has a potbelly and is wearing a striped tie. This will simply not do.

"You're just making it hard on the guy, and hard on yourself," Bruce tells Michael. "It's not going to work out. He's just not the image of the place. He's got a potbelly, for chrissakes. I'd rather have a beautiful woman make a mistake than get good service from a guy with a potbelly."

Michael darkens. He wants to save this guy's neck, as thick as it might be. "Trust me on this," he whispers back. "He's a great waiter. He's reliable, he's good."

Bruce turns away. He will not hear of it.

"I don't care. He could be the greatest fucking waiter in the world and I still don't want him, 'cause he doesn't look right. He's not the image. We're trying to project a certain image here, and from now on, we're going to try to hire pretty girls."

IT'S MILLER TIME

TWENTY-SIX

The name on his American Express card is Michael Simon.

But you do know him. His real name is Bryan Miller of *The New York Times.*

He's thin. That's what everyone wants to know: Is he fat or thin? He's thin. A short shock of black hair with a touch of gray. Handsome in a low-key kind of way.

He has a good metabolism, and an excellent job with which to measure it on a daily basis. He is the restaurant critic of *The New York Times,* and therefore eats out two meals a day, five days a week. He does not eat breakfast, and he does not eat in restaurants on Saturday nights, partly because he thinks restaurants are too crowded on Saturday nights to be judged properly; and partly because he and his wife, Mireille, a petite French woman and shrewd food critic herself, like to go to their country house on the weekend, which involves a lovely drive up the Taconic Parkway to a little town near Massachusetts.

During the week Bryan Miller of *The New York Times* lives in a midtown apartment that is over a restaurant he likes. It is not particularly close to anyplace that delivers Chinese food, but Bryan Miller of *The New York Times* does not order in Chinese food, so what does it matter?

He keeps a list in his briefcase. It tells him all the places to go. It reminds him if a friend has mentioned, "Try the buffalo burger at Jackalope," because before long you're going to forget something like that, if you're smart. The list is ten pages long, some typed, some scribbled. There is, after all, not nearly time enough to try everything new. Also in his briefcase is a pocket calendar that would strike one as a tad small for Bryan Miller of *The New York Times,* a guy with a lot of dates and times and places to keep in his head. It is what most people would call pocket-sized; yet still he manages to keep track of a constant schedule of lunches and dinners. One is impressed by this display of subtlety; a man with far fewer social obligations might still be inclined toward a larger date book.

He likes to steal menus and put them in his briefcase when no one is looking, and then look up at his companions and proclaim, "Done!"

He likes to take notes. He likes to quiz waiters. He likes to eat dessert. He likes to play in a Zydeco band called "The Pinballs" occasionally, even though it doesn't do much for his anonymity. He likes to talk softly, so you're not quite sure what he's saying all the time. He likes to use words like "neat" when he is talking about food, and words like "whimsical" and "piquant" when he is writing about food. At restaurants all over New York, they are waiting for Bryan Miller of *The New York Times* to walk in. There is a French restaurant in New York owned by a man who does not like failure. He owns several other successful establishments, and—or so the legend goes—he had made a decision that his new restaurant would also be successful.

However, for this to happen, Bryan Miller of *The New York Times* had to give his new restaurant at least two stars in his review, or so the owner had himself convinced.

And so the owner had a plan. If Bryan Miller of *The New York Times* gave his bistro one star or less, he would immediately close the doors, throw away all the French stuff and turn it into a steakhouse.

Bryan Miller of *The New York Times* gave the place only one star, as it turned out; but it was a *strong* one star, strong enough for the owner to throw away his contingency plan and allow his French baby to live.

Imagine! A steakhouse waiting in the wings if one lousy guy doesn't like your food!

It's fun being Bryan Miller of *The New York Times.*

/The Falls has been waiting for Bryan Miller to come. They know that they will know when he does. They will do for him what no restaurant has ever done.

They will blow him fucking away.

Bryan Miller has been spotted before. They are not completely crazy when they say to themselves, We can spot him, we can nail him. Not to brag, but, *ahem*, Bryan Miller has been spotted by some of the finest restaurants in town.

Once, a few years ago, Bryan Miller was reviewing Huberts, which had just opened on fashionable Park Avenue. Fancy place. It had opened three or four weeks before, a fact Bryan Miller learned subsequently from a friend of a friend in the kitchen. He got to the restaurant and it was packed, people were having a great time and it was just really crowded and lively, and it was such a new restaurant, this place had just taken off, and he wrote in "Diner's Journal" (a weekly short review he had created) about the food and everything he had there.

He said, by the way, it's awfully lively in there for a restaurant that's been open only a short time.

It turned out that they had half a day's notice that Bryan Miller was coming. Usually when he calls and makes a reservation he gives a phony name. Mr. Gannatt is one of his favorites. But then sometimes he will give his real phone number just in case they need to call back to confirm it. So he's always getting phone calls, Mr. Kerr, Mr. Wilson, he just says yes, whoever they ask for. And in this case Len Allison and Karen Hubert, the owners of this fancy Huberts, knew Bryan Miller's home phone number. Somewhere he had once asked them to call him back about something or other and they had noted it and when they saw it on the reservation book they knew he was coming and it was an absolutely dead night.

So Huberts called all the investors and told them to come to the restaurant with all their friends, get all dressed up and act like you're having a great time, so he would be impressed. And he fell for it entirely.

"They got me," Bryan Miller says.

It wasn't like this in the old days.

Back in the 1950s and 1960s, restaurant reviewing—even at the *Times*—was something that had more to do with the ad department than anything else.

"They would just send somebody out," Bryan Miller says, "somebody from the newsroom, and say, 'Write me a nice little feature story about a restaurant' that happened to be advertising. It was very cozy between advertisers and the newsroom . . . And that was restaurant reviewing until about 1960 when Craig Claiborne took over. He was the first person to ever criticize a restaurant."

In the 1970s, the process became elevated by one Mimi Sheraton of *The New York Times*. She became the first restaurant critic to have the kind of influence now basically assumed. Her power had quite a lot to do with her writing style—bold, tough, never hesitant to slam. She took on the establishment and won. She championed the causes of oddball joints like Sammy's Romanian Steakhouse, a restaurant that today one cannot possibly imagine possibly having a good meal in without being wildly drunk. She loved Sammy's, and you had to love her for loving it; and she loved Peter Luger, and did she create the Chinese food phenomenon single-handedly by praising the Empire Szechuan Gourmet on upper Broadway? No one will ever know. But she loved it, before it was fashionable, which was a period that lasted up until about 9:00 A.M. on the morning her review came out.

She left the *Times* after the accumulation of several unhappy experiences. Her first replacement, Marian Burros, came from *The Washington Post*. Her term lasted less than a year; she left claiming that she'd had enough of the grind. This proved fortuitous for a young freelance contributor to the *Times* named Bryan Miller.

This pleasing fellow, friendly but awfully quiet for a heavyweight influence peddler, had been happily contributing articles to the *Times*'s Living section for years. Nobody thought much about Bryan Miller except that he knew a lot about food, had worked as a chef, worked with Pierre Franey, and that, if you scanned the scenery awhile, there seemed to be nobody else quite right.

Bryan Miller started reviewing restaurants in 1986.

By 1990 he was Bryan Miller of *The New York Times* . . . hated and awaited.

In the interim Bryan Miller had done some important things. He gave Le Bernardin four stars. That heralded a whole new revolutionary kind of thing in food. Something about not cooking fish all the way. It tasted good, Bryan Miller thought. He described the broiled Louisiana shrimp as "a high-kicking chorus line." He wasn't crazy about the star system, he once even got himself in a fair amount of trouble at the *Times* for publicly complaining about it, but what the hell, as long as he had four stars to give, he was going to give them to Le Bernardin. With that he announced to the world, Here I am, I know good food when I taste it . . . read me!

He went to a little tiny place downtown that nobody could find called Montrachet. It hadn't been open too long and the kinks were *still kinks* when he handed it three stars. Owner Drew Nieporent— who now runs Tribeca Grill as well—thought of his three stars as a curse. The phone exploded. He couldn't handle the business. He couldn't control a three-star restaurant! But somehow he managed, and it remains a brilliant discovery even today, even after his three-star chef, David Bouley, went to open his own fancy downtown restaurant called Bouley, and created an irreparable feud that Nieporent has not yet tired of discussing. Particularly when Bryan Miller chose to wave his magic wand of discovery over Bouley and give it four stars.

But here it is late July of 1990, and Bryan Miller has still not discovered The Falls.

If the truth be told—and now it must be—Bryan Miller would never have discovered it, or gone there, had it not been for the efforts of this reporter to insinuate himself in the process and practically drag Bryan Miller into the place. Miller does not allow himself to be dragged into places very often. But he became curious about The Falls for several reasons. For one thing, he was surprised that a new restaurant had been open for several months and that he had never heard of it.

Now *this* is something of a surprise. Peter Himler, The Falls's friendly publicist, had insisted that he contacted Miller several times regarding the restaurant. Letters had been mailed. Calls had been placed. What happened? Had Miller ever heard of Himler?

"Oh yes, *that's* the Peter Himler who's been calling all the time," Bryan Miller says one day over lunch at a Chinese noodle shop. "You know the problem with Peter Himler? He calls all the time and it really pisses me off. I don't like publicists to call me. Send the release and make it an intelligent, well-edited, to-the-point release. I don't need a big package of 8 × 10 glossies. I really can't stand it when these guys, either they'll call up and say, if I get on the phone . . . 'Just wanted to check and see if you received so and so'—well, Jesus, the U.S. Post Office still works. Don't call me, I don't like it. It's so much work to do during the day. If you talk to every PR person who called that's all you would do. They really do call all day. That's why I have a secretary. I'm the only person I know on my side of the newsroom who has a secretary. I couldn't get anything done. This guy I think kind of irritated me by calling too much."

But Bryan Miller is curious. He has been told that The Falls is a restaurant struggling to survive. He wants to find out why.

/On July 27 at 12:45 P.M.—"I couldn't find the place, I didn't know about the scaffolding, sorry I'm late," he says breathlessly—Bryan and Mireille Miller enter The Falls for a leisurely lunch. It is the Friday before a summer weekend, and this will be his last working meal before Monday.

Or Tuesday, actually. He's going to Yankee Stadium Tuesday night to review the food there. "Yankee Stadium had a raw bar last year," he says, spreading a napkin evenly across his lap. It would not do for Bryan Miller of *The New York Times* to spill food on his lap. "Can you believe that? It just became unmanageable. In between innings you'd have eight thousand people and one guy's shucking clams."

Finally he takes a look around the room. "Obviously this really has the look of a nightspot," he says. "I like it!"

He reads the menu and the wine list.

"The wine prices are good. I've seen this wine"—pointing at a dry white Italian 1988—"go for as high as $29. Kind of a hot chichi wine at the moment. And that's the cheapest I've seen it anywhere. It's a very good wine list. Nice, easy menu to read. Which seems like a trivial point but we were at Bouley—you remember how hard the menu is to read? A bad Xerox."

Miller orders a cranberry juice mixed with soda water. He does not like to drink wine at lunch.

"What is dog sauce?" Mireille asks sweetly, referring to the sauce chien offered with the fish entrées.

Bryan Miller has found his own item on the menu to laugh about. "Omelette du Lour," he says, laughing at the misspelling of "jour" on the menu.

"I'm going to try the capon, because it has the pesto and everything else going with it," he says. Then he pauses for another scan. "Maybe the shrimp and fennel brochette. I keep smelling soy."

The waiter arrives to take their order. He is the potbellied waiter that Bruce so wanted to get rid of. If Bruce knew he was waiting on Bryan Miller, he would have either fired him or killed himself.

"I'll have the capellini with sea scallops," Mireille says.

Miller finally decides. Sort of. "I'll start with the crab and fennel brochettes, and then have the capon. Shrimp. Shrimp. I don't know. Should I have the capon or the whole baby chicken?" He looks at the potbellied waiter hopefully. "What would you have?"

Without a blink of hesitation, the potbelly replies: "The capon."

"All right. The capon."

Remember how Brian Moores said the capon breast would never last?

"Mashed potatoes?" the waiter inquires. Mashed potatoes have replaced french fries as everyone's preferred potato at The Falls. Brian makes them with new potatoes.

"Sure."

The waiter disappears with Bryan Miller's order.

Mireille clasps her arms around herself. She is sitting against a banquette, toward the back of The Falls at a table that offers an outstanding view of the half dozen other people eating lunch today.

"The wind is blowing," Mireille says.

Bryan Miller quickly agrees with his wife. "It's kind of strange the way it blows right at you. It's not suspended." He glances upward, looking for a wind source that he doesn't find. "What do you call these lights hanging above? What shape are they?" He refers to those cone-shaped missiles that hide the amber light bulbs that give The Falls its special, night-for-day glow.

"Art deco," Mireille replies absently.

"You know what it is? Something like a black Odeon." Bryan Miller is referring to that quintessential 1980s restaurant a few blocks away, the Odeon, that became the cultural icon of trendy hangout when it appeared on the cover of *Bright Lights, Big City*. The Odeon was the ultimate restaurant for people dressed in black. Bryan Miller has hit upon an unstated but determined goal of The Falls: to be for the 1990s what the Odeon so successfully became ten years earlier. The Odeon still survives. Will The Falls make it till 2001?

Bryan Miller gives his opinion of the menu at The Falls. "Obviously straightforward American . . . They're going to have to pull that off exquisitely well because there's nothing very scintillating on it, there's nothing—it's so middle-of-the-road . . . I think they need a little bit of pizzazz in it—not much. I like the size of it. I think a few things, maybe a couple of interesting pastas, they should probably have a couple of interesting pastas. Couple of really good pastas. One or two grill items that are interesting. That's it. Just a little bit more. It's a little bit too much like a bar menu."

He thinks about it another moment, glances again at the menu—which he has already pocketed in his briefcase for future reference—and keeps going.

"A place like this would be smart to have an excellent vegetarian plate for women who love to come and nibble on vegetables."

Mireille now offers her opinion. Bryan Miller listens very closely to his wife, as well he should. She possesses extremely good taste in food, and operates on a seemingly more instinctive level than her husband. She also seems to relish contradicting his opinion.

"I like the menu. I think it's good. If it's good they don't need anything else. If what they do is well done they don't need anything else."

A brief conversation ensues about celebrity restaurants and their appeal. This is a subject that has been on Bryan Miller's mind lately, as he has been visiting the Tribeca Grill in preparation for a review. He concedes that Drew Nieporent knows him. However, he still believes that his presence is a surprise because of the fake name thing. "Our last night at Tribeca Grill we did sit next to Robert De Niro and Al Pacino," he says, quite certain this was completely by accident.

The appetizers have arrived. The moment of truth.

"Do you want ground pepper?"

"Does it need it?" Bryan Miller asks.

"I don't think so."

"Okay, fine. I'm fine."

Bryan Miller takes a quick few bites.

"It's fine. The shrimp was well cooked. They weren't overcooked. Good. I love fennel."

As they eat, Bryan Miller returns to the subject of the Tribeca Grill. He appears to be fascinated with the place, and believes firmly that it will survive and prosper. Could this have something to do with the fact that in today's *New York Times*, his review of the Tribeca Grill appears with a glowing two-star review?

"I think six months from now they'll just be doing nice, steady business," Miller says. "And they'll have slow days like everybody else, and they'll have busy days, but they have—first of all, the food is quite good. It's nice, good, solid food. There's quite a population down there. They could probably survive on the Battery City, Wall Street, that crowd, without all these uptowners racing down there . . . I'd like to know how many he [Drew Nieporent] turns down tonight. He will not accept more people. He's too smart for that."

Miller is asked whether he is concerned about the power of his reviews.

"I waited a long time to do Park Bistro," he says, referring to a tiny French restaurant on lower Park Avenue on which he recently bestowed three stars. "I had done a 'Diner's Journal' on it in the beginning and that blasted them off. And I just thought I would wait. Other people reviewed them. Gael [Greene] went in, and *Newsday* did something. I just kept waiting and waiting, let's see what happens. The problem is I can't go in right away and do a review because—not that I have any sympathy for the restaurant because I feel that as soon as you open your doors and are charging the public, you're game. You're game the next day. Philosophically I feel that way.

"In practice I don't do it. Because our stars—besides being very important—hang over the door for two or three years. If I do go the second week and write something like Gael does—her stuff comes and goes, that's it. It's usually very equivocal. Because she's there so soon. I can't write one of those things. I'm forced to put a star on it. I'm forced to eat that star every day for the next two or three years. For my own self-preservation I wait at least a month."

The entrées have now arrived.

As Miller begins to wrestle his capon to the ground—those little birds are a struggle, no question—those brown eyes continue darting around the room. "That's not a Keith Haring, is it? It is? And it is chalk? It doesn't look as if it's been laminated or anything."

Mireille is ready with her comments on the capellini. "This is very bland. I don't like this at all," she says. She points to the mashed potatoes and adds, "*That's* good."

Now Bryan is getting annoyed by the chill of the air conditioning. "In order to air-condition *them*"—he points to the scattered customers across the room—"is it necessary to blow us off the banquette? Let Matt Dillon sit here."

/Miller has reserved comment on his food. He is being a thoughtful, reserved restaurant critic. One cannot blame him. It would not behoove Bryan Miller to rush to judgment.

First he will try a slice of pecan pie.

Then he will take several bites.

Okay. *Now* Bryan Miller of *The New York Times* will render an opinion about The Falls.

"The desserts are very sweet. Very sweet. Wow. Killer. It's hard to say based on one meal. They do grilling well. It's good bar food. We didn't try anything more sophisticated. The capon was quite good. Yours was fine. That pasta we had was very poor. They have to have a good pasta here. I think it has potential. Combined with the scene here and the nightlife I think it's a good place. The salad looked pretty good."

Okay, sure . . . but how many stars? Come on, Bryan, give it your best shot.

He shoots a look that says, *Must* I? But he gives an answer that says, I love this. I really do.

"The way—after all the calculations—I give stars is—after all the agonizing and counting dishes and adding things up—basically when I assign stars I say, I'm on the street corner and I bump into you and you say, 'How is that place?' And if I say, 'You know, it's okay,' that's a 'Satisfactory.' If I say, 'Hmmm—it's pretty good,' that's a 'One.' If I say, 'Hmmm—that's good,' that's a 'Two.' If it's *really* good . . .'"

He stops for a second. Clearly we are not dealing in the realm of really good at the moment.

"I would say," he goes on, "just based on this, I'd say it's pretty good. That's just based on the things we had here."

Is that one star, or satisfactory, or what?

"Maybe—it's hard to say. Based on what—" He stops himself. Smart guy. He's not going to lock himself into an answer.

So . . . is it a place you'd write about?

"Mmmmm . . . based just on food? I came in here checking it out as a possible review. I don't think it's review quality right now—but that also has to do with my needs at the moment. I don't need to do another place à la Tribeca Grill, à la Odeon, unless it's compellingly good. Which I don't think this is. 'Diner's Journal'—if I'm doing something on hot nightspots—because this neighborhood isn't written about all that often—that would be maybe one reason to put it in 'Diner's Journal.' I would come back and see what the scene is at night. And recommend a couple of dishes. Sort of a qualified 'Diner's Journal.' And see how the steak is. But just on the basis of this I wouldn't be compelled to come back and write about it."

He wipes his mouth with his napkin.

"We'll drop in. 'Cause I'm down here every once in a while. I'll drop in in the evening to see."

The check has arrived. Bryan Miller of *The New York Times* removes his wallet and places his "Michael Simon" American Express card on top of it. A few minutes later he leaves. Maybe he will come back, and maybe he won't.

DOWN, DOWN, DOWN . . .

TWENTY-SEVEN

It is now the middle of August. The scaffolding must come down.

It has been up for more than three months now. Bruce is getting mighty pissed. As protest, he has stopped paying any of his $5,416.67-a-month rent. He's also called on a powerful lawyer friend. He says his pal has put him in touch with some top officials at the Buildings Department. "They'll come over here and inspect," Bruce says. "I think it's scaring these guys. Something's going to happen."

The landlord has called. That is Bruce's only clue that action is imminent. "They want to meet with me tomorrow morning at 10:00 A.M. I think they're gonna want me to sign something. That's my guess. It'll probably be something that makes me responsible if someone gets hit on the head. I'm not going to sign that."

The next day he goes to the meeting.

It ends somewhat badly, with Bruce saying, "I'm not paying my rent," and Maltz the landlord saying, "Well then, I'm going to sue you," and Bruce saying, "Great, let's sue each other," and leaving.

Then Bruce went and called a new guy at the city, this time a High-Ranking Buildings Official, who explained that there was really no need for the scaffolding, he'd see what he could do.

So Bruce went back to Maltz for another meeting.

By this time Maltz had gotten wind of Bruce's calls around town.

"I'm not asking the city to do anything they're not supposed to do," Bruce said to Maltz. "I'm just—I happen to have a little bit of access not just to talk to Joe the Jerkoff on the phone."

So now the scaffolding is coming down. Tomorrow.

"I told Himler to call up the *Post* and try to get it in the paper," Bruce says. "From the moment it is down for twenty-four hours it's half price for drinks and food. I told Maltz about it. He's not a bad guy, actually. He's not a bad guy."

Bruce smiles. "I'm happy. When I'm happy everybody drinks."

/On August 22, 1990, the scaffolding comes down, as predicted—at least directly in front of The Falls. It continues, a monument to clout, all the way around the entire building.

Page Six of *The New York Post* wasn't interested in the item about twenty-four hours of half-priced food and drink. "They saved me a hell of a lot of money," Bruce says. His second idea was to give anyone who asked "What happened to the scaffolding?" a free glass of champagne. That also seems to have died somewhere between conception and reality.

Bruce spent the morning shopping, and has bought the landlord a present to express his gratitude: six glasses from Orvis, a fishing supply company. Bruce knows the landlord likes to fish. They're heavy, round glass—the type Bruce likes—and each has a different fish on it. His favorite is "cutthroat shark."

"That's perfect," Bruce says.

Whenever Bruce ventures into the retail arena—as he did this morning in search of his little gift, at a huge sporting goods store near his apartment called Paragon—he returns with an opinion. "I should write a letter to Orvis," he says. "They don't know how to sell what they have. The stuff doesn't look good in the catalog but it looks terrific in the store. They gotta fix their catalog."

/Tonight Bruce wants to celebrate. Free drinks for me! So he ends up having dinner with a beautiful blonde at the Primo Table, and asks the waitress to bring over a bottle of $120 champagne. The blonde happens to be Alexandra, Philippe's girlfriend. Philippe is still working on the pool in St. Bart's. She's in town alone for a modeling assignment for Victoria's Secret. The Falls is the perfect place for her to go to dinner by herself, being a beautiful blonde and all. And she has presented Bruce with a wonderful idea: How about a Victoria's Secret Halloween alumnae party?

Wow! Bruce really loves this one. He is imagining the place packed solid with Victoria's Secret female models and cannot even begin to fathom how huge the reaction will be. "That'll have 'em lining around the block," he says. "We can get the waitresses to wear lingerie."

Alexandra and Philippe have been involved for months. Maybe even a year. They met when she went down to St. Bart's to find a place for herself and her boyfriend to live. She met Philippe and asked him to help. He said okay. A week later they were involved. By the time her boyfriend got there, she told him it was over. Philippe was her boyfriend now. So the boyfriend went back to New York and called Philippe's girlfriend and the two of them got involved. The boyfriend told Alexandra they met on an airplane, but she doesn't quite believe it.

/Early September 1990: Everyone thinks that after Labor Day everybody will come back. They don't. Several nights of the week, the restaurant is dead. Weekend nights still draw crowds, and the occasional celebrity drops by. Parties still come in. Hope remains. No one has discussed the idea of closing. When it comes up, Bruce dismisses it. Brian Moores tries out a new menu. Lots of wild game. Venison. Duck. Very California. Brian had taken a brief vacation to the Coast and come back inspired. Prices go up.

Mid-September 1990: Bruce sends the following letter to the investors:

T   H   E
F A L L S

CONFIDENTIAL

Dear Shareholders,   September 12, 1990

Unfortunately the brisk few months that we had in the beginning were wiped out by the lack of business in the summer. No one is more disappointed in our summer performance than we are.

Our options seem fairly simple:

1. An overcall of 10-20% of all investors, this means if you have a $20,000.00 dollar investment it's an overcall of $2,000.00 to $4,000.00. These moneys would be paid back before any dividend would be paid.

2. Certificates of deposit to be put in the bank by the investors to cover overdrafts to $35,000.

3. To sell a share or two, which would reduce ownership by 1 or 2 pts.

4. For a loan to be secured by someone or some entity to 150 Varick Inc.

An informal meeting will be held 9/20/90 at the restaurant at 3:00 p.m. to discuss these problems.

I am doing the best I can under the circumstances, but I feel it is important to inform you of the situation.

Sincerely,

Bruce Goldstein
Terence Quinn

No loan was ever secured. No share was ever sold. No overcall was ever made.

At least one shareholder did create a certificate of deposit at Republic National Bank to cover overdrafts.

Seeing the potential for a loss, some shareholders had taken it upon themselves to unload their burden. The new buyers they found—who often identified themselves as "shareholders" to get a better table— were never presented to 150 Varick Inc. in any formal way. Still, Bruce was eager to keep any shareholders (real or potential) happy. So he accommodated them, even though he never saw any evidence that they owned a piece of the pie.

But it made Bruce angry. Here was all this newfound cash going into the pockets of frightened shareholders and not into his dying restaurant.

"It's like the proverbial sinking ship," Bruce says. "People are trying to find lifeboats wherever they can, and some people don't recognize the rules of the sea. The first thing they should be doing is help plug the leak."

Right now, all that mattered to 150 Varick Inc. was getting more money. Fast.

/October 1990: The California menu hasn't worked. Bruce changes the menu to a spare, simple version of the original. New pastas, new desserts. Mashed potatoes for everybody. This will work. He is convinced that everything needs to be simpler, cheaper. Nobody wants to spend a lot of money on food anymore. Cheaper eats, remember? He tries to get publicity for new, lowered prices, and fails. Halloween was a slow night; there was no Victoria's Secret reunion, and the waitresses all came to work fully clothed. According to sources other than Bruce, The Falls has come perilously close to shutting its doors, for lack of money. Bruce denies this. "We'll make it work," he says. "It's the recession."

/November 1990: Brian Moores quits. Two weeks have gone by where paychecks have bounced, and he is tired of not being paid properly. He is tired of the new menu. He wants to get back to cooking quality cuisine.

Thanksgiving 1990: Dinner for the Homeless. Bruce wants to help the homeless. It is a tradition he began at Central Falls. Investors come down to help out. There are celebrities and clowns. They feed dozens of people and everyone feels very good about it. Even after they find out that one of the homeless guys has stolen The Falls's cellular phone.

.   .   .

/December 1990: Dead. A few busy nights, but Christmas parties do not materialize. Business is slow. Bruce has begun to speculate a little on the possibility of closing. "It's painful," he says.

New Year's Eve 1990: Packed solid. An investor—who also happens to be one of The Falls's most frequent customers—has made a reservation for twenty people at 10:00. He comes in with his friends and is told they have not saved him a table. They tell him it is his fault, that the reservation is for 8:00 for eight people, he will have to wait or go someplace else. He waits. Finally they squeeze the group around a few tiny tables. They wait endlessly for service, and finally leave to go someplace else.

"It was a terrific evening," Bruce says. "There was just a little confusion."

/January 1991: Business slides rapidly. Any night with more than fifty customers is considered a success. All the food purveyors now demand COD. "They're in this with us," Bruce says. "It's not in their interest to see us close, 'cause they lose their money." Behind the bar—without his approval, Bruce says later—employees now routinely fill premium liquor bottles with cheap booze. In other words, inside Absolut vodka bottles is Wolfschmidt's vodka. It is difficult to do with bourbon and whiskey, since regular drinkers can taste the difference, but with gin and vodka, one employee says, "You can always get away with it."

/February 1991: Bruce is desperate. He needs one last event, one last burst of life to save The Falls, before he will give up on his dying baby. He cannot see it die before its first birthday. He has gone to see *Once Around* and gets the idea to bring Danny Aiello in to sing.

/"It's like selling ice to Alaskans," Bruce said one slow winter night, as a bitter wind and rain blew outside. Two people were at a table, four at the bar. His restaurant was dying; he was trying desperately to understand, to explain, in between the ritual turning of knobs on his beloved sound system.

"But Alaskans just want blubber." He laughed at his joke. There was no way to explain, not really.

On this particular night, Mike Tyson was fighting Razor Ruddock at the Mirage in Las Vegas. The open bell was to sound at 9:00. At 8:45

P.M., far earlier than his usual departure time, Bruce announced that he was leaving to go watch the fight. He threw on his coat and walked out the kitchen door to his car.

A few minutes later, the four people at the bar—three women and a man, all in their early thirties, all drinkers—decided to eat.

Wendy was thrilled. She had been working at The Falls for several months now, a friendly Irish girl who'd managed to survive the countless staff purges. She had been in the United States on a tourist visa that was about to expire, and she planned to stay on illegally. So Wendy needed every possible penny. For a waitress, an empty restaurant translates into an empty purse. "They're going to have a bottle of wine, I *know* it," Wendy thought. She brought them to the best table in the house, the rear corner banquette. A year ago—nine months ago—it was unthinkable that this group of nobodies would be seated in so exalted a location. She passed out menus, told them the specials and excused herself.

"Excuse me!" one of them called out a few minutes later. Wendy rushed over. The man at the table looked ill.

"I think we're going to go . . . there's an *awful* smell."

"What! What? Oh, let me check on that . . . we had a problem with the garbage before," Wendy explained, referring to the fact that The Falls hadn't been able to pay its garbage bill, resulting in the garbage sitting directly outside the kitchen door for several hours longer than usual that day. "Perhaps you'd like to move to another table—if you sit in the front of the restaurant, you won't—"

"That's all right," the man said, his companions already slipping on their coats. "You know, once you've smelled something that bad . . ."

Moments later they were out the door. Wendy was crushed. "That's a hundred dollars gone," she said.

But the departed customers were right. The smell was everywhere. A brief investigation turned up the reason. It seems that the kitchen staff had some food that had gone uneaten, and decided they no longer needed to clutter up the refrigerator with food that no one was going to buy. So they dumped it in the garbage pail.

And that was the smell.

Odd, isn't it? With humans, the smell of death comes after you die. In a restaurant, the smell comes before.

"LADIES AND GENTLEMEN . . .

MR. DANNY AIELLO!"

TWENTY-EIGHT

"It's the tie."

So says Sheila, a waitress, matter-of-factly, a tone of voice she is entirely right to assume, because she is, in fact, right. It is the tie. Bruce is wearing a tie tonight. It is not natural for Bruce to be wearing a tie. But these are not natural times. Danny Aiello will be performing tonight—Live at the Lush Life Lounge, March 4, 1991, One Night Only!—and so, for this very special occasion entirely of his own making, Bruce is wearing a tie.

At the rehearsal this morning, he wore a hat either backward on his head or down at least, pulled far enough that you could barely see his forehead, or his actual head, which has less hair than he would like it to, and more gray. Tonight he has thankfully removed the hat, possibly because Terry kept making fun of him for wearing it. He has replaced it with a dark brown jacket, white shirt and red tie, all of the stylish downtown variety—big shoulders, a nice hang, no collar buttons on the shirt. Oh yes, and dark pants and shoes. But who ever really notices the bottom of a man's wardrobe?

It *is* the tie, most definitely. No doubt. Let's face facts: The guy doesn't wear a tie very much. Hardly ever. He's into trendy pullovers, if that is a fashion category, and it basically works. People would say the guy dresses well. Moe Green goes Manhattan.

People would say Bruce looks especially good tonight. Maybe he popped into a tanning salon for a quick bronzing. He does that a fair amount; he used to do it twice a week, until his favorite tanning salon, the Swiss Center on Greenwich, became another victim of this damn recession. Or, more precisely, Bruce became the victim. Anyway, even when he doesn't go that often, Bruce is a man who is perpetually tan. Even without the aid of constant sunshine or the kind of rays you can buy at your friendly neighborhood sun emporium.

So maybe Bruce is glowing naturally tonight. Or maybe not. He's not talking. He's glowing.

Tonight he will be on his best behavior. The tie, remember? Oh, he might drink a little wine, get a little buzz—but tonight he won't need much in the way of artificial stimulation. Tonight is gonna be fucking hot. Celebrities—imagine who might come! Chris Walken might bring some of those guys from the new Woody Allen movie. Bruce read in *The New York Post* how those guys were all going to Columbus, the New York celebrity magnet in another neighborhood, and that frankly pissed him off. Why are they going to Columbus? The food is shit there. People go there and order *tea*. What is it about Columbus that Sean Penn likes? The fact that people take pictures of him with their stares instead of their cameras?

Fuck Columbus. Tonight Columbus is coming to The Falls. You see, Danny Aiello is what you might call a regular at Columbus. If you were being precise about it, you would say that he is a fixture at Columbus. There once were hot summer nights, in the mid-to-late 1980s, that you could catch a glimpse of Danny Aiello sitting in a lawn chair by the side window of Columbus. Christ, you practically remembered him tending to a Weber grill back there. It was his home away from New Jersey home.

Still, somehow, in a way that Danny Aiello doesn't even remember exactly or he might have changed his mind, Bruce convinced him to make his singing debut at The Falls, where he had eaten only occasionally. He's a George Washington Bridge kind of guy, and The Falls is closer to the Holland Tunnel. Otherwise who knows? He certainly likes Bruce. That much we now know. And he gobbled up the rigatoni with meat sauce they gave him, and the band, for lunch during the rehearsal. And the salad. And the mozzarella and tomato. And even the cheesecake (Italian, of course). He also seemed grateful for the attention paid to his requests for hot tea. One gets the feeling he has been to eating establishments in his life— probably his precelebrity life—where he was denied hot tea for no good reason, or where he didn't ask, because he didn't want to trouble anybody.

There are different levels of celebrity, of course—the kind that necessitates wearing baseball caps and scarves in public, thereby announcing that you are a celebrity but declining to reveal which one; and the kind that does not. Aiello belongs in the latter category. His idea of casual wear is an Everlast hooded sweatshirt and jeans and dirty sneakers. No baseball cap. He likes it if you recognize him, and if you ask him for an autograph, he will sign it "Love, Danny Aiello," like he means it.

On the streets of New York City Danny Aiello is most definitely a star. On Varick Street across from The Falls—where one is not likely to run into Kevin Costner or Barbra Streisand—Aiello has the effect of a Katharine Hepburn sighting, or the Pope. People appear ready to kiss the hem of his garment. Partly this is because he had reason to run out onto Varick Street around 11:30 this morning, and make a rather large stink out of being Danny Aiello.

That is not ordinarily his style; but ordinarily he is not in the company of a friend whose car is about to be towed away by the city for $510 in unpaid parking tickets.

"Larry!" somebody screams to the pianist Larry Fallon, who has been jamming with Danny and the rest of the band in their first formal rehearsal, "they're towing your car!"

Whereupon they all jump up, scramble to the window and observe this fact for themselves. And Danny Aiello—realizing, perhaps unconsciously, that his presence on the street might help Larry's cause with the tow truck—runs immediately out the door to plead with the towing company.

"What's going on, what're you doing?" Aiello says to the couple in the blue Ford sedan parked alongside Larry's car, and behind the tow truck poised for action.

"Hey," says one of them, a man in his late thirties, "you're in the movies, right?"

"Danny Aiello," he says, smiling, hand outstretched.

"*Moonstruck*, I saw that."

"Yeah," Aiello says, "and I was in that Spike Lee movie, *Do the Right Thing*, got nominated for an Academy Award. I'm in this movie right now with Richard Dreyfuss, *Once Around*. It's really beautiful. You should see it."

What is this, the *Today* show?

The other member of this couple, a short young woman with an unappealing frown on her face, informs Aiello—who has now been joined by Larry Fallon, the car's owner—that if he pays $510 in unpaid parking tickets, they will leave his car alone, even though it is parked in a one-hour zone and he had let the meter run out.

"I got eighty," Aiello says, looking at the bills he has in his pocket. Larry does not have anywhere near the difference. But by this time a crowd has formed: several people from the restaurant, including Bruce and Terry, plus a dozen or so spectators who feel they have wandered into something special.

Bruce pulls out his money. He has one hundred-dollar bill and one fifty, and hands it over. Terry pulls out a ten. After some cajoling, the author puts in $100, against his better judgment, but figuring that Danny Aiello is probably good for the money. [*Author's note:* He was.] A few others chip in what they have. Before long the $510 is raised and the tow truck chain is lowered. The car is free.

After a few more minutes of friendly conversation on the street, everyone goes back inside. There is much laughter and merriment; even a man now seated at the bar in a brown tweed jacket is chuckling, although nobody seems to know who he is, or what that official-looking piece of paper is that he's clutching firmly in his left hand.

Once Bruce gets back inside, he goes over to the phone by the back of the bar. Just as he is about to make a call, the man in the brown tweed jacket makes his approach.

"Excuse me, but are you one of the owners?"

That is a question that Bruce doesn't like to answer. He once explained that the reason he would never name a restaurant after himself—say, "Bruce's," or something like that—is that then you have bill collectors coming in all the time and saying, "Where's Bruce?" or, "Are you Bruce?"

Nevertheless, he feels compelled to answer honestly.

"I'm from the Electric Meter Co., which is a sub—meter company for Con Ed, and I'm here to collect the balance owed for your electric bill, which is $1,508.03."

Bruce is not having a good time.

"Don't we have an arrangement for this?" he answers quickly and with an exasperated tone that after many years he has perfected.

"I don't know," the man says, as nicely as possible but still standing firm. "The bill needs to be paid by Wednesday or we'll have to turn off the electricity."

"No, no," Bruce responds, and you know he has been in this position before by the quick, calm, steady manner he exudes. "We have an *arrangement*. The bill gets paid. It'll get paid."

"Well, you can pay it now, or bring the payment in . . ." The man looks at his little slip of paper with the $1,508.03 figure highlighted with a yellow marker.

"It'll get paid," comes the calm voice of Bruce like a gentle wave off Malibu.

"Okay." You can practically hear inside this man's head, where sensible voices are pleading, "No! No! This man won't pay!"

"Okay," he repeats. "Whatever your arrangement is."

And what is that arrangement but the scraping together of enough nickels and dimes?

"Thanks a lot," Bruce says, quite graciously in fact, as he extends his hand. It is the handshake of a man who knows that electricity can be generated from a variety of sources, and that he will have light tonight. Just enough light.

/The Falls looks slightly better at night. During the day the restaurant shares, with its predominately white clientele, a certain pale quality. It probably has something to do with the venetian blinds and all that black paint. There is a voluminous amount of black in the place—though not quite as much as there used to be before The Falls. Its predecessor, J.S. VanDam, actually put black carpeting on the walls in the early 1980s, to maintain its then-solid reputation as a terrific place to score drugs.

Now it is black because black makes people look better. The Falls was designed to enhance the looks of two categories of people: celebrities, and young blondes in tight black miniskirts. To that extent its design is a colossal success. At night—when these nocturnal animals most desperately search out rooms that possess the appropriate amount of dim amber light—some of these souls actually find themselves in a cab to Varick Street downtown. Left-hand side, through the light. Ten dollars from anywhere.

They have not come yet, though. The beautiful people are home taking naps. From 5:00 till 8:00 at night, you will not be able to find a single high-priced model at a restaurant anywhere in New York City, because they are all at home, asleep. Yes, there *is* such a thing as beauty sleep. It involves beauties going to sleep. In other words, you cannot go to sleep at 5:00, ugly, and wake up at 8:00, beautiful. But if you are a beautiful woman in New York City, and expect to be treated accordingly, then you damn well better take a nap. Nobody wants to see a model yawning, or rubbing the sleep out of her big blue eyes.

At about 7:30, they will wake up. The models. They will go to their closet and say to themselves: Must I put on the short black miniskirt *again?* I want to wear jeans. I want to wear slacks. But I dare not. It is expected of me that I will wear a short black miniskirt, and I dare not disappoint. Or else I might have to go without dinner. You see, this is the equation. If you are a model in a short black miniskirt, the odds are extremely good that your dinner will be paid for by somebody else. Most likely it will be the restaurant where you are eating. Or it will be the man who is escorting you—an employer or a manager or a boyfriend.

Tonight there may be models and there may not. Danny Aiello is not necessarily the kind of guy who attracts models. He is a devoted husband, and he is expected momentarily with his wife for a quick dinner before the show.

A table is being held.

/It is 9:15. The guests have arrived. The Falls is spilling over with people.

"This is not," says Bruce, who should know, "a typical Monday night downtown." He walks and runs and greets and kisses. This is not typical either. Normally, on a Monday night at The Falls, you would find Bruce hidden behind the bar, turning the knobs on his stereo system, loud, soft, woofer, tweeter . . . whatever it takes to keep his mind occupied with something other than such mundane matters as the customers. He chooses to avoid the glad-handing friendliness of the typical restaurant owner. He would probably prefer it if he never had to say hello to anyone. This causes many people to assume that Bruce Goldstein is rude. Even his friends love to joke that Bruce does not really enjoy their company, that he would much rather be playing with his knobs.

Tonight he will mingle. He will sit at a table for more than a few moments. He may even address the crowd, welcome them to The Falls, explain the purpose of this evening, and wink at the nuns.

Nuns! There are actual nuns at The Falls tonight. They are the first nuns to have ever come to The Falls. No doubt they feel that people are always staring at them. No doubt they have also taken a nap in the early hours of the evening. No doubt they have also scanned their closets and realized that they would be expected to wear the same black outfit they always wear. Tonight they are models, too, but only of restraint. They will keep the tone of the evening clean and sober. There will be no coke snorting in the bathroom tonight.

The nuns get a very good table. As they should. They are nuns. Also, they are the ostensible reason for tonight. The only reason Danny Aiello has agreed to sing tonight was to benefit something called Providence Rest, a nun-run nursing home in the Bronx where Aiello once considered placing his own mother before her death.

"A wonderful, beautiful place," Aiello is fond of explaining. The nuns smile when they hear this. They are fond of smiling.

At 9:15, the nuns are working on their dinners. They're having chicken and fish. As one would expect, they chew their food slowly and well, and frequently dab at their mouths with their napkins. It simply would not do for a nun to spill mashed potatoes on her habit.

They talk quietly, and occasionally take advantage of their good table position up front to glance at arriving patrons. A glance is all that they allow themselves. You will not catch a nun staring over her shoulder at The Falls. It is entirely conceivable that these nuns—being big-city nuns, after all, with access to *The New York Post* just like the rest of us heathens—recognize at a glance a few of the celebrities gathered tonight to contribute $20 to their worthy cause, and hear Danny Aiello's debut. Celebrities, that is, to people who read the *Post;* because it can hardly be said that Andy Capasso, former boyfriend to beauty queen Bess Myerson, central figure in the Bess Mess of 1988, is a genuine celebrity to anyone outside the reading radius of the *Post.* And yet there he is, Andy Capasso and his new girlfriend, at a center table at The Falls tonight, behaving like a celebrity because he is being treated like one. Bess Myerson's boyfriend . . . wow! What was it he did exactly? No one seems to remember.

Of course it is fitting that Capasso shares his table tonight with two of this city's longest-reigning oddball stars—Joey and Cindy Adams. Tabloid celebrities. Twin columnists for *The New York Post.* He of the humor column, she of gossip. Twin towers of influence, or embarrassment. It depends on your point of view. Cindy Adams has been profiled in *Vanity Fair* and ridiculed on *Saturday Night Live.* In the 1990s those are good things to happen to you. Tonight Cindy is hosting; The Falls is told she wants to write a column about having dinner with Andy Capasso and his new girlfriend. Also, Danny Aiello considers her a friend. Or so he says, and you cannot deny that Danny Aiello is the kind of person who means what he says. And look—there she is, center table, nice view, with Bruce and Terry each stopping by for a chat. She is obviously friends with *somebody*, because at The Falls, good tables are *reserved* for good friends.

"Cindy Adams!" Bruce exclaims as she walks in the door. Bruce is possessed of a strong sense of irony, and his smile at the moment reflects that. The fact that she has come to The Falls means, most likely, that she will mention The Falls. That is not ironic, of course. But let's face it—Cindy Adams doesn't hang with the hipsters. Wherever she goes, irony follows close behind.

"Is that a wig?" a waitress asks no one in particular of Mrs. Adams. One presumes it is. Mr. Adams could use one, too; even in this low-key downtown amber light, Joey's head glistens. Inside it are jokes, frequently other people's jokes, that appear under the somewhat misleading rubric of "Strictly for Laughs" in *The New York Post*. Mr. and Mrs. Adams certainly must be the only husband-wife column-writing team in America. New Yorkers are very proud of this fact.

One has to admire the Adamses for being the first celebrities to turn up tonight at The Falls. One thing about being a celebrity is that you are entitled to come late to things. Or not come at all. Or make a reservation for four people and bring twenty and have no one get mad at you. If Steve Martin or Tom Cruise felt like coming to The Falls tonight—felt like walking in unannounced with an entourage—they would be greeted with hugs and kisses, and some lesser individual would go without a table. But a certain amount of realism governs life at The Falls; Steve Martin is not going to show up. Tom Cruise is not going to show up, either.

Let's face facts: Paul Sorvino isn't even going to show up tonight.

The portly character actor—the one who so eloquently sliced a clove of garlic in *Goodfellas*—did at least have a reservation for tonight, and was eagerly anticipated until about 2:00 this afternoon, when his publicist made the unfortunate mistake of confirming the reservation and mentioning, in passing, that Paul was sick. However, the publicist indicated that she was still planning to attend *without* Paul, and would like to keep the table.

This practice is not uncommon in New York restaurants. A business associate of a celebrity will make a reservation under the celebrity's name; then, on arrival at the restaurant, and after being seated, will inform the management that said celebrity is sick or busy or otherwise unable to show up.

This is called "name dropping."

It is indigenous to status-seeking urbanites who do not enjoy sitting in bad sections of restaurants, or waiting for tables, or being treated—The horror! The horror!—like normal everyday Joes.

And while no offense is intended, it is kind of incredible, isn't it, that we live in an age where the mention of Paul Sorvino's name is enough to get a good restaurant table? But is it more outrageous that someone would drop his name, or that a restaurant would stoop to pick it up?

What is the point of saving a great table for Paul Sorvino's publicist? Bruce wonders this aloud, standing by the front desk, ready to call her up and inform her that she will no longer have choice seats for tonight's festivities. "She thinks *she's* going to sit at a table for Paul Sorvino if Paul Sorvino isn't gonna be there!" he screams at Michael Fitzpatrick, who took her original 2:00 call. "I'll call her and tell her she can't fucking have the table, not without Paul Sorvino, the table is for *him*, not for his fucking *publicist!*" He calms down after a moment. "I mean, she can *come*, she can stand at the bar or we can find her another table, but we gave him a great fucking table, no way I'm saving that for *her*." He is fingering a floor plan of The Falls, specially designed to indicate the precise location of all those with reservations for tonight.

All this is taking place within earshot of Danny Aiello and *his* publicist, by the way; and publicists being a competitive bunch, Aiello's publicist has his own opinion.

"She's not *important*," Aiello's publicist says.

"She's not?" This pleases Bruce. This means he does not have to worry about unceremoniously booting the publicist out of her table.

"Definitely. *Not*."

"Okay. Good." At which point Bruce calls up this small-potatoes publicist and informs her that unless Paul Sorvino is miraculously cured between now and tonight, she will not be seated at a nice table.

Hardball!

"Terry, let's go downstairs to the office," Bruce says after blowing her off. He is thinking about this big round table that is now available. He is extremely happy. "Let's call some people. Maybe you can call Chris Walken and get some of those people from the Woody Allen movie."

"I got his number downstairs," Terry says.

"Let's go," he says.

As they walk down the steps to Bruce's private office downstairs, Aiello and his band kick off the second half of their rehearsal. Every so often a face peers in off Varick Street.

"You make me feel so young . . . you make me feel like spring has sprung!"

It's going to be a hell of a night.

. . .

/It is 9:30 P.M. The celebrities have taken their seats.

Let's see, who do we have in the house tonight? Oh look, that's the guy who wrote *Moonstruck*, what's his name, John Patrick Shanley, good guy, good guy. And that's Buzzy O'Keefe, he owns restaurants: the River Café, the Water Club, if it's got liquid in the title it's his. Some guy from Warner Bros. is here, Phil Something. Over there in the back. Griffin is here, of course. Griffin is wearing a blue blazer and khaki pants and a conservative red tie. Griffin has a cool soul, trapped in the body of a preppy. Married a James Bond girl, anyone would be proud to have that on his résumé. She's not here tonight. They never are, are they?

Paulie Herman has come. Paulie used to have a beard. You've seen Paulie, he was the crazy zombie walking across Times Square in that movie, what was it called? He was in all three *New York Stories*. And that's not even counting *The Last Temptation of Christ!* Jesus Christ! Nevertheless, Paulie has not given up his day job, which is really a night job, which is being the host at Columbus. He is the foremost gatherer of celebrities in the New York restaurant business. When the legendary Café Central was alive . . . you know . . . where Bruce "Bruno" Willis first plied his charms as a bartender . . . Paulie was the host. Then they moved to a new space uptown, they failed, some acting, some other shit, then he became the host of Columbus. Guys like Baryshnikov put up the money. And with Paulie at the door, or his friendly brother Charlie, you don't go to Columbus without seeing roughly six celebrities. Go after 10:30 at night and it'll be Eddie Murphy over here, Madonna over there, Danny Aiello *of course*, which is why Paulie came down tonight.

Celebrities! Music! God, it's fantastic! And it is all because of Bruce. Terry had nothing to do with this baby. Oh, well, he might have made a few *calls* . . . brought in a few *models* . . . greeted visitors in the friendly, affable manner that has won him so many friends in this wacky town. But when it comes to a night like this, a night where the Sinatra tapes finally get put away, and *real* Sinatra, live Sinatra, the kind of Sinatra Jilly nods his head to, that's a Bruce Goldstein kind of night.

Yes, Jilly, almost forgot about Jilly. Does Jilly have a last name? Yes, but who cares? It's just Jilly, not Mr. Jilly, not Doc Jilly, not even Jilly Baby, although one presumes that if the Chairman of the Board

DANNY AIELLO
AT
"THE FALLS"
FOR THE BENEFIT OF
PROVIDENCE REST

BACK BAY CLAM CHOWDER
$5.
WATERCRESS AND PEAR SALAD
WITH STILTON DRESSING
$8.
LOUISIANA FILE GUMBO
WITH OKRA, SERVED WITH SAFFRON RICE
$17.
GRILLED YELLOWFIN TUNA
WITH TOMATILLO SALSA
$20.
GRILLED BABY CHICKEN
WITH FRESH HERB SAUCE
$18.

wanted to call Jilly any of these things, he would. And probably has. Jilly seems to have a close personal connection to Mr. Francis Albert Sinatra. He is bald, much like Sinatra probably is under that toupee. His side hair is an agreeable shade of white. He wears a conservative suit and looks slightly out of it, though that is probably just an affectation or . . . something.

"It's great having Jilly here," Bruce says. People seem to love saying his name as often as they can get away with it.

Joe Plotkin is happy to see Jilly. He is standing toward the back of the bar, but he can see Jilly perfectly well from his vantage point. Joe is not a celebrity himself—could there ever be a celebrity named Joe Plotkin?—but he has known many, and Jilly ranks high on the list. Joe Plotkin, in recent weeks, has been booking gigs at The Falls. He has booked gigs for much ritzier places than The Falls, places like Rainbow and Stars at Rockefeller Center; hey, this guy booked the Ritz itself! But Joe has explained that he is helping out The Falls and his old friend Bruce while he is, himself, "between gigs," a phrase that has become something of a euphemism for unemployed, but one that Joe Plotkin uses nonetheless, perhaps because for people in the music business, the word "gig" still holds some serious meaning in conversation.

Every so often a guy turns up right out of Central Casting. Get me Joe Plotkin, the music booker! And down would come this exact guy. Modish brown hair and a goatee. Not too many goatees left anymore, but Joe Plotkin's got one of them. Mod jackets. Dark. Downtown. Cool, baby. Joe Plotkin.

"I got this fabulous girl signed to sing in two weeks," Joe Plotkin says. "Kysia Bostick. She sings as beautiful as she looks. I'm discovering her. That's the joy of this business, going out there and finding somebody like Kysia. Boy is she great. I saw her one night in Wonderland, there were maybe six people in the place. Right now nobody's heard of her, but they will." In fact Kysia is coming down tonight herself to check things out. She'll be hanging with Joe at the bar, toward the back, right where Danny Aiello is pacing right now, nervously, waiting for his moment to arrive.

And why not? For this moment will be yet another leap for Danny Aiello, who until his thirties was just another guy in this world, looking for a larger slice of life. Little did he know that he would someday play the most important slice-cutter ever portrayed in the movies, in *Do the Right Thing*. Since the turn of the last decade Aiello has been . . . is famous too strong a word? He co-starred in a Woody Allen play at Lincoln Center, *The Floating Lightbulb*, not a masterpiece but enough to get him known. Then came the get-me-Danny-Aiello years—through the mid- to late- 1980s, and through today, when the guy actually has two movies out at once, has scripts for *himself* in development, and is going to be playing Jack Ruby, a perfect bit of typecasting except that Aiello wouldn't hurt a soul. Remember, the nuns . . .

Wants to be famous. Enjoys it. Got to meet Tony Bennett last night at the Russian Tea Room. Celebrities like meeting other celebrities. It must involve some kind of secret handshake or something. "I might come by and see you tomorrow," Tony told Danny and Danny told Bruce and Bruce told Terry and, well, word got around: Tony Bennett might be coming tonight.

So maybe that's why Danny Aiello is nervous. Otherwise it doesn't make much sense. The guy's an *actor*. He sings in a *movie*. These are his *pals*.

And yet . . .

Where the hell is he? He's at The Falls, yes, doing a favor for a bunch of nuns. He didn't want to do it, he didn't want to do it. This afternoon he was all over the place explaining how he didn't want to do it. Give it up, Aiello! You wanted to do it! But there he was, doth protesting too much. "Bruce asked me . . . Griffin asked me . . . I didn't want to do it. Didn't have to do it."

Is there anyone in America who would not like to get up, uninhibited, on a stage in a nightclub with a high-quality four-piece jazz combo, a microphone, and sing some Sinatra tunes? Please raise your hands.

Which is why Danny Aiello is walking, faster now, running practically, in what should really be a leisurely backstage pace. It is time for the show to begin, but he isn't quite ready yet. No, not ready . . . thank God there's an opening act, the comedy stylings of Joy Behar, who is quite funny, and Bruce himself, who is going to, in the grand tradition of impresarios, say a few words of welcome, and introduce the entertainment—of course Danny, but also Joy Behar, recruited as an opening act. (At $20 a pop to get in, it was reasoned, one might do well to get an opening act.)

But first a word from those fabulous nuns!

"I would like to take this opportunity to thank Danny," says Sister Joanna, whom Bruce Goldstein has called to the stage. Nuns are not frequently called to the stage, and it shows in Sister Joanna's performance. She is nervously fingering the microphone, perhaps not terribly familiar with nightclub sound systems. ". . . Danny who gave his friendship to the home for many years, his love, his support, his being behind us, his making this evening possible, for you to be here . . . and to you who come this evening, thank you." Was that a hint of a smile?

She's getting into it now, she's not going to blow it by hogging the stage.

"God bless you, enjoy the evening."

Hoots, hollers, wild applause. It simply wouldn't do to not applaud a nun.

And now, ladies and gentlemen . . . Bruce Goldstein!

"You've seen her on HBO, and you've seen her on her own talk show Monday through Friday on WABC. Let's hear it for the great Joy Behar!" Okay, so Ed Sullivan he's not.

"It's great to be here," Behar kicks it off, "watching people eat." You see, comedians do not usually perform in front of an audience with forks and knives in their hands. It is simply too much of a risk. But this being The Falls, where the idea is to get people to spend as much money as possible, it is essential that everyone have food in their mouth while Behar performs.

"This is a very New York happening, isn't it. Jilly over here, we have." Applause. "Jilly, how do you feel? And who's this? *That's* Jilly? Are you Italian, Jilly? Really? Me too. You think there's something funny about that? Most people think I'm Jewish for some reason. It's some stereotype they're working with. Couple of months ago I get a call, Happy Hanukkah. I says, 'Ma, I'm not Jewish.' No one believes me. But with all due respect to Danny Aiello, I do not go out with Italian men. I mean—I love them, they're handsome, but their attitude is, 'Yo—go get the ravioli.' You know? Get your own friggin' ravioli, all right, Danny? Give me a nice tall Jewish guy with an astigmatism. This is what I'm looking for."

A theory was expressed over many cognacs one night at the bar of The Falls—bars being where some of the finest theories in the world are developed, by the way—that all Italians want to be Jews, and that all Jews want to be Italians. Judging from the wild laughter and applause Joy Behar is getting, what sounded rather bogus in a Courvoisier haze now begins to make sense.

"I was married to a Jewish guy." She pauses and looks at the nuns. "I feel like I'm in confession! I was married to a Sephardic Jew. Do you know what that is? It's a status thing. We used to worship at the Temple Julio Iglesias. I was what you call shiksa non grata in that relationship. We did get the Catholic ceremony first, we had the church, you'll be happy to hear this, in the Italian neighborhood, Our Lady of Perpetual Agita." Come on, everybody, laugh . . . she's the comedian!

"It's not that I'm a good traveler. I'm not. I don't know about Danny. Danny. Danny!"

Danny hears his name being called from the back where he has been pacing, and stops for a moment.

"Danny, when you were a kid, did you find that Italians were good travelers?"

"I never left the Bronx," he says quickly.

"See, these are not the Vikings we're discussing. These are the Italians."

You get the picture. Or do you? The room is darker now; scattered spotlights try to present the illusion of a nightclub. One is yellow, one blue. The candles now shoot off a more pronounced glow. Black table-tops, black miniskirts, black sport coats and shoes . . . we are definitely downtown. By the time Joy Behar winds up her act, our eyes have grown accustomed to this darkness. Even Cindy Adams starts to look good.

Up to the stage comes the band, an excellent combo that might have donated their services to this event, but they are musicians and therefore perpetually broke, so they are getting $400 apiece—not counting the cost of the engineer in back who gets $400 and a free steak to turn knobs on a control panel, or the lighting technician, who understands how blue lights and yellow lights combine to make people on stage look beautiful. Isn't that worth the money?

Bruce Goldstein joins the band onstage and takes the microphone. He is no more comfortable now than before. We have arrived at the big moment, *his* big moment to be precise, and literally nothing comes into his head except the most obvious of clichés . . . or are they clichés only because cynics deem them to be?

Tonight is not for cynics. Tonight is for believers. Bruce believes in the redemptive magic of music. He believes that when Danny Aiello grabs that mike . . . it'll be in just a few seconds, he's not quite ready, keep the audience occupied, please, Bruce . . . The Falls will be saved. Bruce will have saved it. Look, the place is packed! Just like opening night, remember? Only now it's been a year, we know what we're doing, the waitresses, *look* at them—each one hotter than the last. Yum! More white wine. It's happening. Jesus.

/"Danny Aiello . . . Live From the Lush Life Lounge"
"You Make Me Feel So Young"

In-Between-Song Banter: "You make me feel so young, baby," to his wife, who will be the audience member he sings most often to throughout this special night—every time he sings a love song.

"It makes it so much easier to know that you have so many friends here . . . it may be obvious to you at this point that this is not my forte, I am an actor and as a matter of fact the class is still out on that. But they say that if you do something for fifteen minutes, which supposedly I did in *Once Around*. I sang a few songs and"—applause—"and because of that people thought that I wanted to be a singer. But I promise you, this is it. My reason for being here is Sister Joanna, and Providence Rest"—applause—"and it's my way of bringing attention to a wonderful, wonderful senior citizens home in the Bronx, that we are so grateful that you came down to support here tonight, and have this Danny Aiello night. I'm truly, truly honored that you came down and I'm thanking you for it.

"I'd like to do right now a song which I did in *Once Around*, it's not the Sinatra version, Jilly"—he nods, as he must, in the direction of the Jillerometer—"but it's close."

"Fly Me to the Moon"

"Thank you thank you. Is it all right so far?"

"You Made Me Love You . . . I Didn't Want to Do It"

"Thank you, thank you very much.

"Can I say something? So help me God, the songs that we've selected tonight were based on them being the easiest to learn. Because we only had a few days to do it, but it's . . . after this song I'd like to—"

" 'Mama'! 'Mama'! " cries the audience, referring to a song from *Once Around*.

"If any of you know Louis Prima, it's a song that I love," Danny says. He does not mention that he is, in fact, developing the life story of Louis Prima into a movie, and that he hopes to star; but he is, and it will someday be necessary to sing this song in a movie, too, so . . .

"It's a song, if we can do it, I know they can, I wish I can, but we'll see, let's try it Larry!"

"Bona Sera, Señorita"

"I'd like to introduce this beautiful group of guys. A wonderful sax man, I just met him for the first time today . . . Wonderful drummer in the back . . . On bass . . . And here's the man who put it all together, my man for a long, long period of time, we go *way* back when I began on Broadway, which is a hundred years ago, Larry, he was nominated this year for a Grammy, he didn't win, but he was nominated, but that's good, too. I know that." Laughter that acknowledges Danny's reference to his Best Supporting Actor nomination in 1990 for his performance in *Do the Right Thing*.

He then gestures at a handsome, beaming young man sitting near the stage. "John Patrick Shanley made my life, changed it. I played in *Moonstruck*, John Patrick Shanley wrote it." Applause. "I'd like to introduce all my friends. Here's Cindy Adams, and of course, her wonderful wonderful husband who's my dear friend for so many years, Joey Adams, thank you so much for coming. I'll probably get around to introducing everyone here tonight, but again I want to take the opportunity to thank you again for showing up, this is a wonderful cause.

"Let me clear it up for a moment.

"The people walking around in here with television cameras are affiliated with the *20/20* show. They're doing an interview of me, an in-depth interview, and part of that interview, of course, will mention the Providence Rest senior citizens home up in the Bronx that I'm so much involved in. And one of my reasons for being involved, of course, Sister Joanna, and Delores Magnota, who introduced me to Providence Rest, and most important to my late mother who I loved so very much, and miss so very much.

"Mama was not in that home, but we did go up there on numerous occasions, usually during Valentine's Day, to have auctions to raise money for this wonderful wonderful senior citizens home. And my mother said, 'Had I ever gone to a home, if ever I was to go to a house other than yours or any of the children's, or of my own, I would want to be at Providence Rest.'

"Okay, Larry, what're we doing, what's next?"

"What I Did for Love"

"You know they do a lot of things for love, you know that, don't you, okay!" Applause.

"This next song is a hundred years old."

"All of Me"

"Take all of me! No!" Applause.

"Not too bad, huh? Let me ask the girls something. Do I have a little sensuality here or what? The nuns are nodding! They see it!

"We did this song also in *Once Around*. It's a different kind of an arrangement, I hope you like it."

"The Story of Love"

"Thank you, thank you very much. We're going to do a little something here that you may remember—it's David Lee Roth."

"Just a Gigolo"

"Boy," he says to the band, "are you guys good.

"Sandy, Sandy, Sandy, my wife, Sandy.

"This is good night. I would only ask, in deference to someone who is very special to me, I did this in the movie, if I'm hoarse during this number, forgive me any cracks, but it's the meaning of this song, and let me just sing it, and see how you feel."

"Mama"

"Thank you, thank you very much, that's it, I thank you all very much." As the audience applauds, and the band plays on: "Thank you Joy Behar, thank you Providence Rest!"

Danny steps off the stage, which once belonged to Boston Garden, where the likes of Larry Bird have played basketball, and became the property more recently of a music promoter who sells pieces of it to restaurants and nightclubs in search of a sturdy platform.

/It is a Monday night, do not forget; a school night. When Danny Aiello leaves the stage and rejoins his wife's table, the population of The Falls drops by roughly 500 percent. The four waitresses on duty take breaks, one or two at a time, by leaning against the wall that separates the dining room from the kitchen. That four-foot wall has served as a leaning post ever since The Falls first opened. It was designed to turn otherwise unappealing table locations into prime corner banquettes; its height allows people behind it—on their way to the bathroom, the kitchen or the bar—to look out across the dining room, to listen to conversations at the banquettes below, or simply to relax, if you are a Falls employee, in a spot where one is not necessarily likely to be spotted by Bruce.

There is, as always, confusion over coats. While The Falls has mastered the art of gracious coat checking, it has never quite gotten the hang of gracious coat returning. A proliferation of furs tonight has made it particularly annoying; there is a vague sense of unease among those turning in their coat checks, created by the confused look on the faces of those assigned to the coat check detail, where one is never pleased to see a look of confusion.

By 11:15, the dining room has been emptied of all but loyal friends. Cindy and Joey Adams have retrieved their coats and left for their Park Avenue apartment. The nuns have departed for the Bronx.

Danny Aiello is finally leaving. He has had a very good time and will now, being one of the more sensible celebrities on the planet, go home to bed.

Joe Plotkin's still here. Cool, baby. Michael Wincott, a young New

York actor who belongs to Oliver Stone's repertory company—you've seen him in *Platoon*, you've seen him in *Talk Radio*, you've seen him in *The Doors*, now here he is at The Falls!—is also still here, having commandeered the Primo Table. He is sitting with three very attractive young ladies, and another man, also handsome. One of the attractive ladies seems preoccupied with kissing Wincott. They have been enjoying themselves over on this side of the bar, away from the action but, in a way, right in the midst of it. That is the essence of the Primo Table.

What few people remain at The Falls at this late hour—Carson just swung his imaginary golf club, Nia Peeples will soon be getting funky with her Party Machine—have done so because Terry Quinn has made them feel so young . . . he's made them feel there are songs to be sung, bells to be rung . . . "I've met thousands of people, literally," Terry had mentioned in passing earlier in the evening, not bragging, just by way of explaining that when he said the words, "I've never met anybody quite like" So-and-So, he felt particularly qualified to make the statement.

But now the evening is wearing down.

Griffin Dunne has loosened his tie. He is holding what appears to be a Heineken in his hand, though it might well be a Rolling Rock. At this moment he especially does not look like the kind of guy who has a Bond girl waiting home in bed.

Way back when, in the late great 1980s, Griffin Dunne was a Yuppie God. Women with a college education swooned over him. He always seemed to be in movies with Brooke Adams, who was a Yuppie Goddess. If you actually lived in New York during those fabulous party years it was highly unlikely that you were not at a party with Griffin Dunne at least once, and the odds are you probably even struck up a conversation with him. If Griffin Dunne were a dog, he'd be a Spotted Celebrity. In those days he tended toward a starched white shirt and blue jeans. Had there been Gap ads in the early 1980s, there is no doubt that Griffin Dunne would have posed.

Griffin is now tilting toward the door. This party's over, babe.

He is huddled now with Bruce. They are billing and cooing, it's sweet.

Together, arm in arm, they whisper their way to the door of The Falls. The night is over. Bruce does not like to say goodbye or goodnight. He likes to leave with a minimum of fuss, and so he and Griffin *slip away to the street.*

Terry sees them leave, and follows.

But by the time he reaches the sidewalk in front of The Falls, Bruce and Griffin have jumped in Bruce's Mercedes 450SL roadster, Rhode Island license plate BG-330, and roared off down Varick Street into the darkness.

"Maybe they'll drive to Thailand in Bruce's car," Terry says, laughing. Baby, it's cold outside. His laugh forms a cloud of condensation that quickly disappears.

OUT OF GAS

TWENTY-NINE

Four weeks later, Bruce has flown to Thailand.

He is not taken with the illicit sex that is so widely available in that part of the world. Other American bachelors travel to Thailand for the explicit purpose of entertaining themselves with exotic Asian women who can shoot darts across the room using their vaginal muscles, or—with those same well-toned muscles—write I LOVE THE U.S.A. on the floor of a bar, squatting down, while Americans gather around and applaud. Or they search out the finest drugs available—cocaine, hash, marijuana, heroin. It's all there on the open market, and American dollars will buy you a generous dose of anything you want.

In another era, Bruce might have gone for such things. So might all of us. As the great philosopher Tone-Lōc once said: This is the eighties, and I'm down with the ladies.

But in April of 1991, Bruce is going for shrimp and cashew nuts. Apparently he has found both to be local delicacies.

He says he will be back in plenty of time.

For what?

Everyone has their theories about why Bruce has left. He says it is a vacation and that he is helping out a friend who is opening a restaurant there.

Bruce has tried to convince Terry and others to close The Falls. Bruce held a meeting at his apartment, and during it Bruce told Terry: I must leave. I need to earn money. But Terry wants to keep the place open long enough to sell it and get one, last infusion of cash.

By a few days before his flight, Bruce was ready to be done with The Falls. It was over. He had tried to convince Terry to close. Sure, his trip was a *coincidence*, but the thing is, who wants to be around to see a restaurant die?

"I just was looking at my ticket today," he says, "and my ticket's a two-day trip to get there, and two to get back, and so I'm away for two weeks. I can't see Terry keeping the ship afloat for two weeks without anything. I don't know what's going to happen. There's a lot of juggling right now . . . I'm of the opinion right now that it's just too hard to do without money and it may not be in everybody's best interests to just keep pissing people off, employees' checks are late, and things like that. And that's starting to happen. I always said what would be the point."

He is dark, beyond pessimistic. He knows that the money is not there.

"You can't operate without any money. You can't keep saying, I hope I have a good weekend. We need fifty grand, sixty grand just to pay off a few things and keep some money around so you can stay open without running scared. The rent's fine. We worked that out with them where we're paying them every week. It's just not enough money there. And business is horrible lately. It's—we're down maybe to $12,000, $13,000 a week. That's $2,000–$3,000 short of what it needs to stay open."

For a moment he speculates that Terry might keep the place open . . . alive . . . somehow. But that sinks his mood even further. "I'm of the opinion that it should just close. I just really am. I don't think he's got the motivation. I don't think he's that type of person.

"If I come back and it's still open—I can't believe that it would be, but . . . if I came back and it was still open, I would stick it out for whatever length of time it was. But I'm just—telling everybody that my feeling is that it should close."

The fear of closing terrifies Bruce. The thought that he is responsible. The idea that it might happen in front of him. Just let it be done! You can hear the sobs in his voice. He cannot leave soon enough, he has rent to pay and needs the job awaiting him in Thailand, even though he knows he cannot escape the fate of The Falls.

"It's an ugly feeling," he says. The deep, resonant voice begins to crack. "You almost feel personally, your self-esteem, your self-worth, any kind of relationship when it comes to an end, you start to wonder about that stuff. Even in a personal relationship you wonder how far you should take it and how far you should talk to the other person and see if you can straighten it out, but at some point you gotta face reality, either it's the right thing for you, or it's not. I'm almost sure that continuing is going to make it uglier and uglier. In a relationship and in life. Any kind of personal relationship. Like they say . . . it's almost like that codependency problem . . .

"When you get fired from a job, the cleaning out of your desk becomes the hardest thing of all. I wish it would just happen behind my back but it can't happen that way. There's other considerations. What assets belong to us, what doesn't belong to us. All those things. There are companies that will come in and say, what's yours, I'll get it out of here, I'll pay—if you have to go that route. I don't know if we want to go that route yet or not. Listen, I wish somebody would come along, come to the rescue. In one way, I'm always the one that has been there to try to, no matter what the situation's been, to try to keep it open. Until I say no, I can't do it anymore, that's what it's going to take for people to wake up. It's just not going to happen. I'm saying now 'cause I'm not getting paid. There's not enough money for me. I'm the last one. And it's been that way for well over a month and a half, two months . . . it's been like piecemeal coming to me.

"It's not that I don't want to stick it out, I just don't see any salvation, any knight in shining armor coming to the rescue. It's happening all over the city, why am I going to be so much different? Places open, they're hot for six or eight months, then the reality sets in. I just don't know.

"Maybe Varick Street is doomed. That's starting to be what I'm thinking. You got S.O.B.'s is dying, you got Heartbreak from what I understand is dinner theater, but now it's going to be the Red Parrot. It's not there.

"It's very depressing to think about this stuff. I wish I could be cold and hard like a corporate executive and say let's cut out the General Motors division in Peoria, Illinois. It's just not that way. It's human beings. I don't see the restaurant anymore, I see the people that work there when I think about it. That's exactly who I see. I don't see the tables and chairs."

Now real tears come forth. Bruce is crying quietly.

"*It's the worst part of thinking about this, is to put people out. I can't tell you what that's like. I really can't. I was up at 4:00 in the* morning 'cause I couldn't sleep, trying to figure it out. You think of things like, maybe we should close the place, wait a month, renegotiate with the landlord, open under another name, but that doesn't solve the basic problems of the place. That there's not enough money, that the location is really rough, that there's nobody walking by the door, and the things I thought could happen, like brunch, and things like that, I don't think can happen over there.

"The economy! I get a kick out of the stock market going high as a kite. That is no barometer of what's going on in the real world. In the beginning people thought things were gonna be rough . . . but I don't even think the recession has really set in yet! That's my honest feeling. People think about the war, all I think that's going to do is bring half a million people back to the United States who aren't going to have jobs.

"So I don't know. I really don't know. I don't know what the future's going to be for—I think that's what has to be here though. I don't want to do it. It's a personal thing. It rips me inside no end to think about it.

"It really does."

A week later he is gone, eight thousand miles away.

/Day by day, hour by hour . . .

The main agenda for April 2, 1991, is to keep the man from Con Ed out, and get everyone else in. See, the man from Con Ed wants to turn off the gas. Something about $500 not paid. A lack of gas can be a serious problem to any restaurant that aspires to serve something other than peanut butter sandwiches.

So the waiters and waitresses are under specific instructions from Terry Quinn, who is holed up this eerily empty spring lunch hour in the basement hideaway office, trying to figure out how to run The Falls by himself, not to admit anyone who looks as though they might be an official representative from Con Edison. This is not as easy as it sounds, since it runs directly counter to the interests of the wait staff to bar potential customers at the door.

Also, how do you spot a utility man? They wear their identity—if not their heart—on their sleeve. So, through The Falls's narrow glass front door, it is often quite impossible to know the identity of a new entry until he or she is well into the bar area. This turns out to be poor planning for a restaurant that fairly quivers every time somebody with a slip of paper makes an entrance.

We're not just talking about gas, either. There's the rent to be paid. And the electric bill. Yes, you're getting the picture. It's darkness at noon.

Down in that office—letters from lawyers staring down at him from the wall, demanding checks for $319.26 and $457.34, threatening legal action, all of them stamped, in big huge red block letters, PAST DUE—Terry Quinn is making a few calls. His ass is on the line, and he knows it. The door stays open or he is royally fucked. To date, Terry has ponied up over $30,000; that includes two grand he put in the week before Bruce went to Thailand—the week Bruce would have closed down the whole damn place, for sure.

Terry is pushing a theory that makes some sense, which is: An open restaurant is worth more than a closed restaurant.

"We shut it, we won't sell it," he is saying. He is muttering, actually. And he is doing that thing he always does with his hair—running his fingers all the way through it, all the way to the back, then smoothing out the back part with his hand. Today he has made it easier on himself by not washing his hair.

"I got three people who want to buy it, and maybe a fourth. This is what you call a turnkey deal. I mean, these are guys who don't want to do anything with the place. They love the place. They love the room. It's a *great* room."

Last night Terry and Patti invited, oh, maybe fifteen people down to kind of fill up the place, see who came, and Patti had a good time. She said to Terry this morning, before he left for work, "I bet you and I could make that place work." But Terry has been thinking about what Patti said, and what she knows, and what she doesn't know. What she knows is that The Falls is a great place, a great room, boy is it pretty at night; but what she doesn't know is, you gotta be there every fucking day and night, and Terry thinks, do I have every day and night to spend at The Falls to make it work? No I do not. And Patti knows that, she's just jumping to the logical conclusion, which is that you could always do better.

You certainly couldn't do worse. That's for sure. On Saturday night ten people came in for dinner.

Friday was Passover, Sunday was Easter, that was the excuse this time. You don't have to be Jewish not to eat at The Falls on a Saturday night.

In between thoughts on the future of the restaurant—a future that Terry will not estimate at lasting more than the next twenty-four hours—he is dialing the phone number of Patrick Fahey, his partner at Peggy Sue's, who wants to buy out his share of the nightclub. He is getting a busy signal, so he keeps dialing and dialing. He even tries the redial function on the phone, but he can't get it to work.

"I thought these redial things . . ." he mutters. That thing with his hair must have something to do with petty annoyances; anyway, there he goes again. He wants Patrick to buy the share. He won't admit it, but he probably needs the money. Dialing dialing dialing . . . the number's busy. "I don't get it, he's got call waiting." More fingers through hair. Is his scar growing, or is it just the bright neon light in here?

Wendy comes in with a cash-stuffed envelope. She places it in front of Terry on the desk. A few moments later, she picks it back up. "You know," she says to herself, since only *she* knows exactly what was in that envelope, "I need $100 for a bank at the bar." So she disappears out the door, up the stairs and out to the old-fashioned stainless steel cash register behind the bar, where she deposits the contents of the envelope so that the evening bartenders will have five ones for a five.

/Terry has a new obsession. Rebecca, the only female bartender who has been there since Day One. She is not his kind of bartender. She is a successful bartender with a large personal following, a fact to which he replies, "That's exactly the problem."

Ever since Rebecca joined the staff of The Falls, there has been a management sentiment against her. Not a groundswell of sentiment, but enough to undercut her position. She had been recommended highly by Henry Hauck, who knew her from other nights at other bars; he described her as a fucking great bartender. This cannot be disputed. Whatever a fucking great bartender is, that's what she is. Which is to say, she's cool. She knows how to smile at the right moment and for the right number of moments.

It is necessary for a female bartender—if she wants to achieve any success at all in the world—to make a certain kind of eye contact with male customers. Bars are dramatically overpopulated by men. This is not one of those facts you can confirm with the Census Bureau; you do, however, need to go to a bar, where you can do your own quick calculations. There will, occasionally, be women, perhaps even lots of women, at a bar, but this does not alter the fact that men do more drinking at bars than women. A woman bartender finds this statistic works to her advantage whether she is attractive or not.

Rebecca is not what most men would describe as a particularly attractive woman. She is in her mid-thirties. Her success as a bartender is not, in fact, a mystery; it is the illusion of mystery—the raising of questions, some of them that may never be answered. Does she like me? Will she smile? Can I make her laugh? May I call her by her name? If I come back tomorrow, will she remember that I like my brandy on the rocks, my beer in a glass? Will she stop me if I drink too much? Does she care about me—*really* care?

You will never know what she is thinking. Sure, she will smile; you will feel deeply rewarded when you see it coming. She has a rich, hearty laugh when you really amuse her—and she is easily amused. She will, on occasion, even lean across the bar toward you to share an intimate thought or two. You will feel honored, legitimately so, because there is something real about her. She has been on the other side of the bar, you *know* that; she has drunk too much, partied too much, spent too much. She has used alcohol to escape, to fantasize. That is the ultimate secret you share with her; you are paying her to make you say, it's okay. Go ahead. Have fun.

"She's not my kind of bartender."

Yes, yes, Terry, we know. You have models and actresses hanging on your every muscle. Bartenders are not your style, are they? Hell, you've been a bartender. You know the deal. At the end of the night, someone is waiting for you. The girl most likely to exceed.

But he is thinking, what difference does it make? Here we are, on the verge of selling, or dying—what the difference is, no one can really explain—so what the hell. Rebecca will remain where she is.

The phone rings.

"Falls."

"Monday night at 8:00? How many?" He jots down a name, a number and Monday on the back of an envelope. "Thank you."

Holy Jesus! A reservation for five days from now!

"I didn't know what to tell 'em . . . maybe there won't be a restaurant here next Monday." He laughs and punches twelve on the phone intercom. "Cassandra, we got a reservation for next Monday night at 8:00, two people. Levin. Put it in the book." Pause. "Yeah, planning way in advance." Laughs. Hangs up.

Who are these people? Don't they know you could waltz into The Falls any night of the week, anytime, and get the table of your choice? If you hurry, that is.

/Last week, The Falls had a gross revenue of approximately $6,000.

If you assume that the average person spent $20 in the place, either on food or drinks, that means three hundred people walked in the door.

The Falls is open six nights a week and five days; so we are talking here about roughly thirty customers per meal.

If you include the bar, the more accurate figure would be somewhere around two dozen. Maybe less.

And yet: The Falls is open for business. In fact, nothing much has changed about the place. The service still sucks. As Terry mopes around the office downstairs—dialing and dialing; that damn phone!—two customers at table 10 leave in a huff; the kitchen has failed to serve their lunch promptly enough. The Falls has been serving lunch for over a year; their kitchen staff presumably knows the importance of speedy cooking for men and women on the go. And yet, with barely a handful of customers clustered around the corner banquettes, The Falls still cannot serve food properly.

The news of this tragedy is delivered to Terry along with a plate of rigatoni, which he desperately wishes were on the dinner menu as well as lunch. "We need *more* pastas," he mutters. But it turns out that at The Falls, even the *news* is delivered poorly.

"Ten people just left because their food was late," Wendy tells Terry as she clears away the office desk to make room for his rigatoni.

"Ten people? I was just upstairs . . . there weren't ten people up there."

"Oh . . . maybe it was table 10."

Maybe. Definitely. Their waiter tried to speed up the kitchen but failed. Instead, hoping to salvage some positive vibes from the episode, he gave the table a free round of cappuccinos and dessert. So they will come back, maybe, if there's a place to come back to, that is.

Terry is beginning to comprehend that any gesture that extends beyond tomorrow is rather empty. Which is why—when a phone call comes during lunch, asking the management of The Falls to make a generous donation of two free dinners for a charity raffle—Terry quickly agrees to the deal.

"They'll be pretty surprised when they get here for their free meal and there's no restaurant!" He is gloating, and why not? It's fun to give things away, and it's easy when you're doing it at no personal cost. Terry Quinn has a generous spirit to begin with, and—no doubt about it—were The Falls a raging success, he would still be giving meals away to charity. But there is something perversely funny about all this, and he is smart enough to recognize it, and he is sweet enough to laugh about it.

Hell, it's his money, right?

All told, Terry's $30,000 investment in The Falls isn't really much by restaurant standards, but you have to realize—at least one third of that was intended solely to keep the door open. For all his financial success over the last five years with Peggy Sue's, the guy has three children to clothe and feed. One of them is his and Patti's little baby girl, Emmelyn. The last thing Terry needs is a wailing restaurant to pacify!

The rigatoni is good. Of this much Terry is certain. However, it is made with Italian sausage. This fact may thwart Terry's plan to keep it on the menu for more than a few hours at most. "We only got a little bit of sausage left," replies Patrick, one of the cooks who took over for Brian, to Terry's praise for the pasta, "maybe enough for two or three orders."

Oh.

Sausage is meat, and meat is expensive. Many of the people who sell food to The Falls do so despite mounting debts. They have become tacit investors in the restaurant; they are continuing to deliver food to The Falls so that it can remain open . . . so that people will come there and buy food . . . so that The Falls will be successful again . . . so that there will be money enough to pay them. It is a cycle that keeps many restaurants open well past their apparent breaking point.

In healthy times, of course, it all works differently. Food is bought on credit—as though the kitchen slapped down its Visa card every time the meat man came around. Bills come in once a month. The accountant pays said bills. As a restaurant begins its decline—when the food purveyor sees that his bills are not being paid, his orders are dropping, both key signals of distress—he often chooses to switch to COD payment, which means, I give you meat, you give me money.

This is what happened at The Falls. This is what happens when you open with a huge burst of overconfidence. You pay your bills. Meaning you only consider how much you're spending *after* you've spent it.

Big mistake.

"If we had been COD right from the start . . ." muses Michael Fitzpatrick a few days after he quit The Falls, finally, after the weeks and months of torturous negotiations with disgruntled bill collectors became too much, "if we had done that, then maybe we'd . . . sorry, *they'd* have more money now."

But now they cannot go back and change. They must deal instead with the piles of paper that surround Terry Quinn and his rigatoni and his Day-At-A-Glance: bills bills bills. Bills that will never be paid.

Letters from lawyers that will be ignored. Posted on the wall over Terry's head is a letter from Andrew Kulak of the firm of Kulak and Kulak. He wants $400 *right now*. "You will send us a check immediately . . ." he writes.

No we will not, reads the expression on Terry Quinn's face. No we will most certainly not.

What is going to happen now? Terry remains calm. He chews his food carefully, like a good boy. He knows that no matter what happens in the next several days, The Falls will not exist much longer. It cannot. It owes too much money to survive—close to $300,000, Terry says, maybe even more if you think of every little penny. This leaves The Falls with a distinct lack of options.

Two options, to be exact.

One is to sell the restaurant. This is really the only preferred option. If The Falls is sold—meaning that a purchaser would get the lease, the fixtures, the phones, the kitchen, basically everything except the liquor license—then Bruce and Terry could use the purchase money to pay off those horrid debts.

The advantage of this arrangement is that it would be the one most likely to save Bruce and Terry from the fiery IRS dragon. You see, a major portion of that debt (how much nobody really knows, probably not even The Falls's trusted accountant, Frank) is Tax Money. Some of it is Income Tax Money. Some of it is Tax Money for employees' Social Security. (FICA tax—something every employer is required to pay into Social Security, on behalf of all employees.) All of it has not been paid for quite a while—perhaps since the onset of winter. Some former employees have started calling about it; hey, it's tax time—the law requires employers to send W-2 forms by the end of January, and The Falls hasn't gotten around to doing that, either. Rumor has it a couple of former waiters have reported The Falls to the Department of Labor or the IRS. Anyway, somebody has been calling, Official Business. Not paying your taxes is a big problem, or at least it can be; eventually, if the IRS or state tax authority chooses to chase down its money, liens could be put on the property of the principals.

"A lot of money is owed to a lot of people," was the plaintive sigh of someone who knows a lot about The Falls's tragic debt situation. "But you don't really *have* to pay other people. They can sue you but that can take years. They don't bother. But the IRS has some legal clout. They can nail you. So The Falls *needs* that purchase money to pay off the IRS and save themselves. If they close and don't get it, then they'll have to get the tax money someplace else."

That is something no one likes to think about. Least of all Terry.

"We'll sell," he says.

Yes, three people have expressed interest in the place. One of them is a principal in the New York Hard Rock Cafe, or is it one of those Hard Rocks in Sweden or someplace? Terry isn't sure. His name is Marshall. According to Terry, he has a three-star chef ready to put in place, an idea for a certain type of cuisine, a crowd he can guarantee. Too bad he can't get a liquor license right away, but he'd be crazy to let the place close. Once you turn out the lights . . . You can't mess with the minds of the masses. They need to know where they can get their food, and when a restaurant shuts down, they *know*.

The other two people . . . one of them doesn't like the kitchen, thinks it's too small. The other isn't right, either. What are their names again? Terry can't quite remember. But yes, *three* people are interested: better hurry! Offer ends soon! Terry understands well the principle of excitement, of heat; he knew how to get people in the door of The Falls, he damn well ought to know how to get people out! You keep saying it, over and over and over: Three people are interested. Three people, three people, three people. A bidding war . . . who knows? The price might even go up!

This is not high-stakes poker for Terry. He has already lost his $30,000 bet on The Falls. If it sells, the first thing a new owner will do is change the name and the image. The whole idea of The Falls will disappear. No, this is more like a valiant late-night attempt to avoid leaving the Caesars Palace blackjack table empty-handed at 5:00 in the morning. You are asking yourself, can I turn my $5 chips into $100 chips? Is this dealer on my side or not? Can you ever make money gambling? Oh, the questions; it's a good thing Terry's head is so big. Maybe the pain never reaches the surface.

Anyway, Terry has worked out a sales arrangement with Marshall from the Hard Rock, with whom the figure of $100,000 has been bandied about.

Here's the deal.

"He'll loan me $100,000," Terry says. "I'll take the money and spend it—paying back the debts, the taxes, you know. Then in about three, four weeks, he'll foreclose on the loan. I won't have the money to pay him back. So he'll get the restaurant and I'll get the money, and it'll be clean. There won't be any debts and he gets a clean slate."

That's what it's all about. Pass the rigatoni while we still got the noodles. Nobody wants to buy bills. And it's legal, too!

The other option facing The Falls is to close.

On the surface, you would think closing a restaurant might be an attractive option to one in crisis. After all, it immediately stops the bleeding. No more restaurant, no more expenses. The Big Four—Rent, Phone, Lights and Gas—no longer matter. In the case of The Falls, you don't even have to turn out the lights when you leave; chances are this service will have been provided by the utility company. (When and if The Falls decides to close, you can bet they won't bother to send in their final bill payment to Con Edison.)

But closing the doors means several things to a restaurant, none of them pretty. The most important result of closing a restaurant is the immediate loss of leverage. Suddenly your restaurant is merely your landlord's space. A potential buyer need no longer seek the privilege of buying the place; he then need only give the landlord a buzz. No leverage, no money, no disbursements. No bills get paid. No investors get their money back. No, no, no . . . that is what it means to close. No nothing.

This is not the preferred option.

To close a restaurant is to close your options.

"We close," Terry mutters, "we lose it all."

/Obviously more subtle issues prey on Terry's mind, like the small matter of pride. After lo these many months—who knows how many Page Six items later?—Terry Quinn's name has come to be closely associated with The Falls, perhaps even more so than Bruce's, for the simple reason that he made it so. He courted the columns, and though he often objected to their content he seemed to delight in their ability to promote. A recent flurry of items in Cindy Adams's column in the *Post*— ones he pursued after Danny Aiello night, hoping to "correct" the misinformation of earlier reports she'd published about the Paramount bar that was Terry's next project—were allegedly screwing him up.

On the morning of Danny Aiello night, Cindy had this to report in her *Post* column about Terry's plans:

■

ACTOR **Matt Dillon,** who owns assorted watering holes, got the go for W. 46th's Paramount Hotel bar. It's six months' free rent, half a mil in decor, open by April, strictly booze—no food. The money man is a real-estate broker.

■

This item highly displeased Terry. For one thing, he wasn't mentioned. For another, Matt Dillon was mentioned. Matt doesn't like being mentioned. Terry does. Also, the item was not entirely accurate in dates, amounts and so on. So Terry sought her out for a correction that night, when Cindy arrived at The Falls, and a correction was promised.

It followed three weeks later in her column.

■

I RECENTLY reported every brilliant breathtaking detail of the brand new barroom to be operated by **Matt Dillon** & Co. and to be built at **Ian Schrager**'s brand new Paramount Hotel on W. 46th. Comes a minor snag. Ian so far ain't getting a liquor license thus Matt so far ain't getting a barroom.

■

No correction there; only some mistakes about Ian Schrager; it's not his bar, it's Terry's bar. But the real problem for Terry is that, you know, those guys at the Liquor Authority, they read the *Post*, they clip that shit and put it all in your file. Terry's sure of that.

If he's right—seems doubtful, but okay—the Liquor Authority has been kept busy recently by the wild mass onslaught of Matt Dillon profiles by the voracious entertainment press. Since early March, our handsome young investor has graced the covers of *Interview*, *GQ* and *American Film*. He may not like interviews, but he clearly loves to say cheese. Inside the pages of *Premiere* and *Elle*, among others, articles on Matt have also appeared. He is promoting his new movie, *A Kiss Before Dying*, which is finally coming out (Or is it? It's now weeks after these stories appeared, and *still* no sign of it in your local theater), and this is what happens when you have spent as many years as Matt has avoiding the press. They want you even more. Matt does not respond particularly well to interviews, or even questions, so these articles—profiles would be too substantial a word to describe them—fail to offer any real insights into The Man Behind the Chin.

But why oh why does Matt so hate to be asked about The Falls? When *Premiere* asked him about The Falls, Matt practically jumped off the roof of a building. What's his problem, anyway? Robert De Niro doesn't complain about *his* restaurant. One wonders whether Matt has somehow gotten wind of the fact that The Falls is in trouble. Any man of intelligence, after all, might choose to sever his public ties with The Falls at this particular moment in its history.

Is it such a blot on an actor's résumé to have his investment go sour? Must be. Terry can think of no other reason for Matt to be so positively ridiculous about The Falls. You can tell Terry was pissed, he even blabbed on to *GQ* about it.

The *GQ* piece by Lucy Kaylin went into some detail about the whole matter. It identified Bruce as one of Dillon's close "pals," along with Terry Quinn, who is referred to in the piece as a Manhattan club owner. After reporting that Dillon loves New York, and is "stuck on its air of edgy sophistication," Kaylin went on:

"Of course, Dillon can be tediously elusive when it comes to other, seemingly innocuous aspects of his life, such as the fact that he's an investor in The Falls. 'He doesn't want to be known as someone who invests in restaurants—I think he thinks it cheapens him,' says Quinn. 'Like, it means Matt Dillon can't hack it as an actor.' "

Quinn went on to tell Kaylin that Dillon wasn't going to settle down with his then-current girlfriend, Emma Woollard. "He's not ready," Quinn was quoted as saying. "It's not soup yet." One wonders if Terry has perhaps been hanging around restaurants too long.

Now it's been a couple of weeks since *GQ* came out, and Terry is relieved that Matt is holed up in Seattle making a movie called *Singles,* and not calling him to complain about his quotes in *GQ*.

Still, Terry doesn't need these problems. Christ, the other day he lost the keys to his navy blue four-door Dodge Lancer, and it screwed up the whole day. At this point he can't afford to lose whole days. Time is money. And there is no money left.

/Money flowed at The Falls. Into a computerized cash register at the bar one day. Out the next in an envelope for deposit at the bank. And then there were expenses. Things that had to be paid for in cash.

In the days that preceded the opening of The Falls, there were numerous expenses. The need for cash arose. Food. Flowers. Plates. Menus. Matches. Cleaning. Five hundred dollars here, $800 there, $1,200 here . . . so much so that on the day before The Falls opened, there existed some question whether there was enough money to make it to the opening night. It fell to Terry to fill the gap. He pleasantly forked over $2,000 more, allowing The Falls to have a few crisp new bills in its cash drawer as opening night approached.

Once The Falls opened, the cash flow got easier, of course. People paid in cash. For the first week or so, before American Express got around to approving charges at The Falls, the restaurant had a cash-only policy. That turned out to be handy, because cash played a crucial role in those opening days; it gave the owners the illusion of success. They'd opened the restaurant, after all, put sweat equity into the place. Was the money not theirs to take?

Cash! In the opening month of March 1990, The Falls took in $109,483.14—close to half of that in cash, the rest in credit cards and house accounts. Which amounted to cash—you could turn an American Express charge into cash overnight in New York City, and The Falls most certainly did. If you go by the *Zagat Guide*'s per-person estimate of $32 for a meal at The Falls, that means 3,421 people sat down to eat there in The Falls's first month, more than a hundred a day. Pretty impressive, huh?

Especially when you look at the books.

The Falls kept at least two important logs of its finances: a cash disbursement journal and a log of daily cash receipts. In the case of receipts, the word "cash" is a misnomer, really; those records included credit card charges and house accounts, so they included all the money coming in to The Falls as payment for food and drink. The cash disbursement journal was a different story. There, The Falls kept a record only of the cash spent and recorded on paper—which does not necessarily equal the cash amounts that actually changed hands on a day-to-day basis.

An examination of that journal for The Falls's first eleven months— if anyone has been keeping track of these last few disastrous months, there are no charts to show for it—reveals exactly when the cash left The Falls, and with whom.

According to the column in the chart entitled BRUCE'S DRAWINGS, which refers specifically to the cash Bruce took from The Falls's cash revenues, Bruce took a total of $29,477.02 from the cash drawer during the first eleven months of The Falls's life. That comes to an average of $2,679.73 a month. Of course, he didn't draw that much every month. In the early days he went for larger chunks; on May 11, back when things were bubbling over, he pulled out $3,000. Later, as things got rougher, he lowered his draw to $200 here, $300 there.

Bruce was paid a salary, too—of $700 a week. He made many long-distance calls at The Falls. He ate most of his meals at The Falls. It was his second home, essentially, and he treated it as such, the way most restaurant proprietors do.

Bruce's explanation of all this was simple and forthright. "I signed a slip for every dime I took out of The Falls. A lot of that was to pay for bills and expenses. I was always stopping at the store to pick things up. It wasn't like I was taking all the money and putting it in my pocket. And the fact is, with my salary and the cash put together, it came to something around $50,000 a year salary—total." And as for his meals being paid for, he says: "You end up paying for that in the end."

Employees at The Falls got paid much the same manner as Bruce—a combination of on-the-books salary and off-the-books cash. The only difference was that they did not control the amount of their draw. Everyone at The Falls—from Bruce to the lowliest dishwasher—took some salary in cash. This is standard operating procedure at all restaurants, and The Falls was no different. Under the category LABOR KITCHEN, the cash disbursement journal recorded more than $5,000 a month in cash going to the chef and cooks and dishwashers—reaching a high in June of 1990 of $9,193.45, when nearly a dozen different people worked various shifts to feed the burgeoning crowds. LABOR SERVICE, which covered waiters, waitresses and busboys, varied wildly from month to month—from a high in March of 1990, $8,369.50, to a low in July of less than one third that amount, only $2,565.17.

The odd thing is that no one's salaries were all that high; Michael Fitzpatrick never earned more than $600 a week. The chef made $1,000, the cooks $500 apiece, the dishwashers $400.

Then there was food and liquor. Always a major drain on the cash supply. The first month food costs were dramatically high—more than $15,000 in cash went to pay purveyors, with another $2,600 for booze. By April the kitchen got the numbers down a little—to $7,600 for food and $790 for liquor. Those numbers stabilized for several months, until November of 1990 when they jumped up again. That was when all the food purveyors stopped taking checks and stopped sending bills. Everything came COD, and that resulted in a December cash disbursement of $18,300 for food and $6,900 for liquor, and only slightly less for January.

Cash went out as fast as it came in.

If not faster.

And by the spring of 1991, there was no money left to follow.

/Nightfall on a hot Thursday night. New Yorkers crawl out of their apartments, two by two. They have their haunts, all of them, and this is the night to haunt.

It is hot . . . very hot . . . perhaps *too* hot.

Every year there is one of these nights. The first hot night. You walk down any strip of New York street, and the entire rat-through-the-python population appears to have had the same idea at the same time: Let's Go Out. Let's get out of this stinkin' python and get some *action*. Okay! Let's let *them* pay for the air conditioning, and we'll pay for the food. The young couples dodge each other, jumping ahead, looking for an edge. Nobody wants to be last on line. It's a two-hour wait at Carmine's. They are packed as tight as sardines at the bar, though it's possible sardines have more elbow room inside their little tins.

Daylight Savings Time is still a few days away, thank God. So it's dark out. Black is beautiful. Nobody wants to go out in the light.

The sun sets around 7:00, and, yes, even at The Falls, more than the usual number of people have shown up, including one customer who has chosen the bar at The Falls to privately celebrate his tenth anniversary. That is how long he has been living in New York City, and it is an occasion that no one he knows would have much interest in sharing. Even his wife has begged off. So he has taken his usual seat at the bar—yes, he is a regular; yes, he has his favorite seat; no, he has no one regular drink, he is torn constantly among the hundreds of choices this bar, any bar, affords him—and is now spending an extra moment or two pondering his drink.

He is happy that it is such a warm night. He is happy to be thirty-five years old, living in New York City, and with enough discretionary income to order himself—damnit, it's a special occasion!—a glass of champagne.

"I'll have a glass of your finest champagne," the customer says. Rebecca is on duty, and she knows this regular to tend toward beers and wines. Red wines and Rolling Rocks, to be precise. He has been to The Falls, oh, too many times; and though he's never ordered a glass of champagne in this establishment, he knows they pour Perrier-Jouët, a perfectly lovely French champagne, and he is more than happy to pay the $8 for the privilege.

"Well . . ." Rebecca says, with an I've-got-bad-news-and-bad-news expression on her face. "We recently switched champagnes. Let me show you what we're serving."

She walks slowly down the long bar, delaying as long as possible. The customer can sense that there has been a quiet but perceptible change in the quality of his bar; still—the champagne! Something must be sacred.

Rebecca has returned, and with a flourish she holds the bottom of the bottle against her left forearm, so that the customer may see it. It *is the* way sommeliers hold a bottle in a fine French restaurant. It is not the way bartenders hold a bottle of swill at The Falls. Perhaps this is Rebecca's way of diminishing the shock of the news: The Falls is now selling, by the glass, a "champagne" known as Cordoniu Brut.

Isn't that the crap everybody got drunk on in college?

In case there is any doubt about the swill-like properties of this beverage, consider that pasted on the bottle is a liquor store sticker price of $4.99—right there on the bottle. The customer must pass on this champagne. He is a man of some standards when it comes to champagne, and this is not champagne. He's not one of those fussy oenophiles who believe that "champagne" refers only to the French region where champagne grapes are grown. He has been known to ridicule just those very people. It's just that bad champagne is not something you want to drink when you're happy, or have any intention of becoming happy, and that is his situation.

And so he declines the offer and switches to Heineken.

"A wise decision," Rebecca says.

It is possible, of course, to chart the decline of a restaurant in customers served, dollars earned, bills paid; and of course those numbers have declined, make that *plummeted*, at The Falls. On the opening Saturday night in March of 1990, more than two hundred people came in for dinner; last Saturday, thirteen months later, less than a dozen turned up. Last week's total revenues for The Falls were maybe $7,000—the place now needs a bare minimum of $12,500 a week to keep the doors open. On graph paper, the customer-per-night chart of The Falls looks something like a Black Diamond slope in Aspen.

But remember, The Falls is still open.

You don't notice, right away, that the huge bouquet of flowers once brightening the back of the bar is no longer there; it cost $200 a week, roughly $200 a week more than The Falls could afford.

Or that cheap Italian house wines have given way to even cheaper California vintages.

Or that Amstel light beer has been replaced at the bar by Coors Light.

Or that matchboxes have been replaced by business cards. (What exactly are you supposed to do with a restaurant's business card?)

Or that once-fluffy and coveted mashed potatoes, made from new potatoes and with a minimum of butter, now taste greasy and look just a little too gray.

Or that the French onion soup is prepared days in advance, refrigerated and then reheated when someone orders it, with a soggy piece of bread floating near the surface under a tiny sliver of cheese.

Or that the vegetables now consist of a couple of fat, ugly carrots on a side plate.

Or that the heavy, hard-bound reservation book of 1990 has been replaced, for 1991, by a spiral-bound notebook one quarter the size, lying unnoticed most nights as the maître d' waits patiently by the door for walk-ins.

Or that the red, green and blue Christmas lights strung up over the restaurant's gray awning remain there in April, an eerie image of an earlier, happier time.

It is the only sign, from a distance, that The Falls is alive at all.

THOSE LIPS, THOSE ISLEYS

THIRTY

It is April 15, 1991. A Monday night. Always slow. And taxes are due at midnight tonight, remember. Ordinarily, that would be the excuse. Yes, that's it! Everyone is home paying taxes!

Always a bad night for restaurants, right? Right? Right?

No.

It is too late for excuses.

By 8:35 P.M., the last meal was served. Five people ate at The Falls tonight. Three girls—pretty girls, actually; Terry Quinn noticed that right away—drank at the bar for a little while. All together they spent a total of $380.67. Most of that, $262.53 to be exact, was charged on American Express.

That left a grand total of $118.14 in cash.

Terry Quinn has been here since 7:00 tonight. That's early for him. It enabled him to get a perfect parking space, right outside the front door. He is wearing a black-and-white sport jacket with shoulder pads and a T-shirt. Nice pants, too. He dressed up thinking people might come in. He is slightly bitter about that. He doesn't like to dress up if he doesn't have to.

At 8:35 The Falls was completely empty. The word "dead" comes to mind; though you might try to dismiss it, it lingers there a while, too.

272

For a half hour, not a single person passed through the front door. No one sat at the bar. No one lingered over coffee. Just two waitresses talking to each other; a busboy staring off into space; two cooks and a dishwasher watching the Mets lose; Wendy, now the manager, who stopped in to say hello; and Terry Quinn.

Bruce is, of course, still in Thailand. He called to say he'd be staying a little longer. Terry doesn't care anymore. I'll run it myself, he thinks. Let him eat Pad Thai.

The subject of taxes is raised. "Maybe we should invite all our former employees down here and tell them we've got their W-2 forms," Terry says. "*That* would fill the place."

Terry walks around to the back of the bar, where he has put a large Fortunoff bag with CDs and tapes in it. Bruce is away; the mice can play. He reaches in the bag and pulls out a cassette of *The Isley Brothers Greatest Hits, Volume One.* Within seconds, the usual mellow sounds disappear and are replaced by the funky jive of "That Lady, Parts I and II."

The waitresses tap their feet.

The bartender mouths the words.

Terry orders a Caesar salad and a plate of rigatoni.

At 9:00, a man walks in. He is youngish, maybe thirty. Nicely dressed in a gray sweater and jeans. He takes the corner seat at the bar and orders a martini. As the bartender mixes it, the man goes downstairs to use the bathroom. He returns after a minute and starts sipping his drink rather quickly. Meanwhile someone else walks in. A trend! This new customer—also male, also in his thirties, not quite as well dressed but does anyone care?—orders a Coors Light. Two people are now drinking at the bar. This is a very exciting development.

"It's Your Thing" comes on the sound system. Those lips, those Isleys! "I used to hate this kind of music when I was a kid and now I love it," Terry says. He is referring to the funky rhythms of black groups like the Isley Brothers, and to their musical antecedents. For instance, he has also developed a strong affection for the stylings of Sam Cooke. His albums are also among those in the Fortunoff bag.

While everyone else bounces to the beat, Terry is drowning his sorrows in Poland Spring bottled water. The days of red wine are over.

Nothing is said. Nothing is done. Nothing can be done.

What is the matter here? The question hangs. People walk past the door and they see that no one is inside and they walk past. The ultimate nightmare. Or they sit at the bar for one drink, and leave.

Where are all those pretty girls when you need 'em? Another question worth pondering. Plenty of time to ponder at The Falls. This is the Ponderosa.

Wendy is the first to suggest closing the doors. "Maybe we should close," she says to Terry. She is sitting at the Primo Table while he is playing Bruce at the audio controls. It is not so bold a suggestion, really—even though at 9:30 in the evening, when she says it, it does strike one as a rather early time to lock up for the night. Had she asked, "Why are we open?" she might have unwittingly raised a more pertinent question, one that only Terry could answer, and perhaps not even he.

Terry cannot answer her statement, so he says nothing, because Terry is not one for wasting words. She waits a few long beats.

"I guess it doesn't cost us any more to stay open," Wendy says. Terry remains silent. "I mean, everybody's here and working and all . . ."

Terry has returned to his seat at the end of the bar—the one Bruce likes, by the end near the service area and the tape deck. He has picked the wrong time to do so, because the Isleys album has just come to an end, and no tape has been put in to follow it—which means something almost unheard of at The Falls, totally so when Bruce is present: dead silence.

While the music plays at The Falls, there is always hope. The sound system is designed so that music bounces off the walls, reverberating back and forth, and, on its journey, passing through one's soul. Even during dinner. What music does elsewhere it does better here. There's so much *more* of it. Is that the reason? Or is it that it matches the spirit of the room, enhancing it, enlarging it somehow? Who knows. Whatever music means, its absence means more.

When the music stops at The Falls—particularly on a night when there are no customers at all in the place—there is a feeling of death so powerful and all-consuming that you want to throw a sheet over the place and walk away. This is true despite the fact that on this particular night, when the music stops, no one makes the slightest motion toward the components. For at least a minute or so, absolutely no music is being played and boy—is this strange! It would not surprise anyone if the phone rang (though it might wake up the busboy) and it was Bruce from Thailand calling to say, FLIP THE FUCKING TAPE!

Finally, Terry gets his butt over there and flips the tape. Life has been restored. The sheet has been removed. Code Blue has been canceled.

. . .

One of the guys from R.E.M. almost came into The Falls tonight. Almost, of course, being a meaningless concept in this business. But Leo tried, he really did. He's been their chauffeur all day—drove him and his three pals to a Yankee game, the season opener, and then tried to help 'em decide where to eat. First choice was Peter Luger, the nineteenth-century steakhouse under the Williamsburg Bridge in Brooklyn, an excellent choice for a group of hungry men in search of cow flesh. Perhaps for that reason, Luger's is not easily cowed by celebrity, and told the group that they would be welcome for dinner at 10:00 P.M.

This being too late for a 1990s rock star, the group then settled on the Odeon, after rejecting Leo's suggestion of The Falls. They opted for a drink first at El Teddy's, a hip Mexican joint near Odeon and The Falls, leaving Leo some time for a drink himself. He dropped them off and took the limo over to The Falls, where he is having a drink with his fireman friend Terry Quinn. Leo is a former fireman himself.

It seems that limo drivers can steer a certain amount of restaurant business—in that some celebrities, visiting New York and lacking the contacts necessary to command superior tables at peak hours, depend on their drivers for help. Leo has done this on several occasions, including a recent experience with a world-renowned rock star who could not get a table at Il Cantinori, a chic Village Italian place, until Leo dropped the name of a mutual friend from the Fire Department ("Oh, is *Pat* with you?" the maître d' exclaimed) and swung a table immediately.

So Leo is sitting at the bar of The Falls and having a drink. He realizes now just how silly his suggestion was. He is a pleasant enough chap, really . . . but he's not enough to save The Falls, and he knows it.

/Eventually even Leo has to leave. He does have a job to do.

Now The Falls is empty.

Terry knows about this neat new bar on East 15th Street.

"Wanna go?" he says limply to Wendy and Susannah, another waitress working tonight.

"Now?" Susannah asks weakly . . . wondering if he means *now*, as in, *Let's lock these doors and go party.*

"Yeah."

A smile is shared among the three. No one will know. Bruce is in Thailand. Fuck it. Let's get out of here!

All right, ten minutes later the doors are locked and Wendy and

Susannah are piled into Terry's car. The Falls is shut tight at ten minutes past ten. And as they speed away toward their destination, each of them knows that it will not make a damn bit of difference to anyone in the world that it is closed.

They get to the bar at around 10:30. Terry knows the bartender, naturally, another old friend who used to know this guy and that guy. Jesus, how does he keep track of it all? It's a decrepit old tavern that has little in the way of charm, and yet tons of it.

On the TV set above the bar, they are showing *Last Tango in Paris*. A good-looking young man is reading a hardcover copy of *Light in August* by William Faulkner. Terry orders a glass of wine.

"Nice place," he says to no one in particular.

IT SHOULD HAVE BEEN

ROAST BEEF SANDWICHES

THIRTY-ONE

On the first day of May, Landlord Richard Maltz and Tenant Terry Quinn had it out.

According to Terry, Maltz played it tougher than he ever had. [AUTHOR'S NOTE: Maltz had previously declined to discuss his conversations with The Falls.] "Terry, when I saw you the other night, I didn't know that you didn't pay last week's rent or this week's rent. I wouldn't have been so nice."

"Oh," Terry replied in his usual understated way, "I thought you were just being a nice guy."

"I'm not a nice guy when it comes to other people's money," he said. "I'm a nice guy with my own money."

The purpose of Maltz's call was to get Terry to sign a stipulation, a legal agreement that would essentially allow Maltz to throw The Falls out without going to court first. Terry doesn't want to sign it. The main reason is that he is already in violation of the stipulation—so by signing it, he would merely be giving Maltz immediate rights to throw him out.

"Look," Terry said, "if I don't sell the place, I'm just going to walk, and you're going to lose the thirty." He is referring to the $30,000 in back rent Maltz won't get if The Falls closes. They actually owe

$45,000 in back rent, but Maltz would keep the $16,000 they put down fourteen months ago as a security deposit.

"Get the stipulation signed," Maltz insisted, "and give me the money tonight, I'll be there at 7:00 P.M."

Terry called him back later that afternoon.

"Listen, I'm not going to be there," Terry said. "I've been thinking about it, and why should I, first of all, sign a stipulation? That would be stupid. That'd make it easier for you to throw me out of there. Second of all, why should I give you the rent if I'm going to leave? If I'm going to walk away from the place and my investment, why should I go out of my way to pay you?"

They went back and forth awhile; still no resolution. Terry continued to try to reason with Maltz.

"I tried to be a nice guy, Bruce wanted me to strip the place clean, have an auctioneer come in there and just take all your stuff that doesn't belong to us, and sell it."

"I'd throw him in jail," Maltz replied.

Terry said, "I'm sure that's the least of our problems. You suing us for selling some stuff."

Maltz said he knew Terry was trying to be a nice guy. They both knew Terry was scrambling. He'd told potential buyers of The Falls that they had to straighten out the landlord before they had a deal. And Terry said they agreed to do that. But they're kinda dragging their feet and he was trying to put a flame under their ass. The longer I'm open, Terry thought, the more likely the marshals will come in and nickel and dime me to death. A thousand dollars here, a thousand dollars there . . . I don't want to pay it. I'd rather Wendy keep the money.

The other day Wendy from Ireland had become the manager, at least unofficially. Wendy had taken over the job because, to be perfectly honest, there was really nobody else.

So finally Terry said to Maltz, "Listen, meet me at 9:30."

Maltz said, "I'm through with you, we're through."

Terry knew that he wasn't through with Maltz. "I don't trust you," Terry said, meaning he worried that Maltz would simply shut the place down and throw him out.

"I'm a man of my word," Maltz said, "I wouldn't do that."
Maltz added, "You gave me your word you would sign that stipulation."

"I just don't think it would be prudent to sign a stipulation," Terry said. "Come in tonight and I'll give you the $1,500, I'm not going to sign the stipulation. If it makes it easier for you, when I leave I'll sign a stipulation. But I want to go over another option. Suppose I form a new corporation. Would you be willing to assign the lease to my new corporation if I straightened you out with the rent?"

Sure, Maltz replied. But he asked: Why would you want to do that?

"I think the space could work," Terry said. He then explained about his roast beef idea.

"A place that I grew up in Brooklyn with was a kind of a roast beef sandwich place, it's called Brendan & Carr, it was on the corner of Avenue U and Nostrand Avenue," Terry went on later, after Maltz said he'd support the idea and hung up. The concept was still percolating, and Terry was all fired up to talk about it.

"They just served roast beef sandwiches, that's all they did. Roast beef, french fries and some hamburgers. It was easy—it was a place you went to eat. It was a small, corner place. But they served the best roast beef sandwiches. Everything was perfect. The rolls were soft, and the gravy was poured on top, it was really a nice little place. I'm saying, I never heard of such a place in Manhattan. It was special. That's all we would do. And I'm thinking maybe if I serve creamed spinach and home fries . . . or something like that.

"I would do it myself. I'd leave the bar scene as it is. It would cut the kitchen costs down, it would cut the whole thing. New corporation, other name, other investors, small capitalization, you don't need anything. What I need is some booze and I need two Mexicans in the kitchen. I'll show 'em how to do everything. I'll have to get a new liquor license. I don't mind that because it's certainly worth it. I think it's a nice space and I think people would come and it would be a hangout."

But wouldn't it be better to hang on to what you've got? Couldn't Terry keep The Falls open a little while longer . . . just until a buyer comes along?

"No, I can't," he said, definitive and defeated. "It's $100,000 outstanding. It probably is more. Plus the rent, plus little things that I haven't taken into consideration. It's not just the money. It's all these agencies sending you forms, it's nonsense. To do business like that is just totally absurd. To do anything legit in this city is totally absurd. You start putting people on the books, unless you're doing gangbuster business, and you don't mind cutting into your profits by giving away the stuff—there's no reason to do it. At the first point that you start to struggle they both push you right over the edge, right over into bankruptcy . . ."

He paused for a moment. Terry Quinn was not the type to cry, but hell, this was a sad moment, wasn't it?

"I'm going to leave it till Saturday. I'll call Michael Zimmer, tell him to get the paintings out of there, and depending on what's going to happen I may take the stereo out of there. Nothing else, there's really nothing else of value. I'll just put a sign in the window. Send our liquor license and our corporate papers in, and—Saturday night will be the last."

Bruce called Terry yesterday or the day before. He said he's going to try and come back next week. He's working on a flight. He told Terry he's working on a deal with the Galloping Gourmet of Thailand. He told Terry he felt bad that he left him with the whole thing.

Terry is still sorting out his feelings. "I'm not as angry at him as . . . Patti says how can you speak to him? I know him better than she does. I don't think he's a malicious guy. He's certainly not a guy who should be running a restaurant. He's more of a guy who should be handling the promotion of a restaurant. An ideas person of a restaurant. But not somebody to hire employees, not somebody to run day-to-day matters, and not somebody to manage and—he just doesn't have those skills. He doesn't apply himself to those skills. He's got a great imagination. He's a great ideas person. There's probably none better. I've never met somebody with . . . He's great at getting out of things, he loves to get himself really in over his head."

This roast beef idea came to Terry last night. He went out with a friend and checked out some menus. If you're gonna do meat, Terry decided, you might as well do roast beef, do the best you can buy.

"I can hype the place up," he says now, while the idea is still fresh, exciting, new. "I can get a new name, put curtains in the windows, make it look a little cooler. I would even take out—downstairs I would take out that junk in the room next to the refrigerator, put a table down there, make a little card room or something, put pictures on the wall, make it like a little men's club, a little hangout or something. Have somebody stand at the door . . . people would get a kick out of being allowed in there."

A VIP room in a roast beef sandwich joint?

"That's where we'll serve the rare roast beef." He laughed, for the first time in several days.

A KISS BEFORE DYING

THIRTY-TWO

At 11:30 P.M. on May 4, 1991, the last of The Falls's four hundred thirty nights of life, Bruce Goldstein called his restaurant from Thailand, collect.

Terry Quinn adjusted his navy blue sport jacket around his broad shoulders, and stretched his legs out from under the tiny round table. These damn tables were always too small. Or maybe he just couldn't get comfortable tonight. There went those fingers through his hair. It's amazing the guy has any left. He had just arrived a few minutes ago himself, in the company of Seymour Cassel, a profoundly craggy middle-aged actor best known for his work in John Cassavetes movies like *Faces* and *The Killing of a Chinese Bookie*, a gregariously friendly man who'd spent much of his youth in joints just like this with Cassavetes and Falk and Gazzara, drinking hand to mouth. He'd been on the wagon for years now, proud of it, too, but he still liked the lure of a cool, dark place. Tonight a pretty, dark-haired young woman was with him. The three sipped strong black coffee—plenty of caffeine, thank you—and sat at the Primo Table.

So Bruce talked to whoever he could get on the phone, and Terry sat right nearby, listening, possibly, he sometimes managed to do that without anyone noticing, but more likely thinking how important it was for him not to take the call. I guess I could have called a bunch of people myself, Terry thought, but what would be the point? There's nothing to celebrate. It's sad. It's tragically sad. People are getting fucked. *This* is what happens.

Meanwhile, Bruce was complaining on the phone. "Where's Terry? Where is he? He should be there."

Terry kept shaking his head. I'm not here.

"Does anybody know where he is?" Bruce didn't believe it. That instinct. That sixth sense of what's happening. He knew he was being lied to. It's surprising he didn't notice the distinctly un-Bruce-like music pouring forth through the sound system he loved to manipulate. Stevie Wonder, Joe Jackson . . . he'd be throwing up his Thai noodles if he knew the flagrant abuse his favorite plaything at The Falls had endured in his absence.

Although perhaps he did know. Right before he called The Falls, Bruce had gotten through to the guy who installed the stereo system, told him to get his ass over to The Falls and work something out with Terry about getting his stuff out of there. No sense leaving it for the next guy. The guy would be there in a few minutes, Bruce was saying, so where the hell is Terry when you need him?

Funny, that's exactly what Wendy was saying a little while ago about Terry.

Must have been around 7:30 or so, when they discovered that every single goddamned copy store in the entire neighborhood, and probably the entire city of New York, was *closed* (nobody Xeroxes on a Saturday night, apparently), plus that damned recession, and how was Wendy ever going to make copies of the handwritten menu she'd put together for tonight? They had to figure out something. Thanks to some judicious ordering and careful planning, the kitchen had managed to get itself down to just what it had left, which amounted to one soup, three appetizers and six entrées. Of those only a few orders of each were available. Wendy had taken a black felt-tip pen and block-printed a final-night menu for The Falls, and was now wondering whether it could simply be read aloud to each and every table:

APPETIZERS

Soup du Jour	$5.
House Salad	
with Mustard Vinaigrette	$5.
Mozzarella and Grilled Red Peppers	$6.

Bruschetta $5.

Goat Cheese and Spinach Salad $7.

ENTRÉES

Linguini with Clams $12.

Steak au Poivre $16.

Chicken Francése $13.

Bucatini with Broccoli Rabe $12.

Grilled Red Snapper $15.

Steamed Seasonable Vegetables $11.

We are pleased to accept American Express.

This is bad. This is very bad.

Here it is the final night of this fucking restaurant, Wendy thought. And we have no menus. We have no copying machine. Wendy could hear the complaints already. You're out of this? You're out of that? Don't tell me you're out of *that*. Jesus Christ. Never mind. We're leaving, we'll find a *real* restaurant, thank you.

Wendy didn't know things could get this bad. She thought yesterday was as bad as it got.

Yesterday was pretty bad. No question. Yesterday it looked as though the restaurant might just keel over and die prematurely. Her mission, really, was to keep the place open long enough for Terry to close it. But yesterday it did not appear that The Falls was going to make it.

Right around 3:00 in the afternoon, when the ice machine passed away.

Ice to a restaurant . . . need this be explained? Think of how much ice you need to function inside your own home, then multiply it by a very large number, and you'll have some approximate idea of the level of panic that ensued when Wendy learned of this technical failure, this glitch that on any other day might have seemed less an act of God. On this particular day, the Death of the Ice Machine seemed a portent of tragedy. No, this was not going to be a quiet, simple death. This was going to hurt.

Oh, damn damn damn damn DAMN!

Somebody please help me!

Wendy shuffled through the answer cards in her brain. Stay calm. There's an answer here. Keep looking. In the background the busboy was muttering to himself, "Doesn't the fax machine make copies?" Wendy heard him and gave it a moment's thought. Yes, that's it. I'll give it a shot. She ran down the stairs, past the nude Madonna photo and the bathrooms, past the broken ice machine, past the pounds and pounds of pancake flour still sitting on the shelf from a year ago when visions of Sunday brunches and jazz combos still danced through Bruce's head. She leapt into the office and practically shoved her makeshift menu into the fax machine.

It worked!

One by one, painfully slowly, copies of the menu came through the Sharp US1 fax machine. They looked pretty decent, Wendy thought. After she made a dozen copies, she tore back upstairs.

"All right," she commanded to her minuscule staff, "let's stuff these into the menus." Tonight Wendy had two waitresses on duty. If Bruce were here he would have been horribly depressed. They both wore tight black miniskirts, but the choice of outfits did not flatter either of these women. One waiter was also on hand, a well-meaning young man who looked as though someone had tied a board to his back to make him stand up straight. His hands tended to shake a little as he carried plates across a room, though on a night like this a little nervousness could easily be forgiven. Two of them had worked at The Falls for less than a month, the other only a little longer.

They stuffed.

Within a few minutes they had put together a dozen menus. That would probably be enough.

This left the small matter of the bar. It seemed that they had also run out of certain things like vodka, whiskey, gin and cognac, not to mention red and white wine.

Inside Wendy's head a hammer had started to pound away. Bang, bang, bang . . . it was going to be pounding all night, she knew it. She had been up till noon the night before, partying with some waiters. Champagne was involved. And while champagne provides a most pleasant short-term high, it also activates the hammer inside the head. Bang, bang, bang. She rubbed her temples. It was difficult to think objectively about alcohol at a time like this.

"Maybe you should have a beer," Frederick the bartender said.

Frederick was not a regular bartender. Nor was he a regular guy. Well meaning, but a bit of a nerd. He got the job as a fill-in bartender at The Falls a couple months ago. His brother worked here, and slipped him past Bruce. Frederick most definitely was not the type of bartender Bruce wanted. To be perfectly honest, he was not anybody's type of bartender. He didn't really know how to pour a drink. He was the type that was always walking by and pouring your beer into your glass for you, a job that you can handle pretty well yourself, can't you? Or he was taking away your wineglass when you still had a few sips left in it. Or he was putting way too little vodka in his gimlets. You get the picture. Add to this a truly painful amount of singing. He had a tendency to sing along with whatever happened to be on the sound system; and if that happened to be an album of his liking, the singing could be so loud you wanted to go find refuge in another state.

Yes, Freddy was the perfect bartender to be on last-night duty.

"All right," Wendy said, "I'll take a beer." He poured her a Heineken. It sat on the bar for most of the night. Here was one drink Frederick did not want to clear away.

Wendy and Frederick sat with a piece of paper and came up with a list of booze they needed. The idea was that they would buy just enough to get through the night, although this was a dangerous calculation since perhaps no one would come in . . . or perhaps hundreds would. One never knew at The Falls; not even tonight.

"We need one vodka, one scotch, one bourbon," Frederick said. "And one good bottle of vodka, Absolut or something, since it's the last night and I want something good to drink behind the bar."

For some months now, ever since The Falls began to suffer economic troubles, you could not be certain what kind of booze you were getting out of the bottles behind the bar. If the bottle said Absolut, that meant only that you were guaranteed vodka. Tonight at The Falls, it would be standard operating procedure. The bottle of Absolut would be Frederick's personal stash.

Freddy planned to get good and drunk tonight.

/The wind blew through the front door, and the candles at the bar flickered.

In walked a beautiful couple. Spectacular, really. The man had a thick shock of jet black hair that set off his pale white skin. He wore a lightweight sport jacket and khakis and a big broad smile. The woman had several feet of legs, most of which were exposed by a purple minidress. It was a warm night, probably sixty-five degrees, and you could go bare-legged in New York if you wanted to. She did. No one was at the door to greet them. They took a seat at the bar but by the time Freddy got down there, singing and humming and filling up beer glasses along the way, they'd gotten up already. Back to the door.

The man cast a look back at the restaurant as they walked back through the door. Never mind, it said.

"Damn," said Wendy, looking out over the scattered customers who had ventured, without knowledge, into the final night's festivities. Bang, bang, bang. That damn headache would not stop.

"I need an Evian." Freddy obliged her.

It was 9:30, and amazingly enough, a fair number of people had shown up. Maybe thirty people eating dinner. Three tables had gotten up and left after they had a look at the menu for tonight. Sorry, sorry . . . Who could blame them? The steak au poivres had already sold out. So had the linguini and the red snapper. Basically, you had your choice of the appetizers, the bucatini, the chicken (better hurry, only two orders left) and the vegetables.

God forbid Terry should walk in now with a group of hungry celebrities. Bang, bang, bang. Where the hell was Terry? Wendy couldn't decide whether to be mad or glad. She would close The Falls herself if she had to. She had the key and the lock and the gumption, certainly. Terry had promised to be in. He told her yesterday he would. Terry's plans for the day included a celebrity cruise around New York City. Some kind of benefit for the Irish Republican Army, sponsored by Mickey Rourke. Free Joe Doherty! Free booze! Terry had been invited, being Irish and cool and all that. Matt was supposed to be there. And there had been some discussion of a party afterward at Peggy Sue's. "Maybe I'll get everybody over to The Falls after," Terry had mentioned to somebody.

Even Patti D'Arbanville didn't know where the hell he was. She called from Los Angeles, looking for him, and Wendy said, "Try Peggy Sue's," although she really didn't have the slightest idea where to find him.

It didn't matter to Wendy. Not really. She had already started working at another restaurant during the day, all this past week. A place around the corner from The Falls, called Café, owned by somebody named Picasso, a relative of the real Picasso. It's amazing when you think about it, that it took more than a decade for someone to open a restaurant in SoHo that attempted to capitalize on the name of an artist . . . let alone Picasso! Now *that's* a big name.

Wendy needed to work, she'd been living on the edge of fiscal responsibility for a while now. Not to mention the edge of sanity. Keeping a restaurant alive isn't exactly the best way to keep a level head. For the last two weeks she'd spent most days fending off phone calls from bill collectors. Sometimes they'd come into the restaurant, and she'd have to give them a few bucks from the register. How much should I offer? How much do they want? When the calls would come to her in the basement office, her momentary refuge from the on-slaught—"Wendy, the produce guy is here," "Wendy, the marshal is here"—she'd trudge back up the stairs and deal with it as best she could.

But every so often she couldn't.

Like yesterday. Friday—oh most horrible of horrible days that was!—at 2:30 in the afternoon, the man from Micros Computer showed up while Wendy was taking a moment's break downstairs. She had only just finished supervising the removal of the artwork from the walls. Per Terry's instructions, Michael Zimmer had taken down his beloved Keith Haring from the wall, along with the rest of the artwork—he'd carried it out, with a friend, right during lunch—leaving The Falls with painting hooks as its only wall decoration.

"Tell them I'm not here," Wendy told the waitress who'd buzzed her about the Man from Micros. The restaurant was still several thousand dollars away from paying off its bill for that damn computer. Nobody ever liked that contraption, what a waste of money it turned out to be. A printed record of disaster. Who needed it? Wendy knew they needed more money for the Micros Man than she could possibly scrape together. Many thousands of dollars were owed. She waited downstairs. The waitress buzzed her again and said, "He's right outside the office door . . . he's on the pay phone . . . don't go out now if you want to avoid him." So she didn't.

Ten minutes later, sure that he was gone, she went back upstairs. Something was different . . . what was it? Not just the dearly departed paintings. Not just the empty restaurant on a Friday afternoon. Not just the first day of sunshine after a week of solid, driving rain.

The computers were gone.

The Man from Micros had unplugged them and taken them away.

Only in America, right Wendy?

Tonight was going a little easier. If only because bill collectors don't call on Saturdays. And after tonight it was Terry's problem, not hers. The throbbing continued, it was getting worse, but there was always tomorrow, when it would all be over. The headache would be gone.

/Look who's here . . . Mugsy and Johnny!

Like clockwork, in walked the produce men. They have been coming to The Falls many Saturday nights since the opening for a drink. Sure, Bruce owes 'em money, but so what? That way they get a free drink or two. Johnny orders a double Glenlivet, straight, and Mugsy has a vodka. Both of them have been drinking steadily all night, and it shows. Mugsy downs his drink fast, but Johnny—after a short, painful sip—waves Freddy over.

"What the hell is this? I asked for Glenlivet."

Glenlivet is a top-shelf whiskey, one that most bars would never dare to substitute. Whiskey drinkers know their poison well.

But The Falls is, you know, kinda low on beverages.

Freddy takes down the Glenlivet bottle, holds it up so Johnny can check the label—for whatever *that's* worth—and pours him another. Johnny takes another cautious sip. No way it's Glenlivet, but the man's thirsty, so he takes a passionate gulp.

"So I guess you're here for the last night?" Freddy says.

Oh, Jesus, Freddy. The man's a creditor!

"What are you talking about?"

"It's the last night," Freddy repeats. "No more. We're closing."

"You're *closing?*"

Freddy nods, like it's a funny coincidence or something.

"All right." Johnny's face has turned bright red. One imagines that he is slightly annoyed to learn, in this fashion, that The Falls's outstanding debt to C&S Produce is about to become permanent. He swallows the last of his unfortunate drink, and with no gesture to either his wallet, Freddy or even Mugsy, storms out the door.

Mugsy, being a bit more amiable, stays around an extra moment or two. "So, you're closing," he says.

"Yep!" Freddy beams.

Mugsy may not understand the broader implications of the event, but he does realize this means he can walk out the door without leaving a tip. Which, after having another free vodka, he does.

/At 10:30 P.M., Roy the busboy quit. He couldn't take it anymore. He became the last employee of The Falls to quit before there was nothing left to quit.

It had something to do with Shelley. The fact is, Shelley wasn't really very competent. Roy was right to be mad. It's tough to be a busboy when your superiors fail you in fundamental ways. A busboy's job is built on faith. Roy depended on the waiters and waitresses, hoped that they'd done their job right, got the orders straight, kept things moving. Shelley did not keep things moving. She slowed things up.

Roy was sick and tired.

Plates were his life. He carried them with as much grace and elegance as he could muster. The job required him to do that, and it rewarded him with $10 a shift plus a percentage of the tips. Tonight that wasn't going to mean very much. Maybe sixty, seventy bucks. Maybe less. Most nights Roy could deal with it. The job was a little demeaning, sure, but you did get to sit awhile. Free dinner, too. Sometimes free drinks. And pretty girls depended on you, there's no denying that. The implications were enormous.

But tonight, as he hovered around the pass-through window of the kitchen, waiting for the final orders of chicken and steak and pasta to come his way, it all became just a little too much to bear. He disappeared for a moment and came back with a black jacket over his black shirt and pants.

"I'm leaving," he announced.

"You're *what?*"

"Where are you going?"

"I'm going home. I can't take it."

Wendy took him aside and whispered into his ear. Nothing was settled. He did not remove his coat. Within a minute he was gone. The customers did not notice, their plates came and went at basically the same speed. The waiter and waitresses did not mind, their tips were their own to keep. Wendy felt bad, she'd hoped to keep this group together for the night, close the place with good feelings all around, but Roy wasn't going to stick around just to make people feel good. What had The Falls done for him, anyway?

Shelley wasn't going to let it affect her. She was too busy chatting with a friend of hers at the bar, a woman who'd come in by herself, dressed provocatively in a miniskirt, who had been ordering a steady stream of champagne cocktails throughout the evening. This friend looked to be in her mid- to late thirties, but she told Freddy the bartender that she had a son who was seventeen years old, you figure it out, Freddy couldn't. The fact is, Freddy had the hots for her. The minute she left the bar to go make a phone call, he filled up her empty champagne glass with a complimentary refill.

"Let's see if she notices," Freddy whispered as she sauntered back to the bar a few minutes later. He stood down the bar a bit and watched. This was Freddy's type, yes indeed, the kind of woman he could get very excited about.

The woman took her seat and without any hesitation took her free drink in hand and started swallowing.

"That's odd," Freddy said. "Maybe she didn't notice." A bartender likes his gestures to be noticed, especially when they involve impressing a woman. Frederick had become a total love slave.

Come on, buddy, slap yourself! Have an Absolut!

Freddy did, in fact, pour himself a drink. And as he did so, a low-level New York celebrity named Chuck Pfeifer walked into The Falls. Terry Quinn, who in fact knew him personally, seemed surprised (and a little embarrassed, frankly) that the guy—whose name appears most frequently on Page Six—had stopped in on the final night. How did he get here? What was he doing here? And why did he leave? So many questions, so few answers, isn't that always how it is?

He left. That's the tragic part. He got to The Falls shortly after 10:00, with a beautiful brunette on his arm. He was meeting a friend who'd been waiting at the bar. They went immediately to a table, not a particularly good table either, took one look at the menu and must have figured, hmmm, there must be something better than this. More food, more wine, more *something*.

Ten minutes later he was gone. A streak of light through the door.

A sigh could be heard. It came from Veronique.

Veronique was the other waitress. She had no friends at the bar. Tonight, like all nights, she devoted herself purposefully to the task of serving her masters. She seemed to please them, some liked her smile and others liked her legs. She displayed both in abundance. Especially tonight.

"That's four," she sighed, meaning four tables that had abandoned her when they saw the menu. Four groups of people who had sat down, given the situation some thought, and realized The Falls was not for them. She paced back and forth by the bags of bread near the kitchen, then into the kitchen, then past the sink, then through the side door and out to the street. She paced. She smoked. She sighed. It was only 11:00. This was going to be one very long, very slow, very depressing night, and she wanted desperately to spend the rest of it right here on the sidewalk, any sidewalk, as far away from The Falls as she could possibly get.

/It was never made entirely clear, but you kind of figured that the four women who took a seat near Terry Quinn's corner banquette at midnight were friends of his. The prettiest of the four, a blonde in black leggings and a flowery top, kissed him hello on the cheek. This did not necessarily mean close friendship with Terry. He has probably kissed several thousand women on the cheek in his life. He is, in fact, one of the great Cheek Kissers of our time. He always seems to know in exactly which direction the woman's cheek is headed, so as to avoid those painful and embarrassing cheek crashes that occur among inexperienced or untalented Cheek Kissers. His strategy is to eye the woman's approach, and determine ahead of time exactly which way her cheek is headed.

The other women didn't kiss Terry's cheek. However, they did continue to give him the hairy eyeball throughout the time they spent at The Falls that night. Of course they probably didn't realize this when they walked in, but they were about to become a part of history. No reason to be coy. These women would eventually be the final customers of The Falls. They seemed worthy of the responsibility, at least at first. Four women, each of them reasonably attractive, are always worthy customers at The Falls.

At first, they kept to themselves. Ordered some drinks, had some laughs, blah blah blah.

After a while, Seymour Cassel took off. Wired for sound. The man drinks enough coffee to be an astronaut.

At 1:00 in the morning, the wait staff had some champagne at the bar. This cheered up everyone, including Veronique. Why, it was reasoned, should a perfectly good, perfectly chilled bottle of Taittinger Brut go to waste?

The kitchen staff had some champagne at their posts. There were, after all, a few orders of goat cheese and spinach salad left to serve.

Frederick was making his move on Shelley's friend. You know a bartender is making his move when customers elsewhere at the bar are waving frantically to get his attention. Freddy had eyes only for Mom in a Mini. He was actually leaning across the bar into her drink. His nose practically descended into her champagne glass.

Way to go, Freddy! *Someone* was going to get lucky tonight.

Those four women, though . . .

They were drinking fairly steadily. You had to give them that. The Falls always looked kindly on women who drank fairly steadily. Even on a night when the bartender had to supply himself from Astor Wines & Liquors, a retail establishment ten minutes away, the profit margin looked fairly good. You could always make an extra buck on the booze. After a while, as has been known to happen to people who spend more than a couple hours sitting near a bar, it could safely be said that these four women were now feeling the effects of alcoholic beverages.

They were drunk.

This created a rather awkward situation for Terry. And that was not good. Terry does not like awkward situations. But this is what he was faced with. Here were four women looking for fun, and at this particular moment, Terry was their only hope.

Be fun for us, Terry! Make us laugh!

So Terry told them a story about a restaurant that was about to close. It was a true story. He left out many of the details, but he did tell them that the story didn't have an ending yet. He said that the restaurant that was going to close was only the first part of the story. He said that after a while, maybe a month, maybe two, there would be another restaurant where the other one was, and it would serve roast beef sandwiches, and it would be good, just like Brendan & Carr, at the corner of Avenue U and Nostrand Avenue, where Terry used to eat all the time, it was a place you went to eat.

"What are you going to call it?" One of the women, with medium-length black hair and an intense, thoughtful manner, raised a perfectly good question. Terry had no good answer for them.

This is where things got a little ugly.

The problem was, Terry is at heart a good-natured fellow. He does not like to say to people, Fuck off, leave me alone, I'm tired, I'm busy. Oh, he'll say those things if he has to. It is in the nature of being a businessman. You must be able to say *no*. But here were these women, and they were nice, basically, and more than that they were paying customers. The cash would come in handy. And so for many valid reasons Terry could not say to them what he was feeling at this exact moment, which was:

Leave me alone. I'm sad.

So without meaning any harm, the women launched into a discussion of restaurant names. For five minutes they threw out the kind of pointless ideas that tend to come up when you have had a bit too much to drink. Which is to say, bad ideas, unfunny ideas, painful ideas.

"I know, I know," bubbled one excitedly. "This will be great." Terry is listening. He is trapped. "Why don't you call the place All the Lonely People. You know . . . like the Beatles song."

She sings. " 'All the lonely people . . . where do they all belong?' "

Terry nods aimlessly. Does she think she is cheering me up?

"It'd be great," she went on. "You could have a whole ad campaign, you know . . . 'All the lonely people, where do they all belong? *Here!*' "

Oh for chrissakes, Terry's expression cries out; do I have to listen to this? But he is sweet, charming, gracious as always.

"Funny," he says.

. . .

/It ended around 3:00 in the morning.

The four girls amused themselves a while longer. Terry finally found a means of escape. They finished their drinks and paid their check. The restaurant had begun to close around them, perhaps they felt it. On the other side of the partition, Wendy sat with a pile of cash and receipts and a cash register. She added up the totals and concluded that there was not going to be enough money to pay everybody. She owed the two chefs their salaries for two weeks, or $1,200 apiece. She owed the kitchen help $150 apiece. But there was only $1,600 to go around.

The three Mexicans who worked in the kitchen—Manuel had quit months ago, by the way; one day he just stopped showing up—spoke not a word of English. They could only read the expression on Wendy's face, which suggested bad news, and they immediately looked depressed themselves. To these three, $150 in cash represented a substantial amount of money.

"You three all live together, anyway, right?" Wendy asked. She was hoping they'd say, don't worry about it, just give us the proper amount of bills and we'll be happy. But they wanted their money, each of them, counted and distributed appropriately. Wendy understood this, being an illegal alien herself, and gave them their money. One of them did have to settle for one twenty, three tens and a hundred singles, but he seemed to get a kick out of the large number of bills.

The chefs were a different story. There just wasn't enough left to pay them. The only solution was going to be the American Express money. There were $1,700 in charges from tonight, and on Monday Wendy could go to the bank and get cash back. "I'll pay you on Monday," she told Larry and Patrick, the cooks. They looked unhappy. They knew that this was it; who wanted to wait until Monday? Who knew if the money would be there? Who wanted to trust people anymore?

"I promise," Wendy said. It was dark. It was late. She was tired.

Larry and Patrick believed her. They smiled and returned to the kitchen. There were three orders of bucatini left, so they put them out, along with a large plate of mashed potatoes. They also carried out two cakes from the refrigerator and put them out. No sense letting them go bad, or throwing them away. The four women, still not out the door, each got a free slice of cake. While everyone was nibbling away, Larry and Patrick went downstairs, retrieved the remaining fruits and vegetables from the walk-in freezer and carried them out of the restaurant, along with some plates and silverware.

One of the waitresses took a piece of chalk to write a final message on the "86" blackboard near the kitchen, where usually one could find a list of the things that were no longer available. Under the circled "86," she had written, in large block letters, "THE FALLS."

The four women finally got up to leave.

"I'll walk you out," Terry said. He followed them to the door, and kissed the last one out the door goodnight. It was to be The Falls's last goodnight kiss.

TOO MANY FISH

THIRTY-THREE

The Falls closed its doors at 4:02 A.M. on May 5, 1991. Wendy and Terry were the last to leave. Terry pulled down the steel door and attached the padlock. His car was parked alongside the restaurant. He got in and drove home, alone, to his apartment on East 66th Street. By 5:00 in the morning he was fast asleep.

Five hours later Terry returned to The Falls. He had originally intended to soap the windows as a way of showing the restaurant had closed, and to protect the fixtures remaining inside. But now that the moment had come to do so, Terry chose instead to merely close the blinds a little tighter. This way, he reasoned, no one could tell whether anything remained of The Falls or not.

Right after he arrived at 10:00 in the morning, Terry saw some mice on the floor. They were the first mice to eat at The Falls. Mice are the first to hear when a restaurant closes, Terry thought. They must have their own network of information, a Page Six for rodents. It's just like humans, only smaller and faster. They go and tell their friends: Hey guys, there's some free mashed potatoes at The Falls! Flourless chocolate cake!

Terry flipped on the lights and the mice raced back out.

Two men came by, as promised, to remove the entire stereo system.

By 11:30 A.M. they had completely dismantled the speakers and wires and decks. They loaded it all into a package van and drove away. Terry took the compact discs, there must have been at least a hundred, maybe more, and put them in a box to take back home with him. Still sitting on the tables near the bar were boxes and boxes of Bruce's tapes—old, decaying cassettes from Central Falls and elsewhere, hundreds of hours of music from Bruce's soul.

Larry and Patrick showed up to get a few last items from the kitchen. Terry sat at a table in the middle of the restaurant and talked with them for a while about what went wrong with The Falls.

"Too many fish," Larry said.

Terry did not understand.

"There was too many fish on the menu," Larry explained. "Too many *fish*. In the beginning we had five fish on the menu. Three regular fish and two specials."

"Five fish," Terry repeated.

"Yeah. And not just regular fish. Crazy weird fish. Expensive fish. Like Hawaiian fish, you know? Monkfish, and snapper, and all kinds of sole. You can't make money with that many fish."

Patrick nodded in agreement. "Too many fish," he said. "Bruce loved fish."

Even with the blinds drawn tight, the sun shone so strong that the room looked pale and sick. With no candles or napkins or forks or knives to break up the view, The Falls this morning was nothing but black tabletops reflecting the light. Here and there an empty glass sat out from the night before. Nobody had bothered to clean up the place—the mice appreciated that—and food still sat out everywhere. With nothing but bare walls and silence, there was little to distract these three men from exhuming the body and performing an amateur autopsy. And today there could be no question but that Bruce had been the cause of The Falls's death.

"I remember the time Bruce came into the kitchen and said the soup was bad," Larry remembered. "He came in and tasted it. I used to hate it when he'd come in and taste things. He tasted the soup and said it was awful, to throw it out and make it over. He left, and I didn't have time to do it again. So he came back a half hour later and tasted the soup, the exact same soup as he tasted the other time, and this time he said it was much better."

"Ha!" Terry said.

"You don't go away," Patrick said. "You don't leave six times. He took too many vacations."

"Yes," Larry said. "You stay and you work and you don't take any money until the restaurant is making money. I would go to the bar to get my money and there wouldn't be any cash because Bruce had already taken all the cash."

Terry put his sneakers up on the tabletop.

"This place should have been roast beef sandwiches and creamed spinach," Terry said.

/The next morning Terry came back to begin the process of dismantling The Falls. It was Monday morning. He had a two-page handwritten list of people he had to call, and sat down in the office, dialing on the speaker phone. He called lawyers and friends and people involved in his new bar at the Paramount Hotel. He wore his usual workday outfit of a T-shirt and sweatpants and sneakers. As he made calls, Larry and Patrick and one of the Mexican laborers worked upstairs to clean up what remained of the place.

As he dropped in and out of conversations, Terry used his nimble fingers to stack the large accumulations of change that had been stuffed away in the office. Some of it was in a basket on the desk, and some was kept in a zippered bag, hidden away behind a bunch of files in the back of a drawer. He took it all, and spent ten minutes stacking it all up. Too bad most of it was nickels and dimes. Nevertheless, he applied himself diligently to the task, stacking and straightening and counting and scrounging.

"There's more than eight bucks here," he announced proudly. He had that sardonic smile on his face, the one that removed the menace from his scar. "Eight whole bucks! We're saved!"

He pondered the pile for a moment.

"You know what I should do?" he said finally. "I should open a fucking wishing well. Jesus, what a great racket. You get people to throw money in all day, nickels, dimes . . . I bet you get a lot of quarters in wishing wells. Then at the end of the day you take all the money out and you take it to the bank. The guys at the bank would hate you bringing in all those bags of change."

He leaned back in his chair and laughed.

EPILOGUE

Kimberly Jones continues to live in Los Angeles and work on *Evening Shade*, where she met and married a member of the camera crew. Four months ago she gave birth to a red-headed baby girl named Carson.

Henry Hauck is living in Miami Beach, where, at this writing, he is the general manager of the bar and restaurant at The Clevelander Hotel on Ocean Avenue. It is, by Henry's count, the forty-seventh restaurant where he has worked. He predicts that the fiftieth restaurant will be his own.

Brian Moores moved to northern California in early 1991, where he lived for several months until disappearing from sight. He was recently discovered working as a chef at a new restaurant in Santa Barbara—by Kimberly Jones, who walked in one day for lunch with her husband and daughter.

Philippe Dumont remains in St. Bart's. He and Alexandra are no longer engaged. He is renting out his villa as a luxury accommodation for $5,000 a week, a business he says is going very well. Philippe's friendship with Bruce ended after his experience at The Falls.

Brian Wry moved to Los Angeles. He has given up plans to be an actor; now he's working in public relations and art direction. "I'm still searching," he says. He is still writing his play about Bruce.

Wendy still lives in New York City. She has been working as the day manager of a popular bar in the Broadway theater district. "I miss my home," she says, "but I don't want to leave New York just yet."

The space at 150 Varick Street is now occupied by Patric, a restaurant created by chef Patrick Robertson, formerly of Le Cirque and other noted establishments. A lavish remodeling job turned the room into an art deco vision, designed by a member of the team that similarly transformed the Royalton and Paramount hotels.

Robertson's menu is more expensive than The Falls—dinner with wine is likely to cost close to $100 for two. The food is also more adventurous, aimed at aficionados of haute cuisine in romantic settings. There was an early rave review from *New York*'s Gael Greene. A review by Bryan Miller has not yet appeared.

Terry Quinn opened The Whiskey, a trendy nightspot in the lobby of New York's Paramount Hotel, in the summer of 1991. It was a smash success, and he says all the investors have made their money back. Now he plans to open a new restaurant on the Upper East Side to compete with Elaine's for the celebrity crowd. It will be called "Emmelyn's," after his daughter, with Patti D'Arbanville, and it will serve, among other things, roast beef sandwiches. Patti now lives with Terry in New York, and is pregnant with their second child. Terry has also gone back to work for the Fire Department, and works out of a firehouse on the Upper West Side.

Terry has found a new partner for his "Emmelyn's" venture. For the first few months after The Falls closed, Terry and Bruce barely spoke to each other. Recently, though, the two have been mending their relationship. Occasionally they meet for a meal at the Coffee Shop, a restaurant that also opened in 1990. It caters heavily to beautiful women and celebrities.

Bruce Goldstein returned from Thailand with an idea to promote a chef he'd met there. The chef's name is Chalie Amatyakul, but Bruce calls him simply "The Thai Chef," a title he recently trademarked. He put together a press kit and got an article about the chef published in the Living Section of *The New York Times*. He says he has raised "substantial" funds from Wall Street types for a book and other projects related to the chef. Bruce also developed, with some friends, a proposal for a television comedy series called *The Doormen*, about a New York City apartment building. He is still trying to interest a producer in the project.

Not long ago Bruce ran into Julie, one of the waitresses he fired from The Falls, at a seafood restaurant a block from where The Falls once stood. He asked her out on a date, and she accepted. They went to the movies.

"To me," Bruce says, "the restaurant business has been not so much a job, but more like a family I created. We'll always be a part of each other's lives. I gotta say . . . I'm very proud of that."

—April 28, 1992

ACKNOWLEDGMENTS

Many people nurtured me through the reporting, writing and editing of this book.

The idea grew out of a decade of obsessive newspaper and magazine writing about people and institutions, during which time I was lucky enough to have editors who took a chance and trusted me: in particular, Dick Martin, Steve Rubin, Adam Moss, and Peter Herbst.

As I first developed this particular idea, certain people provided suggestions, connections and introductions that led me down the eventual right path: in particular, David and Susan Liederman, Randy Rothenberg, Drew Nieporent, Tim Zagat, Noel Behn and Warren Hoge. John Whitesell's ongoing generosity was of particular help.

At The Falls, several people opened their lives to me, enriching this book with their enthusiasm for the project: in particular, I owe thanks to Brian Moores, Henry Hauck, Kimberly Jones and Michael Fitzpatrick.

Good friends offered me their wisdom about restaurants and people that I was fortunate enough to hear. For interrupting my rambling monologues about the nature of restaurants with insights, I owe thanks to Bill Abrams, Ann Brennan, Susan Egbert, David Frankel, Nicole Giroux, Julie Hartenstein, Leslie Larson, Gene Stone and Emily

Whitesell. Special thanks go to Jon Meyersohn, Matt Wagner and Tony Gilroy for their particularly patient and supportive brand of friendship.

I could never have finished this enterprise without the help of friends who had written books and shared their secrets. Fortunately I am blessed with the friendship of some very talented writers, and I am eternally grateful for their inspiration and advice: Don Katz, Jonathan Kaufman, Jane Mayer, Tricia Morrisroe, Julie Salamon and Susan Squire.

Larry Rout helped shape my thinking about journalism and writing. Peter Cohn offered good friendship and smart editing. David Hirshey gave me support and advice when I most needed it. Jonathan Feldman helped me through the toughest moments. Norman Steinberg gave me an office to work in, and Tiffany Rocquemore made my life there easy and pleasant.

I am blessed with an agent, Suzanne Gluck, who always knew what I was doing, even when I didn't.

My editor, Bob Asahina, brought his intelligence, calm and fresh perspective to the process at all times, and saved the world from my first draft. Thanks also to Sarah Pinckney, and copy editors Fred Chase and Florence Falkow.

My parents-in-law, Joan and Howard Minsky, have given freely of their love and support throughout this project, as have Jeffrey and Maura.

At first I wanted to write a book so I could follow my father, Albert Blum, in the card catalog. His creativity and brilliance awed me at first, then inspired me. My mother, Roslyn Blum, taught me the value of passion, and of style; she has an abundance of both. I am grateful for all they've given me. Thanks also to my brother, Steven, who first taught me how to fight for things I care about.

Oh yes, and about Terri Minsky:

Without her this book would simply not exist, along with many other, far more important things. With her my life has been more exciting than I ever imagined.

ABOUT THE AUTHOR

DAVID BLUM *was born in New York City, and grew up in East Lansing, Michigan. He graduated from the University of Chicago in 1977, and has since written for several publications, including* THE WALL STREET JOURNAL, ESQUIRE, VANITY FAIR, NEW YORK *and* THE NEW REPUBLIC. *He lives in New York City with his wife, Terri Minsky. He has recently resumed eating out.*